Lived Theology

Lived Theology

*New Perspectives on Method,
Style, and Pedagogy*

Edited by

CHARLES MARSH

PETER SLADE

SARAH AZARANSKY

OXFORD
UNIVERSITY PRESS

OXFORD
UNIVERSITY PRESS

Oxford University Press is a department of the University of Oxford. It furthers
the University's objective of excellence in research, scholarship, and education
by publishing worldwide. Oxford is a registered trade mark of Oxford University
Press in the UK and certain other countries.

Published in the United States of America by Oxford University Press
198 Madison Avenue, New York, NY 10016, United States of America.

© Oxford University Press 2017

Library of Congress Cataloging-in-Publication Data
Names: Marsh, Charles, 1958- editor.
Title: Lived theology : new perspectives on method, style, and pedagogy /
edited by Charles Marsh, Peter Slade, and Sarah Azaransky.
Description: New York City : Oxford University Press, 2016. |
Includes bibliographical references and index.
Identifiers: LCCN 2016021263| ISBN 9780190630720 (cloth : alk. paper) |
ISBN 9780190630744 (epub)
Subjects: LCSH: Christian sociology. | Theology. | Christian life.
Classification: LCC BT738 .L53 2016 | DDC 230—dc23
LC record available at https://lccn.loc.gov/2016021263

Contents

Editors' Preface

THE FIFTEEN ESSAYS in this book cluster around a set of questions that yields new perspectives on method, style, and pedagogy in theological and religious studies: how might theologians engage the lived experience of Christian persons and communities with the same care and precision given to reading and interpreting texts? How might storied accounts of life with God inform the methodology, style, and teaching of Christian theology, and in turn illuminate a new model for bridging the widely lamented and discussed division between the academy and the congregations? Answers to—and explorations of—these questions shape the mission of the Project on Lived Theology at the University of Virginia, and provide a narrative arc to this collaborative volume.

As an academic discipline, theology has often ignored the lived consequences of its commitments. To be sure, we have seen in recent years impressive interdisciplinary progress in theological studies—that is, notable and meaningful engagements with ethnography, anthropology, geography, critical theory, oral history, and the social sciences. Such interdisciplinary efforts have enabled theologians, students, and practitioners to think more clearly about the patterns and practices of Christian conviction. Friedrich Schleiermacher, the beloved prince of nineteenth-century Protestantism, insisted that theologians always work in the context of an obligation to think faithfully and critically about church practices; by so doing they would give voice to what "is implied in the new activities and patterns of behavior in the believing community." Schleiermacher believed that critical thinking on the churches' "new activities and patterns of behavior" enlivened theology as a discipline and kept it honest to its original sources. Karl Barth, despite the thunderous criticisms of Schleiermacher, spoke of the theological vocation as an awakening to "the movement of life."[1] Theology's task remained, however, dynamic and unscripted: to sketch "the bird in flight," to follow the trail of the "portable tent," that is to say, to venture a word about God, who transcends human speech.[2] Theology aspires to an art of impossible ends, and yet must labor to render the impossible possible in language.

The essays in this book inspire a confessional reinvigoration of lived experience and illuminate a way beyond the Schleiermacher–Barth impasse. By affirming the methodological centrality of faith's redemptive practices, shared spaces of collaboration emerge across the ecumenical and theological spectrum. *Lived Theology* clusters around the conviction that the revitalization of public theology in America needs a theological culture that is both robustly public and confessional. By "public" we have in mind the generous sense of Dietrich Bonhoeffer's conviction that grace-formed and authentic discipleship fortifies "civil courage" and "ultimate honesty." This volume maps a variety of strategies for engaging the lived experiences of Christian faith communities as theological texts. Our hope is to exemplify in method, style, and pedagogy a model of the theological vocation that remains structurally open to life.

The book springs from two gatherings convened by the Project on Lived Theology at the University of Virginia. With more than a decade of workshops, conferences, seminars, and site visits, which have convened theologians, biblical scholars, sociologists of religion, historians, ethicists, pastors, and community development workers, the time seemed propitious to take stock of the lessons learned and insights gained. It should be noted that the contributors to this volume represent only a fraction of the more than four hundred people who have been involved in the Project.

This volume could not have been completed without the support of our research community, especially Kris Norris, Shea Tuttle, Kelly Figueroa-Ray, Rachel Butrum, Kristina Garcia Wade, and Nathan Walton. Thanks are also due to Willis Jenkins who was involved in the early stages of the editorial process. Finally, the editors wish to thank Cynthia Read, senior editor at Oxford University Press, for her generative presence at our 2013 conference and her ever-sharp editorial insights. We are deeply grateful to the Lilly Endowment for its generous support of the Project and its commitment to theological education in North America.

Notes

1. Karl Barth, *The Word of God and the Word of Man*, trans. Douglas Horton ([1928] Gloucester, MA: Peter Smith, 1978), 290–91.
2. Ibid., 317.

Notes on Contributors

SARAH AZARANSKY is an assistant professor of social ethics at Union Theological Seminary, New York. Her publications include *The Dream is Freedom: Pauli Murray and American Democratic Faith* (2011), and an edited volume, *Religion and Politics in America's Borderlands* (2013).

JACQUELINE A. BUSSIE is director of the Forum on Faith and Life professor of Religion at Concordia College, Moorhead, Minnesota. She is the author of *The Laughter of the Oppressed: Ethical and Theological Resistance in Wiesel, Morrison, and Endo* (2007) and *Outlaw Christian* (2016).

DAVID DARK is an assistant professor at Belmont University. He is a voracious consumer of popular culture and the author of books including *Life's Too Short To Pretend You're Not Religious* (2016) and *The Gospel According to America* (2005).

SUSAN M. GLISSON, the executive director of the William Winter Institute for Reconciliation at the University of Mississippi from 2002 to 2016, is the co-founder and principal of Sustainable Equity, LLC specializing in community trust building and social justice. She edited *The Human Tradition in the Civil Rights Movement* (2006).

JOHN W. DE GRUCHY is the Emeritus Robert Selby Taylor Professor of Christian Studies at the University of Cape Town, South Africa. De Gruchy has authored or edited more than thirty books on Dietrich Bonhoeffer; the church in South Africa; contextual, public, and Reformed theology; social history; Christianity and the arts; reconciliation and justice; and Christian humanism.

LORI BRANDT HALE is associate professor of religion at Augsburg College, Minneapolis. She is the author of *Bonhoeffer for Armchair Theologians* (2009).

SUSAN R. HOLMAN is an independent scholar and consultant in poverty studies in religious history as well as in health and human rights as it relates to international poverty, religion, and nutrition. She is senior writer at the Global Health Education and Learning Incubator at Harvard University. Susan is the author of *God Knows There's Need* (2009) and *Beholden: Religion, Global Health, and Human Rights* (2015).

WILLIE JAMES JENNINGS is associate professor of systematic theology and Africana Studies at Yale Divinity School. He was the winner of the 2015 Louisville Grawemeyer Award in Religion for his book *The Christian Imagination: Theology and the Origins of Race* (2011).

WILLIS JENKINS is associate professor of religion, ethics, and environment at the University of Virginia. He is the author of *The Future of Ethics: Sustainability, Social Justice, and Religious Creativity* (2013) and *Ecologies of Grace: Environmental Ethics and Christian Theology* (2008).

JOHN KIESS is assistant professor of theology at Loyola University, Maryland. In addition to his work on the ethics of war through the lens of the Democratic Republic of Congo, he is also interested in political theology, political theory, and philosophy, and wrote *Hannah Arendt and Theology* (2016).

JENNIFER M. MCBRIDE is associate dean for the doctor of ministry programs and continuing education and assistant professor of theology and ethics at McCormick Theological Seminary in Chicago. She is the author of *The Church for the World: A Theology of Public Witness* (2011) and co-editor of *Bonhoeffer and King: Their Legacies and Import for Christian Social Thought* (2010).

MARY MCCLINTOCK FULKERSON is professor of theology, Duke Divinity School. Her book *Places of Redemption: Theology for a Worldly Church* (2010) is on ecclesial practices that enable resistance to racism and other contemporary forms of social brokenness.

CHARLES MARSH is the Commonwealth Professor of Religious Studies at the University of Virginia and director of the Project on Lived Theology. His recent work includes *Strange Glory: A Life of Dietrich Bonhoeffer* (2014), and *The Beloved Community: How Faith Shapes Social Justice from the Civil Rights Movement to Today* (2005).

PETER SLADE is professor of the history of Christianity and Christian thought at Ashland University, Ohio. He is the author of *Open Friendship in a Closed Society: Mission Mississippi and a Theology of Friendship* (2009), and co-editor of *Mobilizing for the Common Good: The Lived Theology of John M. Perkins* (2013).

TED A. SMITH is associate professor of preaching and ethics at Emory University's Candler School of Theology. His work includes *Weird John Brown: Divine Violence and the Limits of Ethics* (2014), and *The New Measures: A Theological History of Democratic Practice* (2007).

Lived Theology

Introduction

LIVED THEOLOGY: METHOD, STYLE, AND PEDAGOGY

Charles Marsh

When I first studied theology, my idea of it was quite different, rather more academic probably. Now it has turned into something else altogether.

DIETRICH BONHOEFFER TO HIS BROTHER KARL
FRIEDRICH BONHOEFFER

IN THE SPRING of 1989, I finished a doctoral dissertation at the University of Virginia on the early philosophical theology of Dietrich Bonhoeffer. I wrote the thesis under the supervision of Robert Scharlemann, an exacting, inscrutable Lutheran theologian, whose semester-long seminar on Fichte's *Wissenschaftslehre* (*auf Deutsch*) remains a cloud of unknowing in my fairly unhappy graduate student career. Scharlemann would officiously shepherd my exposition of Kant, Hegel, and Heidegger to completion, and for this I remain forever grateful. It would take several more years, however, and many convivial exchanges with a colleague at Loyola University in Maryland, to help me recast the work as a dialogue of sorts with Karl Barth and thus to achieve sharper Christological focus. Without the Barthian intensification, prompted by the aforementioned colleague, James J. Buckley (a Roman Catholic student of Hans Frei), the project would surely have languished in some forlorn series in phenomenological studies and never found a home with Oxford University Press, where it appeared in 1994 under the confident title, *Reclaiming Dietrich Bonhoeffer: The Promise of His Theology.* Bonhoeffer's thought, focused on the theme "Christ existing as community," and the Barthian notes, had come to me as a liberation and a challenge.

Like most church-going Protestants, I had heard Bonhoeffer's name in sermons and Bible studies and knew him as the heroic conspirator and modern-day martyr. I'd read sections of *The Cost of Discipleship* and *Life Together*. As a graduate fellow at Virginia, I had taught sections of *Letters and Papers from Prison*—the provocative ruminations on the world come of age, religionless Christianity, holy silence, and the arcane discipline—in a course called "Faith and Doubt in the Modern World." But it was not until late in my studies that I discovered Bonhoeffer's early philosophical theology; and when I did, out of the malaise of theory-heavy 1980's academe, it thrilled me. For this erudite Berliner and straight-arrow academic had himself struggled mightily to break free of a stultifying intellectual inheritance. The focus of my dissertation (Bonhoeffer's years as a doctoral student and Privatdozent at the University of Berlin from 1927 to 1933) introduced me to a young theologian who came to experience the liberal Protestant tradition as an enervating weight, but found the grace—nowhere more vividly than during his year in America in 1930–1931—to move from the "phraseological to the real," as he would later say.[1]

In my years as a graduate student, first at Harvard Divinity School and then at UVA, I became frustrated—vexed, as many theology students are—by the lack of a vital connection between my academic life and my involvements in Christian social ministry. From September to May, I read modern theology and philosophical hermeneutics; and in the summers, I worked in an inner-city neighborhood of Atlanta in a community-building program for minority youth. Over the course of five consecutive summers I returned to Georgia, running a day camp for young men in which I combined my love of basketball, poetry, and the Bible into a program called Body and Soul. During these months in Reynoldstown, in a half-acre green space surrounded by urban poverty, and buttressed by the abandoned textile mills of Cabbagetown, I received as much as I gave; the daily rituals of the Stewart Center taught me that "concrete, down-to-earth life together" is a great and poignant joy.[2] In the fall, I returned to Cambridge or Charlottesville excited by the prospects of a new academic year, but feeling a million miles away from the inner-city families whom I had served. With the academic monograph published in 1994, I considered taking up a study of the Holy Trinity, but found it nearly impossible to keep my focus on this sublime and magnificent doctrine of the Christian Church. Perhaps I suffer from doctrinal attention deficit disorder, the result of too many contentious debates between my Calvinist and Armenian kinfolk that had ruined more than few Thanksgiving meals in my childhood. There is also the plain fact that the Trinity *is* a mystery, a topic of "awesome majesty and . . . splendor which demands almost reverential silence."[3] It was a relief to leave these matters to more capable minds, and no doubt my theological colleagues felt the same. Instead, my thoughts turned to my evangelical-fundamentalist upbringing in the civil rights-era South, and to questions unresolved and mostly unasked of the theological conflicts that marked that time.

In 1967, my family moved to a town nestled deep in the heart of Klan country, in the meanest season of Mississippi burning. The White Knights of the Ku Klux Klan of Mississippi, housed in a ramshackle building near the Baptist church my father pastored, had embarked on a final desperate campaign of heightened terrorism. Those tumultuous years—the Klan murders and bombings, the FBI investigations, the desegregation of public schools—eventually gave way to the peaceful, easy 1970s; and I had not thought much about massive resistance and civil rights since that time. But now, I could think of nothing else. The fragments of the past became obsessive in character, and I felt the call of the road.

So it was on a morning in the summer of 1994, thirty years after the Freedom Summer Project of 1964, that I headed south with a vague notion to understand the religious motivations of the civil rights movement. I wanted somehow to apply whatever skills I had honed in philosophical theology to a more challenging and irrepressible set of interpretive and theological questions, which meant sorting through the disparate claims of a historical crisis configured largely by clashing and colliding theologies.

Historians and scholars before me had acknowledged the religious motivations of the civil rights movement; but in paying attention to theological details, an expansive field of inquiry appeared, promising fresh insights into Christian thought and practice. Revisiting the civil rights movement as theological drama meant capturing the dynamic particularity of lived faith in its exquisitely varied expressions; it meant bringing the repertoire of whatever interpretive skills I had honed in my academic training to bear on the teeming, chaotic social world of (from the perspective of 1994) the not-so-distant past. I came to see that particular ways of thinking about God, Jesus Christ, and the Church framed the original purposes and goals of the movement, as well as the varieties of opposition against it.

Certainly, these purposes and goals were often supplemented and nourished by other religious and intellectual traditions; but as I explained at the time, the movement burst into life amid the singing, testifying, prophesying, and organizing of people in the pews and pulpits, seemingly compelling one to pay closer attention to the voices of the Church. The task of interpreting the religious and theological sources of the civil rights movement meant capturing the dynamic particularity of its stories and events, trying hard to make them vivid, honest, and inspiring, and asking the question of God with appropriate suspicion.[4]

I spoke with anyone willing to tell their story. I talked with the men who so greatly despised the prospects of black freedom that they organized terrorist cells and committed murder in the name of God. I discovered the ways African American activists, politically liberal clergy from American congregations (both Christian and Jewish), local people gathering in black freedom churches and community centers, and a coterie of white inside agitators, moved in a deliberately united, ever fragile front, to challenge and change discriminatory laws, and inspire and expand democratic participation. The inviting notion of "public discipleship," so named in a different context by Baptist-Pentecostal theologian Clark Pinnock, strikes me as an eloquent summation of their peculiar manner of living, the shape of their hope, dispositions, and habits. The world was God's good creation, most would tell you without hesitating, even when dressed up in Jim Crow's fancy tricks and lies. Victoria Gray Adams called the Student Nonviolent Coordinating Committee (SNCC) an "enfleshened church"; amid this fellowship of dissidents, and always with Bonhoeffer's life and thought as a guide, I found a greater cloud of witnesses, *Doktorvaters,* and *Doktormutters* of a different kind.

The sources available to me were rich and wide-ranging, and included sermons; testimonials; church bulletins and minutes; hymnals and Sunday school curricula; denominational newspapers and the major dailies; Bible studies; published and unpublished autobiographical narratives; interviews with participants and oral histories curated by other scholars; archival recordings; newsreels; photographs, films and videos; participants' journals, letters, and notebooks; unpublished literary and theological manuscripts; published historical and sociological studies; biographies, memoirs, and academic monographs; and organizational and institutional histories. In piecing together such a wide variety of sources, I confronted an irresistible challenge: how to integrate genres and disciplines, modes of inquiry, and scholarly methodologies with the intention of understanding the theological meanings enacted in lived experience.

In early drafts, I inevitably foregrounded the theological insights; but as any decent writer knows, narrative unloosened from theory eventually runs over everything. Graham Greene's memoir *Journey without Maps,* which mostly relates his malaria-drenched four-week trek through the Liberian jungles, came to my mind as a parable of writing lived theology. Still, amid the stumbles and pitfalls, I was inspired to ask questions that would prove illuminative. How do we make theological sense of lived experience in its idiosyncratic presentations? How does one read enacted faith as a theological text? And more broadly, what change might occur in theological writing, research, and teaching, when theologians engage lived experience with the same care and precision with which we read and interpret books, articles, and historical documents? It was reassuring to discover that methodological quandaries were quite often resolved by asking the right questions. As far as the writing went, after a while most of the academic discourse disappeared altogether— and only then, did the characters and stories come to the foreground and sparkle into life. Telling the truth about lived faith challenged my tendency (one shared by many theologians) to fit the idiosyncrasies of lived faith into familiar categories— and to presume that dogmatic generalities render the particular more or less predictable. It's hard to read modern theology and not become uneasy with its demurral on faith's lived complexities. Jürgen Moltmann, the great Tübingen theologian and generous friend to our research community, put it like this: in order to explain who "God the Lord is," we will have to be willing to tell the stories of what people have actually experienced, and to do so with unflinching honesty.[5]

In the company I kept at the time, if a theologian appealed to a nontheological category in thinking about some aspect of the created order, she or he risked betraying the sufficiency of Christian revelation and its superior inner resources; referring to a book written by a theologian as "non-theological" amounted to a stinging rebuke. The "theological" was presumed to be a more pure and elemental way of thinking Christianly than philosophical, literary, historical, or psychological approaches. "Theological" pertained to the grammar of Christian faith, the linguistic rules governing the church's distinctive belief and practice. But as I began to think about the complicated and irrepressible material appearing in my journals, everywhere demanding narrative order, analysis, and precision, I soon encountered the discursive gap between theology and memory, theology and history, theology and lived particularity—a gap which might need to be more fully appreciated by academic theologians before it can be bridged. Telling an honest story is a difficult task.

My own "turning from the phraseological to the real" inspired me to think intentionally—both alone on the road, and in my study and in conversation with engaged scholars and theological practitioners—of ways to encourage others in their own journeys. A graduate research assistant once said that when he described lived theology's mission to his fellow graduate students, they would often light up and say, "That's why I decided to study theology in the first place!"

Over the years, nevertheless, usually in convivial exchange, I have heard colleagues insist that I long ago crossed the Rubicon from theology into history. Why didn't I just admit it? I'd feel a lot better. "Nothing but history and sociology," a postliberal theologian remarked upon reading my 1997 book, *God's Long Summer*. "I see you're now writing journalism?" a systematican said at an academic conference. I would not be unhappy at all to spend my days writing history and journalism. But it is necessary to push back on these claims, as I remain convinced that life narratives written from "a higher satisfaction" remain always and everywhere the enlivening center of theological thought.[6] My journeys into the dense magnolia jungles of wounded memory would illuminate, for me, a new way of writing theology.

Method

Lived theology begins with a modest proposal. How might theological writing, research, and teaching be expanded or reimagined so as to engage lived experience with maximum care and precision? How might the discipline of theology, in its method, style, and pedagogy, appear anew if narrated accounts of faith-formed lives were appropriated as essential building blocks of theological knowledge? Answers to—and explorations of—such questions form the narrative framework of the chapters that follow.[7]

In order to uncover the idea of lived theology as methodology, it might first be helpful to distinguish lived theology from other forms of scholarship concerned with religious practices and material culture. "Lived religion," as exemplified in a variety of insightful papers in David D. Hall's 1997 edited volume, *Lived Religion in America: Toward a History of Practices*, sought to understand the phenomenon of religion by focusing on religious practices in their historical and social contexts. The essays by Professor Hall and his fellow historians clustered around "an empiricist orientation to religion," with the confessional restraint of a social scientist.[8] As one of the authors explained, lived religion "points us to religion as it is shaped and experienced in . . . everyday experience."[9]

These insights are exceedingly helpful. Practices are inherently communicative, and, in the most basic sense, adhere to social settings and particular places. They are both communal *and* individual. We might add that practices, theologically framed, overflow sacred events and sacred spaces, churches and congregations, and religious actions and persons; that indeed all worldly phenomena, within the ontological sweep of creation and redemption, offer multistoried narratives of humanity's shared history with God, or in Barth's words, the history "which God wills to share with us."[10]

It is my conviction that such offerings constitute the unique mission of lived theology (although making sense of the social consequences of theological ideas has merit on its own). Lived religion examines practices, beliefs, and objects to understand more clearly the human phenomenon of religion, while lived theology examines practices, objects, and beliefs in order to understand God's presence in human experience.[11] This might be a good way to differentiate between the two endeavors.

The turn to religious practices via history and ethnography does not in itself produce modes of interpreting the theological field; theology, drawing on the wisdom of confessional, evangelical, and liberal expressions, focuses the perceptions needed to see experience against the horizon of the Triune God. As such, lived theology is an apt expression for the foregrounding of embodied particularity in theological narrative. Lived theology then pursues both a descriptive and an edifying purpose: namely, that of keeping narrative space open to the actions of God in experience, and understanding the social consequences of theological ideas. Because theological ideas aspire in their inner logic toward social expression, the theological interpretation of life should thus be properly and finally understood in a different light than that provided by social sciences or by theoretical discourses within the humanities (although sociological description and theory may supplement and complement the work of lived theology). Interpreting and narrating the lived experience of Christian persons and communities remains a genuinely theological task.

No more or less demanding than philosophical or systematic theology, lived theology is more curious, transgressing disciplinary boundaries as a matter of course, examining circumstance, context, and motivation and, like journalism and history, digging for the truth. Persistence such as this means marshalling every available resource for the sake of discerning God's presence and activity, giving them narrative shape. As many of the following chapters demonstrate (4, 6, 13, and 14), lived theology pushes even further beyond familiar disciplinary partnerships—theology and social theory, theology and ethnography, theology and anthropology—by making space for life-narratives, testimonials, observed experience, and biography in the theological enterprise.[12] Inviting faith's lived singularities into our teaching and research expands the range of academic theologies to include the idiosyncratic transactions and exchanges of lived faith as well as the wisdom, and the voices, of theological actors on the margins or outside of academe, of those who comprise the "church of the outcasts." "Christian faith is ineluctably grounded in random occurrences," Nicholas Lasch wrote in his seminal essay, "Doing Theology on Dover Beach."[13] Lived theology is therefore based on the rationale that the concrete forms of God's presence and action in the world promise rich and generative material for theological method, style, and pedagogy. Sifting through these varieties, forms, and spaces gives the chapters of this volume a thematic consistency.

"I am a victim of eclecticism," Martin Luther King, Jr., wrote in a paper at Crozer Seminary.[14] In his life and thought, King would "synthesize the best in liberal theology with the best in neo-orthodox theology." To speak of method in lived theology is to affirm the same. It is to apply theory in a piecemeal fashion, where it fits, deeming it useful "only if and when [it] illuminate[s] social reality." These are the words of Victor Turner, the anthropologist and distinguished UVA professor whose gift was demonstrating how it is less the researcher's ideas or her theoretical systems that illuminate, than the "flashes of insight taken out of systematic context and applied to scattered data."[15] Still, without interpretations there are no discernible facts, and if we proceed into the field (or into any text or set of ideas) without that awareness, "we are only moving bones from one coffin to another."[16] To accumulate facts without an awareness of theory runs the risk of substituting a rich web of reference and meaning with "putative common sense" and naïve objectivity.[17] Theory is necessary both to construct interpretation and to criticize constructions, but, as Clifford Geertz noted, it cleaves more closely to experience than "tends to be the case in sciences more able to give themselves over to imaginative abstraction."[18] Likewise, a number of the contributors to this volume write as participant-observers, seeking a "thick description"—a multisourced discernment, if you will—of God's presence and actions in the world. Always, however, our goal has been to follow the flow of discourse and actions, to rescue the "said" from "its perishing occasions."[19] Understanding the process is a peripheral, but sometimes necessary, task. For the intuitions, not the tissue of logic connecting them, are what tend to survive in the field, anticipating discovery.

The collaborative work represented herein begins and ends with a certain disciplined attention to the detail and complexity of worldly life. It is amid the diverse and complex interrelations of God's reality and the world that lived theology seeks to perform its task.[20] In this manner, doing lived theology helps adjudicate the perennial theory–practice conflict in its eclectic application of resources to the interpretive task. Our hope is to engage aspects of human experience resistant to theoretical formation, casting light on regions of experience that systematic or philosophical theologies often ignore (and sometimes distrust). Lived theology might then remind us that "the Yes and the Amen" inspires attunement to a deeper mundane, inviting theologians to a full immersion in the insights and exigencies of the field.[21]

A final point on method. The lack of a sense of place has quite often inhibited theology's narrative capabilities. Apropos of geographic influences on religious thought, Bonhoeffer would observe, in a letter written during his year as an assistant vicar in Barcelona, that his understanding of dogmatics and systematic theology had been "unsettled" by the strong impressions of Mediterranean culture. "It's difficult to process them all," he wrote, "but one has become inescapable: Barth could not have written in Spain." Even as a clear *Sitz im Leben* proved generative in Bonhoeffer's contextual approach to writing and teaching, so in our collaborations, the right questions and a sense of place inspired a framework within which on-the-ground decisions regarding the interactions of theory and method became surprisingly uncomplicated.[22] Absent a sense of place, we find ourselves lost in a no-man's land of concepts without footprints.

Style

I like to ask participants in our workgroups and seminars what books inspired their interest in theology. Karl Barth's *The Epistle to the Romans*, Gustavo Gutiérrez's *A Theology of Liberation*, and James Cone's *Black Theology and Black Power* are often cited. Other transformative works might include: Mary Daly's *Beyond God the Father*; Rosemary Ruether's *God-Talk*; Jürgen Moltmann's *Theology of Hope*; Friedrich Schleiermacher's *On Religion: Speeches to its Cultured Despisers*; Søren Kierkegaard's *Fear and Trembling*; Rudolf Otto's *The Idea of the Holy*; Walter Rauschenbusch's *Theology for the Social Gospel*; Howard Thurman's *Jesus and the Disinherited*; and Bonhoeffer's *The Cost of Discipleship*. Each of these books prompts an encounter with theology's power to convict, agitate, instruct, and edify. Certainly anyone who has read Barth's early work (I'm partial to *The Word of God and Word of Man*) knows something of the event-quality that energizes the best theological writing, sets language free, and approximates movement. This is theology that ventures the impossible task of drawing the bird in flight, theology mindful of "its power of awaking pleasure and provoking eager thoughts."[23] And these theological writers, despite what might seem irreconcilable differences, convey to the reader exceedingly more than reports on doctrine.[24] Theology, in its most vital and dynamic forms, should make you feel things.[25] "Algebra" and system have their place, but as Rowan Williams has written, theology ought to think of itself, first and foremost, as "a literary endeavour, as a way of talking," as a way of transfiguring language. Lived theology labors under "the secret heaviness of experience" where stories live their complete lives.[26]

Our hope and challenge is to catch the "light beams" that capture a person's and community's character, a sense of the whole and the parts, and of life with God under the constraints of time, history, and circumstance. Narrative representations of selves and others invite an infinite variety of possibilities. Still, the theologian, if not paralyzed by the question of God in the particular instance, must proceed "like the miner's canary" (as Virginia Woolf said of the biographer's task), "testing the atmosphere, detecting falsity, unreality, and the presence of obsolete conventions," hopeful that from all this variety will come, "not a riot of confusion, but a richer unity."[27]

Lived theology highlights the particularities of experience, narrates "lived life" (Moltmann) with God in its brilliance, depth, detail, and intensity, and affirms the wisdom and detail of these experiences as constitutive aspects of the theological enterprise.[28] It would presume, in its method, style, and pedagogy, that the patterns and practices of social existence are an essential part of faithful theology (and indeed, not just practices and patterns as a conceptual category, but individual narrated accounts of lived life). Our challenge, then, is to keep track of two distinct but interrelated tasks: a disciplined attention to the way theological commitments in their inner logic and integrity, extend toward action; and second, a reconsideration of theology as writing. Lived theology is an inescapably messy undertaking. Crafting a more direct and communicative rendering of the divine–human encounter requires us to place new demands on our discipline, even as it asks for patience with failure. Restoring the power of the individual encounter with God in the concrete situation and in its community to words, into language—this is the task and responsibility given to each generation of theologians, which cannot be abdicated by the fashions of the guild. On precision, discernment, and honesty depends—in a most important and yet I think underappreciated way—the trustworthiness of the narrated encounter of God. On precision, discernment, and honesty depends the trustworthiness of the theological writer, whether he or she is candid with the reader, or fudging truth in a polite deferral on worldly complexity. In the end, how sincere we truly are, how desperate and committed we are, will be demonstrated by how hard we are on our discipline, how willing we are to break with academic fashion when fashion mutes the polyphanies of life, how willing we are to be honest and accept difficulty.[29] The work must be done anew essentially from scratch, taking "the whole situation upon us in the fear of God," as Barth said, and in the fear of God to enter into the movement of the era.

If I might strike a doxological tone: lived theology emerges from the movements, transactions, and exchanges of the Spirit of God in human experience.

It might appear to some readers that the mission of lived theology hopes to return us in some measure to the narrative theology movement of an earlier decade; to those who turned their attention to "theology as narrative." Such theologians as Stephen Crites, Stanley Hauerwas, James McClendon, and Eberhard Jüngel convened, for a time, in the hope of "ensuring that those features of human history which are contra-indicative to highly generalized theories of human nature ... [would] not be forgotten."[30] The narrative theology movement approached the "sheer phenomenality of human history," with postliberal aspirations to concentrate theological grammar against the perceived threat of foundationalist hegemony, and to champion the particular as a "crucial conceptual category.[31] The Baptist theologian James McClendon, in his intriguing 1974 book *Biography as Theology*, implored theologians to acknowledge that "a theology of revelation or of reason, or a theology of secularity or of religiosity, if it does not enter into the actual shape of the lives of the people in its community of concern, is after all irrelevant to [our] lives."[32]

But narrative theology as a disciplinary impulse followed different trajectories and forged positions that were not readily compatible: toward meta-theological explorations, on the one hand, and toward homiletical edifications, on the other. Moreover, the movement's Anglo-American wing mollified Christianity's ontological convictions, which in turn diminished the seriousness of story. John Webster would later speak critically of narrative theology as a "fashionable theological ploy of dubious utility." It had proposed too simple a resolution of complex historical problems, evaded ontological description, and shirked questions about the truthfulness and rationality of faith.[33] John Milbank, a former colleague at UVA (whose lively exchange in December 2000 with sociologists of religion and faith-based activists in the seminar on "Lived Theology and Community Building" remains a happy memory), wrote in *Theology and Social Theory* that "the paradigmatic dimension of narrative"—God reconciling the world to himself in the event of Jesus—shows that an ontological questioning is "always already begun."[34] Narrative theology promised more than it delivered and produced precious few narratives. And in the end, its preference for discourses about narrativity over actual life narratives crushed the wild and crooked tree that characterizes the best theological writing. Appeal to story has never been enough, of course, as if theology might be quaintly transposed into artful testimony. Clarence Jordan, the Baptist minister and founder of the interracial agricultural cooperative called Koinonia Farms outside Americus, Georgia, used the phrase "God-Movement" to describe the new sociality of Christ. Lived theology is what one experiences, sees, and hears with the perceptions and from the perspective of the "God-Movement," which cuts through all other movements for human flourishing "as their hidden sense and motor, the movement of God's history."[35]

Every congregation and Christian community can be read and written as a theological text. In our work in particular, redemptive communities that exist alongside, in partnership with, or independent of church–institutions (that is, communities committed to housing, economic development, and the renewal of civic infrastructures) have offered stories that can be observed, reflected upon, and rendered into multilayered theological narratives. Chapters 2, 3, 7, 8, 12, and 13 consider grassroots communities that pray and read scripture together, work to ensure decent lives for their neighbors, and practice hospitality to strangers. In many respects, the future of any viable public theology lies in the wisdom of communities that "intentionally embody the habits, practices, and convictions of the peaceable reign of God in concrete localities"; communities that would embody "a Biblical counter-narrative of peace and plenty" and insinuate a more humane set of social practices in a brutal market-driven society.[36]

In my own experiences of trying to write lived theology, it has often been the case that early drafts included, in the body of the work, generous portions of analysis and interpretation, breaks for second-order reflection on the unfolding story. But inevitably the conflict between showing and telling arises, and I am reminded that (to put it indelicately) literary narrative interrupted by scholarly hiccups is not a pleasant sound. I might then try locating the analytical material in the footnotes, but such measures, in excess, produce distractions of their own. So I lumber on, trying hard *to show*, even though academic instincts say *tell*, until I begin to experience the calming of theoretical aspirations, which, only then, enables story. Chapters 6 and 10 directly address these challenges of writing lived theology.

Pedagogy

About every other year I teach a course called "The Kingdom of God in America." Though the course is pitched in the academic catalog as a study of religion and social movements in America, it has become an introduction of sorts to lived theology. KOGA—the feral acronym coined by a popular teaching assistant—invites one hundred undergraduates to explore how theological commitments shape the church's relationship to the social order. We study the interactions of doctrine and social existence and ask how modern European theologies influence the American search for "beloved community." Though the historical focus of the semester remains the American civil rights movement (1955–1968), we make time for the countercultural movements of the late 1960s—with Joan Didion, Michelangelo Antonioni, Helmut Thieliecke, and Richard Rorty as our guides—as well as the faith-based community-development movement of the post-civil rights decades (with John Perkins's *Quiet Revolution* as our guide).

Throughout the semester and twice-weekly lectures, I highlight the theological sources of human-rights campaigns in modern American history. We unearth theological treasures in the freedom struggles and in their participants and actions—from the Social Gospel to the resurgence of progressive community organizing. Such characters, actions, and events, we learn, comprise "texts" brimming with insight and wisdom, and present difficult questions about the confounding and complex behavior of theological ideas. In our readings, discussions, and conversations, we discover that the religious genius of the civil rights movement was its ability to ground the pursuit of redemptive community in an ontology of reconciliation; its originating theological commitments expanded the vistas of social hope and inspired robust and transformative civic engagement.

One of the SNCC's most eloquent church-based leaders was the business owner from Hattiesburg, Mississippi, named Victoria Gray Adams. Until her death in August 2006, Mrs. Adams, who served as a Methodist chaplain at Virginia State University in Petersburg, often graced our classroom at UVA; and she never failed to conjure, in testimony and song, in theological reflection and philosophical rumination, in a manner that was direct, palpable, and unforgettable, the spirit of the freedom movement. She recounted her first step into a civil rights life during a church service one night in Hattiesburg, at the conclusion of which she prayed silently, "Here am I, Lord, send me. I'll go." She said she always understood the movement as "a journey toward the kingdom of God." SNCC's founding mothers and fathers, like Mrs. Adams, were quite often radical Christians whose exuberant witness was motivated by diverse theological backgrounds, while keenly attuned to the needs of the concrete situation. "What happened back there in the 1960s with ordinary people, "Adams said, "could not have happened without an understanding of ourselves as spirit-people."[37] If SCLC assumed a professional and preacherly role in mobilizing disenfranchised African Americans for power, SNCC (no less animated by religious convictions) sought to embody what might be called an incarnational ethic in its preference for grassroots organizing among the poor. "Our goal was to reconcile," the activist Diane Nash said, "to create a 'community recovered or fulfilled,' rather than simply gain power over the opposition."[38]

In class, we look at the disciplines of voter registration, political organizing, and community building, at the exquisite varieties of civil courage, and at the energies and convictions of the worshipping communities that sustained them. Reading primary sources, we analyze the consequences of SNCC's resolve, in late 1965 and 1966, to distance its work from the churches, and finally to repudiate Christian conviction. It's true that Anglo-American theologians have been reluctant to treat race as a theological category, even when they have occasionally spoken of racial matters; but it might also be observed that African American theologians have been reluctant to engage the civil rights movement (in all its beauty and chaos) as a reservoir of theological meanings, even when speaking of the civil rights movement, its leaders, and their convictions.

The interpretative task particular to our work in KOGA involves understanding the specific details of religious convictions in their inner-logic and their dynamic particularity, appropriating the movement as a rich source of theological wisdom, and applying our skills in understanding the uses and misuses of God-language in the flow of events. It is difficult to be a Christian without a living example, Bonhoeffer wrote in his late "Outline for a Book." The "church for others," he said, looking beyond the ruins of the German Church, will not only need to "confront the vices of hubris, the worship of power, envy, and delusion as the roots of all evil," affirming the qualities of moderation, authenticity, trust, faithfulness, steadfastness, patience, discipline, humility, modesty, and contentment; the Church will need to make certain it never underestimates "the significance of the human example," whose origin lies in "the humanity of Jesus."[39] "[I]t is not the religious formula, the dogma, that constitutes the church, but the practical doing of what is commanded."[40] Faith gathers authenticity not through intellectual concepts, but by the exemplification of witness. To wit, in chapters 11 and 12, the reader is shown how teaching courses in lived theology enriches the moral imagination and brings into the classroom a more varied cast of theological thinkers and practitioners than would otherwise people the academic canon. A robust humanism and vivid realism frame the stories of those who "refuse to remain spectators of the panorama of injustice."[41]

Conclusion

In trying to set forth a rationale for the distinctive mission of lived theology, I realize that my observations may at times seem reductionist. Such a criticism might be formulated as follows: if enacted and embodied faith is privileged in theological method, style, and pedagogy, and thus theology is left without a grammar of its own, and dependent on, if not parasitic on, extrinsic realities, theology, in turn, is reduced to speaking of God by speaking of social practices in a loud voice. But I think the criticism betrays a failure of nerve—and, one might add, a weak view of the righteousness and mystery of God. In any case, lived theology's attention to the singularities of experience—to doctrine's multistoried expressions in social existence—should not be mistaken as a correlationist methodology or any other approach that would seek to understand the being of God on the basis of some mode or modulation of human experience. Our aim, rather, is to conciliate confessional and liberal convictions around the patterns and practices of lived experience, and thus to inspire an ever-widening ecumenism that at once animates and is animated by faith's redemptive practices. Lived theology seeks to bring to light all that we learn as scholars and practitioners when, as Lasch says, "we attend, calmly and fearlessly, to the actual complexity, obscurity and intractability of our circumstances".[42]

If theologians intend to welcome the voices of ordinary women and men, of everyday saints and sinners, into our peculiar but marvelously capacious discipline, not as categories of "alterity" or "difference," but as crafters of story, style, and teaching, then it will be necessary to ensure that the names of Victoria Gray Adams, Fannie Lou Hamer, Howard Kester, Will Campbell, Ella Baker, Clarence Jordan, Howard Kester, and Yuri Kochiyama are as familiar as Jean-Yves Lacoste, Giles Deluze, Michel Foucault, Jacques Derrida and Slavoj Žižek; that we know as much about the Delta Cooperative Farm as Finkenwalde; as much about the Southern Tenants Farmworkers Union and all those who people Anthony Dunbar's forgotten treasure, *Against the Grain: Southern Radicals and Prophets, 1929–1959* as the Inklings or signers of the Barmen Declaration. "In the absence of demonstrable agents and agencies of social change," Herbert Marcuse wrote in *One Dimesional Man*, published in the winter of 1964, "the critique is thrown back to a high level of abstraction."[43] The German émigré might have paid more attention to the Great Refusal playing daily in the Southern theater.

What we strive for in this volume, finally, is a widening of the lens of the theological imagination to include, as agents of constructive theology, the enacted confessions and commitments of Christian persons and communities. It is not doctrine in abstraction but under the impressions of place, time, and circumstance that form Christian thought and practice. It bears restating that exercise of imaginative energy required of lived theology is strenuous; but measuring theological truth claims alongside faith's social expressions helps strip academic and church theology of its dreamy deracinations. To do lived theology is to accept the finitude, fallibility, and fragmentariness of life situations as the condition of all redemptive research, writing and teaching.

Dare we hope that the lived theologies flourishing in North America, and throughout the global, ecumenical church, might invigorate and reshape the theological vocation in the uncertain years ahead? It is surely my hope that interpreting lived experience from a "higher satisfaction" will not only produce vivid narratives, but also offer encouragement to theologians, students, and theologically engaged scholars to turn our hearts and minds outward, toward the teeming world of history, as listeners to and doers of the Word, reminding us why we decided to pursue the peculiar science of God in the first place.

"Are we still of any use?" Dietrich Bonhoeffer once asked of Christian leaders and theologians like himself. "What we shall need is not geniuses, or cynics, or misanthropes, or clever tacticians, but plain, honest, straightforward [persons]. Will our inward power of resistance be strong enough, and our honesty with ourselves remorseless enough, for us to find our way back to simplicity and straightforwardness?" By creating space in language, and by organizing spaces of conversation and exchange in and outside the academy, lived theology welcomes to the table both friend and stranger.

I realize that these introductory remarks may have appeared at times declaratory in tone, if not sermonic, and that I've promised many things under the banner of lived theology—certainly more than can be delivered in a collection of essays. But I trust that the reader who has hacked her or his way through the dense vegetation of these opening pages will see that the uncommonly generative exchanges in which I have been privileged to take part as director of the Project on Lived Theology, and which are taking place more frequently throughout the guild, both in tandem with our work and for reasons related to a generational hunger, offer perspectives on theological method, style, and pedagogy worth taking seriously. It might be enough for me if this volume accomplishes nothing more than to reassure readers that theology can always be more engaged, vivid, and inspiring than its prevailing guardians allow and with such reassurance, turn our sights to the "wild presence" of God in ordinary and unfamiliar places.[44]

(The author wishes to thank Kristopher Norris, doctoral candidate in religion and ethics at UVA, for his helpful suggestions in early draft stages of this essay, and to Shea Tuttle, my colleague at the Project on Lived Theology, for her sharp editorial insights on the final drafts.)

Notes

1. Dietrich Bonhoeffer, *Letters and Papers from Prison*, ed. Eberhard Bethge (New York: Macmillan, 1972), 358.
2. Dietrich Bonhoeffer, *The Way of Freedom: Letters, Lectures and Notes, 1935–39*, ed. Edwin H. Robertson, trans. Edwin H. Robertson and John Bowden (London: Collins, 1996), 30.

3. Luis M. Bermejo, S. J. "Introduction," in *The Spirit of Life: The Holy Spirit in the Life of the Christian* (Chicago: Loyola University Press, 1989).

4. Charles Marsh, "Preface to the 2008 Edition," in *God's Long Summer: Stories of Faith and Civil Rights* (Princeton, NJ: Princeton University Press, 2008), xii–xiii.

5. See Jürgen Moltmann, *The Spirit of Life: A Universal Affirmation*, transla Margaret Kohl (Minneapolis: Fortress Press, 1994), 10ff.

6. Dietrich Bonhoeffer, "After 10 Years," in *Letters and Papers from Prison*, Dietrich Bonhoeffer Works vol. 8, ed. John de Gruchy (Minneapolis: Fortress Press, 2010), 52.

7. These questions also animate the research programs and collaborations of the Project on Lived Theology at the University of Virginia.

8. Robert Orsi, "Everyday Miracles," in *Lived Religion in America: Toward a History of Practice*, ed. David D. Hall (Princeton, NJ: Princeton University Press, 1997), 8.

9. Orsi, "Everyday Miracles," 8–9.

10. Barth, *Church Dogmatics*, IV/1, 7.

11. I am grateful to Ainsley Quiros for clarifying this distinction in the introduction to her doctoral dissertation, " 'God's on our Side, Today': Lived Theology in the Civil Rights Movement in Americus, Georgia, 1942–1976" (Vanderbilt University, 2014).

12. Lived Theology shares many of the concerns and some of the same conversation partners as those assembled by Pete Ward in *Perspectives on Ecclesiology and Ethnography*. Ward's work—and that of his colleagues editing the Studies in Ecclesiology and Ethnography series—has a narrower interdisciplinary focus than Lived Theology. Specifically it concentrates on "ethnographic and qualitative research" (2) and on bridging the gap between this "empirical [research] and theological analysis of the church within Religious Studies, Systematic Theology, and Practical Theology" (i).

13. Nicholas Lasch, *Theology on Dover Beach* (Eugene, OR: Wipf and Stock, originally published by Darton, Longman and Todd, 1979), 21.

14. Martin Luther King, Jr., "How Modern Christians Should Think of Men," in *Martin Luther King, Jr. Papers*, Volume 1 (Berkley: University of California Press: 1992), 278.

15. Ted Smith, "Eschatological Memories of Everyday Life," see Chapter 1.

16. This is Wayne Meeks's wry observation in his book *The First Urban Christians*. Wayne A. Meeks, *The First Urban Christians: The Social World of the Apostle Paul*, 2d ed. (New Haven, CT: Yale University Press, 2003), 5.

17. Meeks, *The First Urban Christians*, 5.

18. Clifford Geertz, *The Interpretation of Cultures: Selected Essays* (New York: Basic Books, 1973), 24.

19. Geertz, *The Interpretation of Cultures*, 20.

20. Michael Welker, *God the Spirit*, trans. John F. Hoffmeyer (Minneapolis: Fortress Press, 1994), x.

21. Henry James, "The Element of Order and Harmony as Symbol (1902)," in *Theory of Fiction: Henry James*, ed. James E. Miller (Lincoln: University of Nebraska Press, 1972), 281.

22. Not included in this volume, but everywhere present in the first decade of UVA's intiative, is the remarkable work of Mark Gornik, founder and president of City Seminary in Harlem, whose books *To Live in Peace* and *Word Made Global* are seminal volumes in an emerging lived theology canon.

23. Douglas Horton, "Translator's Note," in *Das Wort Gottes und die Theologie*, Karl trans. Douglas Horton ([1928] Grand Rapids, Michigan: Zondervan Publishing House, 1935).

24. In 1935, the Roman Catholic novelist Graham Greene, a writer with a razor-sharp eye for mystery, made a feverish trek across the Liberian interior. He had no clearer grasp of his intentions at the end than when he began—except that in England he had been bored to the point of suicide. His record of these travels, *A Journey without Maps*, is a flawed, vexing, cautionary tale for writers; for we see how the flaws and the failures, and the chronicles of hardship, tedium, and breakthrough, are sometimes the only story we get.

25. Todd Breyfogle, "Time and Transformation: A Conversation with Rowan Williams," *Cross Currents* 45 (Fall 1995): 293–311.

26. Karl Barth, *The Word of God and the Word of Man*, 283–85.

27. Virginia Woolf, *The Death of the Moth and Other Essays* (London: Harcourt Brace, 1942), 195.

28. Jürgen Moltmann, *The Spirit of Life: A Universal Affirmation*, trans. Margaret Kohl (Minneapolis: Fotress Press, 2001), 183. Robert P. Scharlemann, Unpublished Lectures on Modern Theology, University of Virginia, 1984.

29. I am indebted to Jorie Graham's remarks on contemporary poetry. See her "Introduction," *Best American Poetry 1990*, ed. Jorie Graham and David Lehman (New York: Scribner, 1990), xxxxviii.

30. Patricia Hampl, *I Could Tell You Stories: Sojourns in the Land of Memory* (New York: Norton, 2000), 20.

31. L. Gregory Jones and Stanley Hauerwas, "Introduction," in *Why Narrative: Readings in Narrative Theology*, eds. Jones and Hauerwas (Grand Rapids: Eerdmans, 1990) 5; Hampl, *I Could Tell You Stories*, 20.

32. James Wm. McClendon, *Biography as Theology: How Life Stories Can Remake Today's Theology* (Eugene, OR: Wipf and Stock, 2002), 21.

33. John Bainbridge Webster, *Eberhard Jüngel: An Introduction to His Theology* (Cambridge: Cambridge University Press, 1991), 16.

34. John Milbank, *Theology and Social Theory: Beyond Secular Reason* (Oxford: Blackwell, 1990), 390. See also "Theology and Social Theory and Its Significance for Community Building," http://www.livedtheology.org/resources/theology-and-social-theory-and-its-significance-for-community-building-a-conversation-with-john-milbank/.

35. Barth, *The Word of God and the Word of Man*.

36. Mark Gornik, *Participant Reflections of the Conference on Lived Theology and Civil Courage* (Charlottesville, VA: Project on Lived Theology, 2003).

37. Victoria Gray Adams, Interview with the Author.

38. Diane Nash cited in *A Circle of Trust: Remembering SNCC,* ed. Cherly Lynn Greenberg (New Brunswick, NJ: Rutgers University Press, 1998), 18–19.

39. Bonhoeffer, "Outline for a Book," *Letters and Papers from Prison,* 561.

40. Bonhoeffer, *Letters and Papers from Prison,* 504.

41. Christopher Rowland, *Radical Christianity: A Reading of Recovery* (Cambridge, UK: Polity Press, 1988), 161.

42. Nicholas Lasch, "Criticism or Construction: The Task of the Theologian," in *Theology on the Way to Emmaus* (London: SCM Press, 1986), 15.

43. Herbert Marcuse, One-Dimensional Man: Studies in the Ideology of Advanced Industrial Society (Boston: Beacon Press, 1964), xliv.

44. Stanley Hauerwas, *The Hauerwas Reader* (Durham, NC: Duke University Press), 382.

Part One

Lived Theology as Method

I

Eschatological Memories of Everyday Life

Ted A. Smith

WHEN PREACHERS PUBLISHED sermons in the nineteenth century, they often included a note that made it clear that others had taken the initiative to move the sermon from oral to written form. Sometimes the title page simply contained an indication that the sermon had been "published by request of the church." And sometimes preachers felt the need for more elaborate backstories. In the frontmatter to the published version of a sermon preached against the Fugitive Slave Law in 1850, Charles Beecher of Newark included the text of his correspondence with those he claimed had requested publication. "DEAR SIR," three parishioners wrote. "At a meeting of the members of the Free Presbyterian Church of this city, the undersigned were appointed a Committee, to request a copy of your Sermon on the Fugitive Slave Law, delivered in said Church on Sabbath evening last." "DEAR BRETHREN," Beecher replied, "I have not been able earlier to prepare my manuscripts for the press. They are now at your service; and if their publication can in in any degree influence public sentiment in favor of truth and righteousness, I shall rejoice."[1]

Prefatory notes like these presented the preacher as a humble servant responding to the demands of a congregation, rather than an ambitious agent eager to be heard. They also legitimated the sermons as something more than the scribblings of one person. The veil offered by such notes was thin then, and it is even more threadbare now. I will not try to cover my vices with such a preface. But I will say that the present chapter began as a spoken lecture at the 2013 Spring Institute for Lived Theology at the

University of Virginia. Its first life was oral; it arose in response to an invitation by Charles Marsh to talk about *The New Measures,* a book I had written some years before. And it came after incandescent lectures by Traci C. West and Willie James Jennings. I have not tried to squeeze all of this specificity out of the text, for I think these origins matter, especially for a book on lived theology.

The Shelters of Indirection

In writing *The New Measures,* I made a series of choices to present it as something of a finished object.[2] I tried to focus on stories about the practices associated with the revivals of the 1820s, 1830s and 1840s. I chose to present these stories without a constant, running commentary on why I wrote them in the ways that I did, and what I hoped they might do. This included a decision not to bog the stories down with complete accounts of their origins. I discuss the academic origins of the project only briefly. There is something like a method chapter. There are signposts to academic conversations in the notes. There is a base of reading in history, theology, and social theory that I hope is there for those with eyes to see. In the book I try to address Christian theologians, ethicists, and preachers interested in questions that can be gathered together under the sign of "modernity." But I tried to keep even these more academic conversations in a secondary role. I wanted the stories to do their own kind of work.

If the academic origins of the book are in the background, the deepest origins are almost entirely submerged. Those deepest origins are in my years as a pastor in two small-membership congregations in rural New York State. The lives of those communities peek through in many places. The book is dedicated to those congregations, for they gave the most to make it possible. And it considers the ancestors of the people in those congregations: those great-grandchildren of Puritans who trembled on anxious benches in Buffalo; worked for women's rights at Seneca Falls; flocked to hear Frederick Douglass in Rochester; and pulled up stakes to move to Ohio. In the book I try to tell stories that get very close to that burned-over ground, stories of what people wore and how they moved their hands and what they read and how they made a living and who sat next to them in worship. This is a description of lived theology, but it is a description—not the thing itself—and it is a description of the lived theology of other people. If those others are the ancestors of the people I worked with in upstate New York, and if they left legacies that have shaped the lives of many of us, for better and worse, they are still at one remove from both me as the author and any potential reader of the book. That remove is defined not by the years that have passed, but by the writing of history, for to write about people historically is to locate them in a time that is not our own. It is to create a gulf between us, and to figure that gulf as temporal.[3] The book does that kind of work. It tells a *history* of lived theology.

I hope there is also something more. I hope the book is animated by theological traces that live more fully in the present tense. These traces do not do their work in the same way that the historical writing does. They are not descriptions of facts about God, the meaning of history, or the nature of hope. They do their work not by description, but by performance. And because they work in a different register, they can live in the same sentences that are doing the work of historical description.

The decision to do living theology in this layered and indirect way has produced mixed results. It led to a book that is sometimes too vague to indicate the conversations I wanted to engage and too allusive to make precise contributions. But the indirectness of the living theology in the book is not—as one of the more conservative members of the New York congregations might have said—because I was *ashamed* of the Gospel. The indirectness arose, rather, from a sense of the *demands* of the Christian Gospel, which I take first of all to involve speaking of a God who enters history fully without ever becoming simply identical to mundane historical realities. Speaking of this Gospel strains the limits of our language, for Christian theologians cannot say all that we need to say through doctrinal speech that hovers above history any more than we can through strictly empirical speech that blocks any references beyond a history defined within an immanent frame. Simply combining doctrinal and historical registers results in the worst kind of historical fundamentalism. More truthful lived theology requires some indirectness, I think. It pushes us to rely on gestures, gaps, silences, and stories that exceed the points they are designed to illustrate. Pressed to such indirection, I did not try in *The New Measures* to describe the theology I learned from and with the congregations in Weston and Dundee. Rather, I tried to perform it. And my hope is that this performance lets it avoid reduction to a discrete object of knowledge and serve instead as a mood, a taste, a scent that infuses the whole book.

Walter Benjamin described something like this in his famous description of theology as like the hunchbacked dwarf who hides inside the robot—the automaton—of historical materialism:

> There was once, we know, an automaton constructed in such a way that it could respond to every move by a chess player with a countermove that would ensure the winning of the game. A puppet wearing Turkish attire and with a hookah in its mouth sat before a chessboard placed on a large table. A system of mirrors created the illusion that this table was transparent on all sides. Actually, a hunchbacked dwarf—a master at chess—sat inside and guided the puppet's hand by means of strings. One can imagine a philosophic counterpart to this apparatus. The puppet, called 'historical materialism,' is to win all the time. It can easily be a match for anyone if it enlists the services of theology, which today, as we know, is small and ugly and has to keep out of sight.[4]

If theology is small and ugly and has to keep out of sight, *lived* theology—scandalously, gloriously particular—must keep hidden all the more. It needs the shelter of a little indirection because, as Charles Marsh has said, it is *real*. That reality can produce discomfort. Academics in the theological fields seem to have developed a certain tolerance for abstract talk about God. We have learned how to sit through conference papers on doctrines that describe God engaging a "history" that never seems to have a date or a place attached to it. We have also become comfortable with genres of history and sociology that offer thick descriptions of the world as if God had nothing to do with it. But when those lines get crossed—when someone says something theological about the world we usually describe in empirical terms, something like, "God blessed this town through the dying of this church"—we (or at least I) don't quite know what to say. We have room for idealist theology and materialist history or sociology. But we do not have conventions for relating the two. And so lived theology can be alarming. A little indirection helps us bear it long enough to take it in.

If we need to be protected from lived theology, it also needs to be protected from us. It is as fragile as it is powerful. It can be co-opted almost immediately into the genres of sermon illustration, where every story makes a point; or tell-all memoir, where the author becomes the real subject; or uplifting biography, where an exemplary person overcomes trials to bring in the Reign of God; or what I call enchanted positivism, a kind of fundamentalist historicism in which events are presented as if they were simply identical to some good, or God, beyond them. Indirection has vices of its own; I have known many of them firsthand. And there are no genres that cannot be co-opted. But a little indirection can shelter lived theology long enough to let it do some of the work that it can do.

Seeing the value of this shelter, my hope in speaking more directly about the origins of *The New Measures* is not to shatter all the mirrors that hide the life inside the automaton, but to turn them just enough to offer a fresh angle of vision. I hope to make possible a perspective in which the connections between the life of a community and the writing of a professor become visible, a perspective that gives a glimpse of the living hand that makes the move.

The Church that Has No Brand

I served as pastor of the Presbyterian congregations in Weston and Dundee, New York, from 1995 to 1999. When I arrived, Dundee was a town of about 1,500 people in a county of about 25,000. The Dundee church had about seventy members and memories of better days with better pastors. Most of its members came from the more stable and prosperous families in the community. They worked as educators, insurance agents, state agricultural extension officers, UPS drivers, retired missionaries, administrative staff, and farmers who held title to the land they worked. Weston was located about twelve miles away at an unincorporated crossroads in a beautiful corner of one of the poorest counties in New York State. The Weston congregation was small but durable, with about forty members on the books, a larger extended church family, and a history that reached back before the Civil War. Weston's members included an interesting mix of folks—administrative assistants, farmworkers, health professionals, engineers who commuted to Corning, people living with long-term disabilities that kept them out of the formal economy, retirees, and more. Both congregations were mostly but not only white, like the communities in which they were located.

Weston and Dundee were far away from any theological school. But this is not the story of some pure "other" to the academy. Learning of many kinds permeated both congregations. And, as one who had never had a full-time job beyond being a student, I inevitably brought the academy with me. I came to the congregations formed especially by undergraduate courses with Elizabeth Clark, who got me thinking about the gendered powers sedimented into theological language, and Stanley Hauerwas, who got me thinking about the church as a distinctly Christian counterculture. At Oxford, Sarah Coakley pointed me toward W. H. Vanstone, whose theological memoirs of ministry taught me the shape of a hope that can live in situations where progress feels out of reach. At Princeton Seminary, a seminar with Jeffrey Stout and Cornel West helped me see how religious traditions might be connected to commitments to radical democracy. Work with the Industrial Areas Foundation in Trenton, New Jersey, helped me understand what it took to make lasting change. And reading Clarence Jordan and Wendell Berry helped me understand the distinct challenges and possibilities for churches in rural areas. I brought all of this good baggage (and a lot more) with me to Dundee and Weston. I hoped to work with the people there to create a proudly rural, radically democratic, gender-conscious, deeply pious Christian counter-culture—a church!—that would work for and bear witness to God's redeeming work in the world.

Of course we fell short of that ideal. The congregations grew by all the numbers that denominations measure. They grew in members and money and mission programs and quantifiable busy-ness. And we had many bright moments. But we were not the Beloved Community. Sometimes this was due to what I think of as ordinary, run-of-the mill sins, like my own lack of courage, attachment to privilege, and simple inability to see what needed to be done. If we had all been a little better, we could have moved a little closer to the goal. But sometimes we could not have done better. Sometimes the enduring obstacles were simply manifestations of finitude. Working with a small budget in a region with many needs forces hard choices. Some grievous wounds go untended as others get treated. But in these situations I could still imagine that—if we only had the time, and the resources, and the people—we might have done a little better.

I had expected such everyday sin and finitude. But there was another deeper and more stubborn failing that surprised me. These were moments when reality was curved in such a way that doing better only would have made things worse. One searing example came when the denomination was offering resources to help us polish up our brand as a congregation. I was talking—probably ranting, really—to some members about the ways in which market logics penetrate every corner of life, and how we needed to resist this, and how we were not a brand but a church. And one teenager said something like, "Yeah, that's right. We don't have a brand. We're the church for people who don't like brands. That's *our* brand. That's cool." He was right, of course. In a culture of Che t-shirts, designer Chuck Taylors, tenured radicals, and nose rings for everybody, there are few things more deeply assimilated to this culture than the desire to be countercultural. It is not like the church could escape that fact by being a little more truly counter to the culture. This is not an everyday failing. And it is not, I think, a condition of finitude. I can only think of it in terms of fall.

Sin, finitude, and fall. We—I—fell short of radically democratic Christian counterculture in an endless variety of ways. And yet I had an unshakable sense that God was at work in the lives of those congregations. I believe this was true not just in whatever parts of our lives might have been least touched by finitude and fall, but exactly in those parts that were most deeply distressed. I came to think that God was at work in our life together in and in spite of these failings. The conjunction is key: redemption happened *in and in spite of* us, like a power made perfect in weakness. As a character in Marilynne Robinson's *Gilead* says, "That's the pulpit speaking. But it's the truth."[5]

The Temptations of Lived Theology

I started doctoral work with a conviction of that truth, but not with words to name it. I also started with a bunch of more properly academic questions. Those questions had been formed especially by what Frederic Jameson has called a "turn to culture." That turn has taken many different forms: pragmatist, postliberal, liberationist, phenomenological, and more. What these turns share is the sense that there is no view from nowhere, that every view is from somewhere, and that that somewhere can best be described as a "culture." If one starts with assumptions like these, then cultural studies of various kinds become necessary. Under the sign of this turn to culture, biblical scholars might turn to the history of interpretation, even as theologians and ethicists turn to ethnography. Someone interested in religion and modernity might write a history of revival practice. A person might even begin life as a philosophical theologian and then find himself driving south, as Charles Marsh did, with a microcassette recorder and a desire to do fieldwork.[6]

In *The New Measures* I consider two of the strongest turns to culture that I know, two turns to culture that have done much to define the field for scholars of my generation: the turn of Delores Williams and that of Stanley Hauerwas. Both Hauerwas—in *With the Grain of the Universe*—and Williams—in *Sisters in the Wilderness*—denounce universal principles that claim to transcend any particularity. Both insist that we need, instead, to turn to some particular culture that stands counter to the dominant culture: for Williams, the community of African American women; for Hauerwas, what he calls simply "the church." They turn to these cultures which embody norms that enable critique of a dominant culture. The trouble is, the cultures don't do the work they are supposed to do. They do not necessarily display the promised critical virtues. And they too often display the very vices they are supposed to criticize. And so both Williams and Hauerwas introduce criteria that will define what should *really* count as part of the relevant culture. They introduce critical principles of selection, bundles of qualities that can mark the true version of the culture to which they made appeal. They both call a counterculture into being by starting with ideals and then using those ideals to select and gather disparate cultural facts into a true and normative church. I argue in the book that, "in each case the critic's initial ideals, 'realized' in the culture of the critic's making, disappeared and then reappeared with new authority. The cultural elements attained authority through a tautological magic: ideals defined cultural practices that then embodied ideals."[7]

I think Hauerwas and Williams display both the difficulty and the temptations of lived theology. They display the deepest difficulty: we turn to culture seeking norms, but then the culture lets us down. The people don't believe what we need them to believe. The history does not prove our point. And so we are tempted to refashion our account of what we take to be real to get it to do the work we need it to do. Williams and Hauerwas offer one very sophisticated version of this kind of move, using a norm to define the culture that can then successfully ground the norm.

There are many variations on this theme. Consider the examples of two thinkers who worked in the wake of the historicism that pervaded central European intellectual culture after Hegel. That historicism shared many features with the present turn to culture, and we can learn from the ways that it played out. Ernst Troeltsch, for example, tried to do theology and ethics by telling the history of the church. But he found that the facts alone could not always do the work he needed them to do. And so, responding to Adolf von Harnack, he described an "essence" of Christianity that could give his historical narratives purpose and direction. The essence helped Troeltsch move from historical descriptions to normative claims. It also helped secure the nature of the claims that could be made. But the subjective, constructed quality of the essence undermined whatever power the history might have had to authorize the claims.[8] Vladimir Lenin, working another branch of this same Hegelian tree, experienced a different version of this problem. Nineteenth-century Marxism had made something like a turn to culture in casting the proletariat as the subject of history, but the actually existing proletariat had been disappointing in this role. And so Lenin proposed to define what he called a "vanguard" of the proletariat that, like a true church, could do the work he needed it to do. The turn was still to history, still to an actually existing body. But this body was not so much found as made by the very norms that it was supposed to justify.[9]

The temptations of tautology are constant companions of lived theology. They are the temptations that arise when we want to move between fact and norm. We know the norms we want, or at least those we don't want, and so we're tempted to find a way to adjust the facts so that they do the work we need them to do. But moves like these give up the fundamental insight of lived theology. For when we select the facts so that they support our norms, we substitute our account of the real for the real itself, often without much self-consciousness. Good lived theology might offer *more* than just the facts. But it must never offer less.

Eschatological Memories

Lived theology makes some kind of empirical studies part of the repertoire of every theologian and ethicist. It also displaces epistemology, at least as conceived in Anglo-American philosophy, as the fundamental discourse of method. In place of questions about how the solitary subject knows what she knows, lived theology forces us to ask how we can move from fact to norm, from history to theology. And so the theology of history becomes a kind of first philosophy. This has been obscured, I think, as those of us with normative interests have been learning how to do responsible work of description. Our conversations have focused on getting the methods of history and ethnography right on their own terms. This focus may have helped us do the work that has been most necessary at this moment. But the bigger and more difficult questions—about how our best descriptions can be involved in anything like theological or ethical claims—have received less attention. These are the questions of the theology of history.

Walter Benjamin and Theodor Adorno have been especially helpful to me in trying to ask these questions with more precision and answer them as best I can. And this is not a coincidence. They worked as heirs to the nineteenth-century turn to culture I described above. Indeed, Benjamin and Adorno worked out some of their core ideas in a seminar on Troletsch led by Gottfried Salomon-Delatour in the summer of 1923.[10] But they worked in a time when history was in the process of discrediting itself, and absolutely. It was not just that the proletariat had failed to play its appointed role; it was that the vanguard had become a wolf to its own people and ideas. And the bourgeois traditions of someone like Troeltsch were joining the death squads or dying without much effective resistance, material or ideal. There was no good history to which to turn—and yet they turned to history, for they refused to trust ideas that claimed to hover above lived, material realities.

That double-bind—of believing that all thinking was historically conditioned, and then realizing that history had become catastrophe—practically defines these two. And it is why I think they are especially helpful in teaching us how to avoid idealizing cultures that are less obviously pathological.

I want to compare two famous passages from these two thinkers to show how they coped with these realities. I'll quote them at some length. First, consider Adorno's luminous paragraph from the end of *Minima Moralia:*

> The only philosophy which can be responsibly practiced in the face of despair is the attempt to contemplate all things as they would present themselves from the standpoint of redemption. Knowledge has no light but that shed on the world by redemption: all else is reconstruction, mere technique. Perspectives must be fashioned that displace and estrange the world, reveal it to be, with its rifts and crevices, as indigent and distorted as it will one day appear in the messianic light. To gain such perspectives without velleity or violence, entirely from felt contact with its objects—this alone is the task of thought. It is the simplest of all things, because the situation calls imperatively for such knowledge, indeed because consummate negativity, once squarely faced, delineates the mirror-image of its opposite. But it is also the utterly impossible thing, because it presupposes a standpoint removed, even though by a hair's breadth, from the scope of existence, whereas we well know that any possible knowledge must not only be first wrest from what is, if it shall hold good, but is is also marked, for this very reason, by the same indigence which it seeks to escape. The more passionately thought denies its conditionality for the sake of the unconditional, the more unconsciously, and so calamitously, it is delivered up to the world. Even its own impossibility it must at last comprehend for the sake of the possible. But beside

the demand thus placed on thought, the question of the reality or unreality of redemption itself hardly matters.[11]

This paragraph is familiar to many. What I want to do, though, is to read it into this conversation about a turn to culture and lived theology.

> Perspectives must be fashioned that displace and estrange the world, reveal it to be, with its rifts and crevices, as indigent and distorted as it will one day appear in the messianic light. To gain such perspectives without velleity or violence, entirely from felt contact with its objects—this alone is the task of thought.

Here's the move like what I have been calling the turn to culture. It comes in a call to work "without velleity or violence," as passively as possible, from "felt contact" with the objects of thought. This, Adorno writes, is "the simplest of all things." And then he gives the theology of history that informs his view, the vision for how he will move from fact to norm: "consummate negativity, once squarely faced, delineates the mirror-image of its opposite." One might call this a negative lived theology, a theology that does not so much negate history as discern the negation that has already happened in history. That "consummate negativity" testifies to its opposite.

The problem, Adorno writes, is that this is impossible. For even seeing this testimony for what it is requires a measure of separation from "the indigence" we are trying to escape. It requires forgetting that we, too, are immersed in that which we are trying to critique.

> The more passionately thought denies its conditionality for the sake of the unconditional, the more unconsciously, and so calamitously, it is delivered up to the world.

Or: the more we insist that we are part of a counterculture, the more deeply we are assimilated to the dominant culture. And so we cannot attain this critical perspective without some false consciousness. But such thinking is demanded of us, even if it involves us in ideology.

> But beside the demand thus placed on thought, the question of the reality or unreality of redemption itself hardly matters.

The *demand* creates the aporia, the fissure, the negativity. And this negativity, remember, "delineates the mirror image of its opposite." Because the

demand does the work, Adorno can remain agnostic about whether anything like redemption actually happens. Because the need itself imposes
a kind of negative revelation of its satisfaction, it does not matter for
Adorno's model of critique if the need is ever actually satisfied. The question of the reality or the unreality of redemption itself hardly matters.

Adorno makes redemption into what Jacob Taubes calls a "*comme si*
affair," something that does its work "as if" it were real.[12] And so it does
not matter if it is real or not. It is because of this indifference to the actuality of redemption that Georg Lukács's famous, mean, funny caricature
of Adorno living out his days in the Grand Hotel Abyss rings true. At just
this point I think that the best instincts of a lived theology must break with
Adorno, not out of some pious defense of a doctrine of redemption, but
out of an insistence that bodies matter, that creation matters, that redemption is not just an epistemological device, something that can do its real
work whether it is actual or not, but rather a granting of new life on which
all life depends. For lived theology, at its best, is not just a method. It is a
series of commitments to the life of the world. It knows that something is
at stake. And so it walks the tightrope without the net of "as if."

Walter Benjamin walks that same tightrope in what has come to
be called, with a nod to Spinoza, his "Theologico-Politico Fragment."
Benjamin probably drafted this piece in 1920–21 or in 1937–38, both times
of acute crisis in German politics. Benjamin's writings reflect that crisis.
"Only the Messiah himself contemplates all history," Benjamin writes,

> in the sense that he alone redeems, completes, creates its relation to
> the messianic. For this reason, nothing that is historical can relate
> itself, *from its own ground* [*von sich aus sich*], to anything messianic.
> Therefore, the Kingdom of God is not the telos of the historical
> dynamic; it cannot be established as a goal. From the standpoint of
> history, it is not the goal but the terminus [*Ende*].[13]

Because the Reign of God cannot serve as the goal of history, the secular
order [*die Ordnung des Profanen*] can never be legitimated in the name of
its realization of, or even approach to, the Reign of God. Theocracy "has no
political but only a religious meaning," Benjamin writes. The secular order
should not pretend to be established on the messianic. It should instead be
"erected on the idea of happiness [*Glück*]." In naming happiness as the rightful goal of the secular order, Benjamin does not elevate earthly happiness to
the status of an ultimate value. On the contrary, he insists that the pursuit
of happiness—the work that the secular order should be involved in—runs

counter to the approach of what he calls the "Messianic Kingdom." It is like an arrow pointing in the opposite direction, Benjamin writes. But exactly in this movement away from the Reign of God, the secular order plays its part:

> But just as a force, by virtue of its moving along, can augment another force on the opposite path, so the secular order—because of its nature as secular—promotes the coming of the Messianic Kingdom. The secular, therefore, though not itself a category of this kingdom, is a decisive category of its most unobtrusive approach. For in happiness all that is earthly seeks its downfall [*Untergang*], and only in happiness is its downfall destined to find it.[14]

Benjamin's philosophy of history rejects any kind of identity between what he calls the secular and what he calls the messianic. Benjamin relies here on the older notion of the *saeculum* as defined by its location in the time between the times rather than by how "religious" it is. Religious institutions, actions, and individuals, like everything else in the secular age, are not simply identical to anything of the messianic age. The people, institutions and practices of the secular order do not even approach the messianic asymptotically. They do not make a pretty good start that just needs a little more effort. They do not approach the messianic in little pockets of righteous remnants or perfect countercultures or resurreciton excellence. They do not even offer symbols that participate directly, from their own ground, in that which they symbolize. On the contrary, the people, practices, and institutions of the secular order are always driving *away* from the messianic. But precisely this—world history's drive away from the Reign of God—becomes the means of the Reign's approach. This world does not become the Reign of God because it lives forever. Rather, it is— even now—"messianic by reason of its eternal and total passing away."[15]

Benjamin's language here is soaked in centuries of Jewish and Christian messianic hope. Exile becomes an occasion for God's deep, wily fidelity. In the cross the world's rejection of God makes manifest God's boundless love for the world. This world finds itself joined most intimately to the Spirit of God not in its perfection, but in its longing, its deepest need, its cries too deep for words. Even two Presbyterian congregations in upstate New York find themselves caught up in the work of redemption exactly where they are bound most closely to a fallen age.

Benjamin articulated the structure of messianic hope with rare beauty and power. He had a hard time giving an account of his hope, though, as many critics have noted. He appealed sometimes to the embers of Marxism, sometimes to Kabbalah, sometimes to Romantic accounts of language. I am not troubled by this in the way that some of those who comment on Benjamin are. The mere fact that he cast about for grounds for his hope shows that redemption was not a *comme-si* affair for him. He understood what was at stake, and so he gives to us the task of giving an account of whatever hopes we have.

The hope articulated in *The New Measures* depends on the old Reformed saw, beloved of Puritans and articulated in the Second Helvetic Confession, that "The preaching of the word of God is the word of God." This confession is the door by which the dwarf climbs into the automaton of the material history presented in the book. (Pointing out the door so baldly only confirms Benjamin's sense that there are reasons to keep such moves out of sight, and not to speak of them directly!) I read this confession as a Reformed corollary to a wider theology of the sacraments. Confessing that the preaching of the Word of God is the Word of God should not involve any claim of simple identity between the things of this age and the messianic. Such a claim would underwrite a fundamentalism of the preacher's words, and so a particularly low form of local tyranny. The true sense of this confession comes only when we remember that all our talk about God is rendered false not only by our finitude but also by our sin, and even by that seemingly bottomless layering of sin that Christian theology has tried to describe with language of the fall. As Elizabeth Clark first helped me see, talk about God goes wrong not just because our language is limited, but because it is shot through with millenia of misused power. The trick is to acknowledge all of this, to see in our talk about God a steady driving away from God—and yet, to name this as the means of God's approach to us. This may well be true of all creation; I think and hope it is. But if I am forced to give an account of my hope, I will limit my case to God's promise to meet us in the preaching of the Word and the celebration of the sacraments.

Animated by this hope, *The New Measures* offers "eschatological memories" of the practices of preaching. They are memories from what Adorno called the "standpoint of redemption." They are memories that see, if only as one sees an image in a photographic negative, the approach of redemption in the drive away from anything like redemption; memories that intimated the faithfulness of God in the infidelities of preachers. Charles Grandison Finney seemed like a perfect subject for this kind of study, for he had not only given up the better parts of Puritan theology but also sold out the radically democratic energies that broke forth in the early revivals at Cane Ridge. There was not much for me to like about Finney. If the practices of his preaching were going to be a means of the quietest approach of God, it was going to be happening like an arrow moving in the opposite direction.

The gift of materialist histories is their messiness. And so attention to the material stuff of Finney's preaching—to architecture, performance, patterns of reasoning, and the new kind of authority that he helped to create—opens into studies of politics, theater, literature, and more. If we think about practice like Alasdair MacIntyre does, as making sense within a relatively discrete tradition, then these connections might catch us by surprise. But if we think about practice via Pierre Bourdieu's *habitus*— if we think of practices as bundles of dispositions, "structured structures predisposed to function as structruing structures," that can migrate across many different social spheres—well, then, we won't be surprised at all. Of course the material stuff of Finney's preaching was shared with people like P. T. Barnum, Andrew Jackson, Edgar Allan Poe, and Elizabeth Cady Stanton, who once gave her life to Christ at a Finney revival. (She later took it back. But she retained fond memories of Finney's sincerity.) And so, if the fallen material stuff of preaching is the means of God's approach, and if that material is shared across many spheres of society, then we might dare to hope for the silent approach of the messianic in all of creation.

Even modernity—for Finney was quintessentially modern. His preaching embodied all the qualities that critics of modernity love to hate: instrumental reason, fascination with novelty, a forced freedom, an abstract equality, a cardinal virtue of sincerity, and a secular vision of the world. What would it be to imagine something like the use of novelty to attract attention—a technique at the heart of both Finney's preaching and Barnum's showmanship—as, in and in spite of itself, a means of God's redeeming work in the world?

This line of thinking is dangerous. My colleague Elizabeth Bounds has done more than anyone else to help me see these dangers. For trusting that God works in and in spite of our failing is just a hair's breadth away from calling evil good. It risks snipping the motivational thread that sustains ethical action. Those are real dangers, especially in these days. I think, in the end, that Adorno fell prey to them more often than not. And I probably do, too, as wary as I try to be. But I think these are risks that we have to run. They are the risks that come with saying, in any strong sense, that it is not all up to us. They are the risks of a hope worth having.

Mindful of these risks, how do we *write* this hope? Or, how do we write lived theology worthy of the name?

Writing Eschatological Memories

I think the question of genre is one of the most pressing questions facing those of us who care about lived theology. Partly this is a question of audience: how can people who care about lived theology write for a wide circle of people who live theology? And partly this is a question related to the theological demands of the task: how can one tell the story of redemption drawing near in history's drawing away? I am naïve enough to hope that there might be some overlap between good answers to these two questions. The work of the scholars and activists associated with the Project on Lived Theology gives me grounds for that hope.

It is easiest to name a few ways this writing should not proceed. There are familiar temptations and collective habits that we need to avoid. One of these is a taste for what Charles Marsh has called the "whipped homiletical froth" of preachers' stories. These are stories in which every narrative perfectly illustrates some point that is already known in advance and can be known perfectly well without the story. If preachers are prone to such stories, lived theologians have not been immune. Another habit to break, as I argued above, is the positing of idealized countercultures. Yet another is the construction of a narrative of decline from some Golden Age, whether it came before Paul, or Constantine, or Scotus, or Columbus, or Luther, or Descartes, or Kant, or Vatican II, or Rorty, or the Human Rights Campaign, or any other person or movement that might be cast as the villain. It is not that we cannot speak of progress or decline; rather, it is that we should not tell narratives of *world historical* progress or decline, for such narratives must be anchored by some moment of identity between heaven and earth, whether that is a Golden Age now lost or a Glorious Future just a few five-year plans away. Scholars in the United States and Europe have found many ways to wean ourselves of narratives of progress. Narratives of decline have a more stubborn hold on our imaginations. But, as Benjamin saw, these seemingly opposite narratives are two sides of the same coin.

If these are habits we should break, what are the habits we should take up? Habits need institutions, and genres are institutions of literary habits. And so I will try to offer a very tentative beginning of an answer by briefly suggesting four genres for lived theology. This list is nothing close to complete. The list is meant to extend conversation, not end it. The list is also not intended to suggest a set of types to which works in lived theology should conform. Almost all of the best works of lived theology cannot be reduced to a single template, but even a limited typology can still facilitate critical thinking. It might be most useful in the places where it fails to describe complex pieces of writing.

1. A first genre for lived theology offers what I call *transparent history*. This is history—or ethnography, or some other art or science of description—that makes no direct claim about God, redemption, or anything to

do with anything messianic. But transparent history is written in such a way that anyone with eyes to see can see the theology at work. The Book of Ruth is like this. And this is how I read books like Charles Marsh's *God's Long Summer* or Marla F. Frederick's *Between Sundays*.[16] Works like these meet every standard of *wissenschaftlich* scholarship. They offer rigorous, attentive descriptions of this world. The theology that appears in them comes primarily through the words of others. It appears in quotation marks. But for certain kinds of readers, the quotation marks fall away. Descriptions of lived theology become intimations of living theology. Moreover, the shape of the narrative often embodies a theology of history, a claim about how this story relates to the story of redemption. And so readers can transform the history into theology in the act of reading. If the text on the page does not demand this way of reading, it yields to it readily.

2. A second genre works in a style like that of Adorno to tell *stories of negation* that trace the contours of catastrophe so precisely that they become a sign of the hope for which they long. The trick is to tell these stories of negation without taking up residence at the Grand Hotel Abyss. One of the grand masters of this genre, and the one from whom I have learned the most, is W. E. B. Du Bois. I think especially of Du Bois's writing in the first decade of the twentieth century, that incredible decade in which he wrote *The Souls of Black Folk*, his biography of John Brown, and other major works even as he helped found the Niagara Movement.

Consider the ending of Du Bois's biography of Brown. The last paragraph ends with an image of John Brown's body. Du Bois does not describe John Brown's body like the familiar song does. He does not describe a body that is mouldering in the grave even as the soul goes marching on. Instead he describes a body that is suspended between life and death, the body of an old man who lies "weltering in the blood which he spilled for broken and despised humanity."[17] Du Bois does not inscribe Brown into a long line of freedom fighters that bring the nation a little closer to the Reign of God. Instead he describes Brown as "belated," an eddy in the main current of history, an "anachronism." Brown's body does not redeem the nation. It does not launch the nation on a new path to justice for all. It speaks instead a word of judgment. Du Bois closes his book with an extended quotation of one of Brown's last speeches:

> You had better—all you people of the South—prepare yourselves for a settlement of this question. It must come up for settlement sooner than you are prepared for it, and the sooner you commence that

preparation, the better for you. You may dispose of me very easily—
I am nearly disposed of now; but this question is still to be settled—
this Negro question, I mean. The end of that is not yet. (238)

The end is not yet. Du Bois's Brown promises judgment and redemption
that cannot be separated from one another. The eschatological dimensions
of the promise come into clearer focus when they are paired with the epigraph to this same final chapter. As in *The Souls of Black Folk,* Du Bois
uses the chapter's epigraph to signal a hope that runs beyond the truth
that must be told on the page. "Ho, every one that thirsteth, come ye to the
waters," the epigraph reads, in an unattributed citation of Isaiah 55 (219).
John Brown's body does not pour out these waters for a nation that needs
them. His bloody, weary body needs the cleansing and refreshment which
it cannot provide for itself. And so John Brown's body does not redeem
the nation or launch a movement for justice. It serves instead as a kind of
prayer for judgment and hope, a sign that the end is not yet.[18]

3. A third genre is the one that I attempted in *The New Measures*. I would
call this the genre of *wishful thinking*. I first conceived *The New Measures*
more as a story of negation along the lines of Adorno's *Minima Moralia*
or Du Bois's biography of John Brown. I wanted to trace the contours of
the craters of modernity as they appear in the moonscape of preaching in
the United States. I slowly moved away from that plan for three reasons.
First, I lacked the artful agility of Du Bois. I kept falling into the craters
I was trying to limn. Second, I worried that readers would too readily
assimilate such stories to narratives of decline. I felt like I needed a different rhetorical strategy to shock myself into hope. And finally, I came
to think that such stories do not do justice to the ways in which God is at
work in the world, however indirectly. And so I decided to risk dreaming
of what the approach of redemption might look like. Benjamin's notion
of the "wish-image" (*Wunschbild*) or "dialectical image" (*dialektisches Bild*)
seemed to offer one way to articulate this hope without slipping into the
fundamentalism that comes from identifying historical processes with
the work of God. A dialectical image sees a phenomenon as testifying
to a hope from which it has fallen away.[19] Informed by this hope, *The
New Measures* conceives a series of quintessentially modern practices of
preaching as dialectical images of the Word of God. In Chapter 3, for
instance, I describe the craving for novelty as—in and in spite of itself,
exactly in its unfulfillment—a prayer for God to do a new thing. I do not
tell these stories of the unobtrusive approach of redemption as if they

were data about a new heaven and a new earth. I separate them from the more strictly empirical material with the gap of a section divide. I deliberately leave them framed as speculation. Their real work is not to describe redemption as an object, but to pry open a space in which such things can be imagined and desired. They can do this work even if they are mistaken, as they surely are, at least on some level. They can do this work even if a reader argues with them, as I hope readers will. But they are not framed within the "as if" of Adorno's redemption, for it is the particular *content* of this redemption that I hold lightly, not the category of redemption itself. On that everything depends.

4. A fourth genre I might call the *prodigal narrative*. I hint at this in the final chapter of *The New Measures*, in which I tell the story of one of Finney's sermon stories. As much as Finney supported education for women, he was always cagey about whether he thought women should preach. But his stories told other stories. A Finney sermon on "The Spirit of Prayer" argued that the Holy Spirit gave people "a spiritual discernment respecting the movements and developments of Providence." That's his point—nothing more. To illustrate this point he tells a story in which a woman in New Jersey discerned that God wanted to send what those in the revival movement called "the latter rain." And God did. The story illustrates his point perfectly. But—in spite of his intentions for it—it makes other points as well. Prodigal details leak out around the edges. The woman's faithful preparations indicate that she was running a house church. They suggest that she was the preacher and that God blessed her work. Finney did not mean to tell *that* story. But he did. The Gospel truth of a preaching woman found its way through the seams of a story designed to illustrate another point.[20]

We are always telling prodigal narratives, I think. Talk of excessive meaning is a postmodern commonplace. But lived theologians might work with the prodigal nature of narratives more self-consciously. We might spot the prodigal details in the stories of others. Willie James Jennings points to some of these in his essay, naming the ways that mission narratives hint at missionaries who "went native" and the ways that the lives of many missionary kids do not quite fit into any of the familiar narratives of empire. We might notice those stories that outrun the intentions of the mission chroniclers. We might even tell stories of our own that are intended to outrun what we can know we should intend.[21]

MY HOPE IS that this introduction can take a form like the one Willie Jennings discerns in the mission narratives. As an introduction, it is too brief to offer a comprehensive overview of all that lived theology can or should be. And it surely goes wrong in some important ways. It might only give new force to Benjamin's argument that theology is best kept out of sight these days. But I hope that some little bit of lived and living theology has slipped beyond the bounds of the arguments I have tried to impose on these prodigal narratives, and that this theology will live a life I do not know how to imagine for it. And if the publication of these thoughts can in any degree influence public sentiment in favor of truth and righteousness, I shall rejoice.

Notes

1. Charles Beecher, "The Duty of Disobedience to Wicked Laws: A Sermon on the Fugitive Slave Law" (Newark, NJ: J. McIlvaine, 1851). For an example of the note that the sermon had been published by request, see Nathaniel Colver, "The Fugitive Slave Bill; or, God's Laws Paramount to the Laws of Men. A Sermon, Preached on Sunday, October 20, 1850" (Boston: J. M. Hewes and Co., 1850).

2. See Ted A. Smith, *The New Measures: A Theological History of Democratic Practice* (Cambridge, UK: Cambridge University Press, 2007).

3. Here my thinking has been shaped especially by Michel de Certeau, *The Writing of History*, trans. Tom Conley (New York: Columbia University Press, 1988).

4. Walter Benjamin, "Über den Begriff der Geschichte," in *Gesammelte Schriften (G.S.)*, 7 vols., ed. Theodor Adorno et al. (Frankfurt: Suhrkamp, 1972), I.2:693. English translation (ET): Walter Benjamin, "On the Concept of History," in Walter Benjamin, *Selected Writings (S.W.)*, 4 vols., ed. Howard Eiland and Michael W. Jennings (Cambridge, MA: Belknap Press, 1996–2003), 4:389.

5. Marilynne Robinson, *Gilead* (New York: Picador, 2004), 91.

6. On the turn to culture, see Smith, *The New Measures*, 15–17. See also Ted A. Smith, "Troeltschain Questions for 'Ethnography as Christian Theology and Ethics,'" *Practical Matters* 6 (2012), http://practicalmattersjournal.org/2013/03/01/troeltschian-questions/.

7. Smith, *The New Measures*, 17–22.

8. See Ernst Troeltsch, "What Does the 'Essence of Christianity' Mean?" in Ernst Troeltsch, *Writings on Theology and Religion*, trans. and ed. Robert Morgan and Michael Pye (Atlanta: John Knox, 1977).

9. On Lenin's politics of the vanguard, see Georg Lukács, *Lenin: A Study of the Unity of His Thought*, trans. Nicholas Jacobs (London: Verso, 2009), Chapter 3.

10. See Detlev Claussen, *Theodor Adorno: One Last Genius*, trans. Rodney Livingstone (Cambridge, MA: Belknap Press, 2008), 97.

11. Theodor W. Adorno, *Minima Moralia*, in *Gesammelte Schriften*, 20 vols., ed. Rolf Tiedemann (Frankfurt: Suhrkamp Verlag, 1977), IV:281. ET: Theodor

Adorno, *Minima Moralia: Reflections from a Damaged Life*, trans. E. F. N. Jephcott (New York: Verso, 1978), 247.

12. Jacob Taubes, *The Political Theology of Paul*, trans. Dana Hollander (Stanford, CA: Stanford University Press, 2004), 74.

13. Benjamin, "Theologisch-Politisches Fragment," *G.S.* 2:1, 203. ET: Benjamin, "Theological-Political Fragment," in *S.W. 3:305*.

14. Benjamin, "Theologisch-Politisches Fragment," 204, ET: Benjamin, "Theological-Political Fragment," 305.

15. Benjamin, "Theologisch-Politisches Fragment," 204, ET: Benjamin, "Theological-Political Fragment," 306.

16. See Marla F. Frederick, *Between Sundays: Black Women and Everyday Struggles of Faith* (Berkeley: University of California Press, 2003) and Charles Marsh, *God's Long Summer: Stories of Faith and Civil Rights* (Princeton, NJ: Princeton University Press, 2008). As I suggest in the body of the text, I do not think the books by Frederick and Marsh can be reduced to a type of "transparent history." Both books are extraordinarily complex. But I hope that the category can serve as a useful tool in the more extended conversation these books deserve.

17. W. E. B. Du Bois, *John Brown*, ed. David Roediger (New York: Modern Library, 2001), 237. Subsequent references to this book appear in the body of the text.

18. The thoughts in this section have been adapted from the final chapter of Ted A. Smith, *Divine Violence: John Brown and the Limits of Ethics* (Stanford, CA: Stanford University Press, 2014).

19. On wish-images, see Walter Benjamin, *Das Passagen-Werk*, *G.S.*, 5.2: 1224–1225; ET: Walter Benjamin, *The Arcades Project*, trans. Howard Eiland and Kevin McLaughlin (Cambridge, MA: Belknap Press, 1999), 893–894. See also Susan Buck-Morss, *The Dialectics of Seeing: Walter Benjamin and the Arcades Project* (Cambridge, MA: The MIT Press, 1989); Margaret Cohen, "Benjamin's Phantasmagoria: The Arcades Project," in *The Cambridge Companion to Walter Benjamin*, ed. David S. Ferris (Cambridge, UK: Cambridge University Press, 2004); Michael William Jennings, *Dialectical Images: Walter Benjamin's Theory of Literary Criticism* (Ithaca, NY: Cornell University Press, 1987); and Smith, *The New Measures*, 33–34.

20. For a more complete discussion of this story, see Smith, *The New Measures*, 254–255.

21. Chapter 4, this volume, 74.

2

The Risks and Responsibilities
of Lived Theology

Peter Slade

IT IS A long road from fieldwork to published book. But, as I have discovered, the journey of lived theology does not end when the book is safely on the library shelf and its title added to one's vita. The author still has a responsibility to those who were the subject of the study. This chapter is a theological and methodological reflection on my particular experience of researching and writing a study of Christian communities in Mississippi.[1] It is a consideration of the location of the lived theologian. It is a reflection, with the benefit of hindsight, on the profound influence of that location on the methodology of research and writing a theological narrative rooted in ethnographic research of religious communities.[2] It is a story, ultimately, of how I came to know my place.

As a theologian, I have learned important lessons from sociologists. Ethnographer Loïc Wacquant advocates for sociology *from* the body.[3] Such ethnography requires a rich and fully engaged approach to the subject. For those concerned with lived theology, this means an awareness not only of social bodies (religious communities, the object of study) but also of our own bodies as fully present in these contexts. This means an awareness not only of what the Apostles' Creed calls "the holy catholic Church" but also of our selves as part of "the communion of saints." Put another way, we should do theology from our bodies as living members in the Body of Christ.

What, then, is the place of the lived theologian? The answer is that the lived theologian is properly located in the Church. But this smacks of a Sunday school answer. It is the right answer, but how one is to *do* lived theology in the Church is far from obvious. These are the questions of method and location that dominate the process of a research project. Before considering these, I want to turn to the questions that come at the end: when the project is finished, the book written, the paper presented.

I will tell a story that illustrates the risks and responsibilities of a lived theologian: how doing lived theology from our bodies in the Body can get awkward.

IN 2011, I TOOK a group of eight students to spend their spring break in Jackson, Mississippi, volunteering with Voice of Calvary Ministries and revisiting many of the people, organizations, and situations that I had studied six years earlier during my doctoral research. This was not my first time visiting Jackson in the two years since the book had been published—but it was the first time since people had taken notice of my published work.

At 6:45 on a Tuesday morning, my eight students from Ohio dragged themselves into a Mission Mississippi prayer breakfast at St. Joseph's Hospital. They picked up some coffee, yogurt, and pastries and—on strict instructions from their professor—scattered themselves through the room to chat with the collection of Mission Mississippi regulars, hospital staff, doctors, and administrators. These prayer breakfasts are intentional, interracial, intercessory prayer meetings that take place in different venues across Jackson every Tuesday and Thursday morning. I had been to many of these prayer breakfasts. They are the central practice of this racial reconciliation organization. As I looked around the room, I saw Dolphus Weary, Mission Mississippi's Director of Development. I had not spoken with Weary since my book had been published—though I had sent him a copy. He gave a rueful chuckle as we shook hands. "Your book has been mixing things up," he said.

When it was time to start praying, Weary called the breakfasters to order.

"Peter, stand up. We have got a young man with us this morning—Peter Slade—and he wrote a book about Mission Mississippi. He is here this morning with his students." I may be wrong, but this did not feel like the usual church greeting, of acknowledging visitors. Rather, Dolphus Weary was calling me out, making me stand out and stand up. I was no longer the researcher. I was no longer the participant observer, quietly taking notes and recording interviews. But what was I exactly? I pondered this as I bowed my head and prayed with my small group of Catholics and

Protestants—black, white, and Hispanic—under the fluorescent lights in
the basement of the hospital.

I knew which part of the book had been "mixing things up." I had
spent a long chapter excavating the reasons why this racial reconciliation organization did not explicitly talk about justice. The answer cut very
deep for whites, particularly the conservative white Presbyterians of the
Presbyterian Church of America (PCA). The roots of the answer burrow
back through white supremacy and Jim Crow to the theological resistance
to the abolition of slavery. The Church is about the business of Word
and Sacrament, they said, justice is not our job. But why did the African
American leaders of Mission Mississippi go along with this? Dolphus
Weary was the protégé of veteran community activist John Perkins and had
been his chosen successor at Voice of Calvary in Mendenhall. I concluded
that Weary and the other African American leaders had not forgotten
about justice; rather, they saw the importance of keeping the whites at the
table long enough to start a conversation. For Weary, Mission Mississippi
was only "Reconciliation 101."[4]

I knew John Perkins had read my book. I was busy not signing copies
at a conference in Cincinnati in 2009, when he took a copy from my table.
I had also learned from friends in Jackson that he had gathered one thing
from it: Mission Mississippi—the organization run by the man he had
mentored—would not address issues of injustice. He was incensed.

As the prayer meeting came to a close at 7:45 and the room emp-
tied, Dolphus Weary sat with my students and graciously talked to them
about the difficult task of bringing the gospel message of reconciliation to
Mississippi's churches, and how hard it is to get Christians to stop talking
and start listening. Toward the end of the conversation, Weary referred to
the strained relationship he now had with John Perkins. "He's my father
in the faith," he said sadly, "but J. P. came to the table not ready to listen.
He just wanted to say his piece."

Driving back in the van, my students wanted to know what on earth
their professor had written that these people actually cared about so much.
As I offered an explanation, we passed the red-bricked and white-columned
First Presbyterian Church. In 2003, its session had first approved giving
me access to the church's archives; but then, after further deliberation, it
barred me from seeing any church documents. If I were so much as to talk
to church members without checking with the elders first then, I was told
to my face, "You will be very sorry."

"I am hoping to write a congregational history: it will only work if people want to participate. I don't want to cause any trouble." I had tried to sound reassuring.

"Trouble! Don't you worry about that, we know how to handle trouble!"

Seven years later, when my book energized the conservative Presbyterian blogosphere, Ligon Duncan, the minister of First Pres', Jackson, accused me either of bias or of poor scholarship. He left this comment on a blog: "There are lots of gaps in his presentation of this story . . . I'll write more to you privately about this, and perhaps post some facts that Mr. Slade has failed to mention in his book."[5]

As the PCA blogs and comments piled up, the chancellor of Reformed Theological Seminary responded with a pastoral letter on his own blog and I received invitations to lecture at both the denomination's undergraduate college and seminary.[6]

I had responded by email to Ligon Duncan's public online comment, but he had never written back. "I was hoping to have a chat with him while I was down here," I told the students in the van.

"Do it now, Dr. Slade!" They were fired up from coffee and their early morning exposure to Christian reconciliation. "You need to meet with him."

I was trapped. Followed by a gaggle of undergraduates, I walked across the Presbyterian parking lot, past the pastel-wearing moms dropping their children off at the day school, past the armed guard, past the security camera. We were buzzed into the church offices. With my students watching, pulse racing, and hat in hand, I said, "Hi, my name is Peter Slade." I dropped my hat on the floor, but continued, "I wondered if I may see Dr. Duncan."

"He is not here right now, but you can talk with his secretary to set up an appointment."[7]

Later that day, my students and I sat down for lunch at Voice of Calvary Ministries with Phil Reed, another veteran of community building and reconciliation. "I agree with what you said in your book," Reed confided, "but you've caused a stir." He went on to tell me of the ugly scenes between Perkins and Weary over justice and the mission of Mission Mississippi. But Reed had more to report than this fractured relationship. "Neddie, Dolphus, and myself, we've been meeting with Ronnie Crudup from New Horizons. We're developing a curriculum on justice for evangelical churches."

MY DISCOMFORT THAT morning in Mississippi was threefold:

1. *I was uncomfortable in my relationship with the Church*: In the setting of the prayer meeting, I was uncomfortable because, despite my prior easy relationship with the community I had studied and in a small way participated in, it was no longer an easy place for me to go. In the case of First Pres', the prospect of meeting with these powerful Christians made me extremely anxious. They had been less than cooperative in the past—they had actually threatened me—and that had been before I had put a less than flattering history of their congregation in print.
2. *I was uncomfortable with the effect of my work on the relationships between people I had written about:* I was sorry that anything I had written would have strained the relationship between Dolphus Weary and John Perkins—both of whom I hold in very high regard.
3. *I was uncomfortable that my work had changed the organizations I had studied.* It made me nervous to hear that what I had written had helped precipitate a significant change in Mission Mississippi. I was not prepared for that kind of responsibility.

What business did I have to write anything? What was my rightful place in all of this? How could I run away and get out of this place?

These anxieties have deep methodological roots in my own academic training. I came to the Project on Lived Theology with some training in oral history and documentary work after studying at the Center for the Study of Southern Culture at the University of Mississippi. One thing that had been drilled into me is that good documentary fieldwork interferes as little as possible with the subject of study. Someone engaged in a good documentary study should have a hyper-self-reflexive understanding of the impact of his or her presence on the subject. There is a great deal of hand-wringing over the unintended impact of the researcher on the communities studied. I also have a background in community development work—I studied the subject at Ruskin College, Oxford, while employed as a community worker for the Church of England. The good community worker is very conscious of her own role and influence on the community, and essentially tries to work herself out of a job. So the best documentarian, ethnographer, or anthropologist *leaves* the subject as he found it. The good community worker *leaves* the community stronger than she found it. What my experiences in Mississippi made me realize is that the faithful lived theologian *never leaves* the communion of saints. Whether we like it or not, we are part of the Body. Even death does not release us from this situation. As the Apostles' Creed affirms, we believe in "the resurrection of the body; and the life everlasting."

In her book *Places of Redemption,* Mary McClintock Fulkerson, quoting Charles Winquist, maintains, "Creative thinking originates at the scene of a wound."[8] In my case, I was conducting my research not just in libraries but also in physical proximity to the wound of injustice and racism in Mississippi: studying the broken and suffering Body of Christ. Fulkerson also points out that Christian theology is creative in the presence of such wounds because theology is "an inquiry shaped by a logic of transformation."[9] This is an important observation and it should make us pause, because it points out the risks and responsibilities involved in such a project. What or who is being transformed? If this is a theological inquiry, then clearly the theology and the theologian are subject to this "logic of transformation." If there is to be no change, then there is no point in the study. But far more uncomfortable for me is the idea that the people I am studying will be changed by this conversation. This is not simply because of my background in documentary work but also because—if postcolonial studies tell me anything—as a white, English man I need to be very cognizant of my latent colonial tendencies.

The lived theologian is located in the Church, but she or he is also located in the academy. There are fundamental differences between the academy and the Church—but moving in and between these institutions means that the lived theologian has to develop a *theological double consciousness.* The one important theological point to note is that despite the temporal ordering of our lives, the Church is our primary and preeminent location. After all, Jesus said, "I will build my church; and the gates of hell shall not prevail against it" (Mt 16:18). There are no such reassuring words in scripture for university presidents!

Now that the lived theologian knows his or her place, how does this influence the method of researching and writing a lived theology? When I started studying with Charles Marsh in 2000, I understood the task of the Project on Lived Theology as collapsing the distance between the academic study of theology (particularly systematic theology) and the lived experience of the people in the pews; to get theologians to study communities with some of the attention they usually reserve for texts; to remind theologians that they should have this theological *double consciousness.* The conviction that I shared with Marsh was that so much academic theology seems to have been dis-located. This is why, in the Preface to my study of Mission Mississippi, I wrote:

> Christian theologians call the Church the Body of Christ, but rarely do they go and look at this body to find what they might learn about Christ the object of their study. Underlying this book is the conviction that they should. Congregations and faith communities develop their own *lived theologies* embodied in their practices and proclamations and theologians need to be in conversation with these lived theologies if academic theology is to stay true to its calling to serve the Church and if local churches beliefs and practices are not to become intellectually impoverished.[10]

But how to set about this task? For me it was not quite a journey without maps, but it was close. I set off with some convictions (modified along the way) that I believe should guide my own work.

The first is that *academic theology needs to be in conversation with the lived theology of Christian communities*. One immediate problem that such a conversation runs into is the great distance in vocabulary separating the lecture hall from the sanctuary. The lived theologian who inhabits both places has to learn to code-switch—to be fluent in both languages. But when it comes to writing a book, one must choose to employ a single voice. A key methodological concern is therefore how to work with both the highly articulate and often obscure vocabulary of academic theology, and the lived theology of the average churchgoer. The written word is the natural habitat of the academic theologian; in this medium, their words tend to carry more authority on the page, thus making any equal exchange very difficult. The temptation is to remedy this imbalance by translating practices and stories of faith into the language of academic theology. To do this, however, is to lose the authentic voices of lived theology and to risk patronizing the subject. Influenced by my background in oral history, in my research I conducted a significant number of extended interviews. When I came to write, I drew on the transcripts of interviews, ensuring that participants in Mission Mississippi retained their own voices in this conversation, and I included descriptions of their practices.

Accompanying my concern of equal exchange is my conviction that, as far as is possible, *the work should be accessible to the people who are the subject of the study:* that theology does not just come *from* the Body—it should be *for* the Body.[11] This is the impulse that can really get a theologian into trouble.

To address these concerns of equal exchange and accessibility, I decided to present both academic and lived theologies using biographical narrative. I was helped in my task by the fact that two of the main theologians whose work I used—Jürgen Moltmann and Miroslav Volf—have fascinating and intersecting biographies. I also found that presenting academic theology woven into a biographical and historical narrative levels the playing field by demonstrating that the academic/lived theology dichotomy is, in fact, false. Just as for the regular person in the pew, theologians' religious beliefs and convictions spring, at least in part, from their reflection upon their own lived faith in their own particular cultural context.

There is a model in place for the interaction between academic theology and the faith of regular churchgoers: professors at seminaries pass on their "good" theology to their students, who then enter the pulpit as mediators of this theology to their congregations. In this traditional model, the flow of theology only goes in one direction. This cannot be the case in lived theology. *For academics engaged in studying the lived theologies of faith communities, the theology must flow in both directions.* We must have the humility to allow the embodied theologies of the community we are studying to contribute to the theological conclusions of our work—even if we think we know better. In my case, participants in Mission Mississippi insisted that the most important practice of racial reconciliation was the prayer breakfast. I decided that I should take this claim seriously and bring an ethnographic study of these prayer breakfasts into conversation with academic theologies of reconciliation. "Of course they would say that," proclaimed a dismissive colleague, "they are a bunch of Baptists from Mississippi!" In the end, I discovered in the prayer breakfasts a practice of open friendship that shaped my thesis and led to my strongest conclusions.

There is, of course, a danger that comes with writing for the community you have studied: that you will moderate or modify the accounts to avoid the risk of future confrontation. The belief that one is inescapably connected with that community through the Church only amplifies that danger. The writing of lived theology requires truth-telling for reasons that exceed the academic expectations of intellectual honesty or the desire to expose the truth held by the investigative reporter and the revisionist historian. As Miroslav Volf points out, "the will to truth must be accompanied by the will to embrace the other, by the will to community."[12] Reflecting on this danger in light of my experiences in Mississippi, I come to my fourth conviction: *writing lived theology is telling the truth with the hope of reconciliation.* In this the writer shares the fundamental posture of all those whose place, whose primary location and identity declared in baptism, is in Christ.

TO ENGAGE IN the process of researching and writing lived theology entails an inescapable engagement with the Church. This place of the lived theologian as part of the Body is tricky and uncomfortable because it requires not only openness to being changed but also an acceptance of the responsibility that you will change others. It may, as Charles Marsh suggests, involve betrayal; but the betrayer cannot escape the betrayed.[13] Indeed, we need to be reconciled to those we have betrayed. We need to have the will to embrace those whom we have angered. The lived theologian is part of the Church, part of the body of Christ. This not only locates the object of study but also locates the scholar and the audience for the work. It then remains the scholar's location after they have shared their work. Taken seriously, this must influence how we first engage in ethnographic research and then write, "an honest story" set against the distant "horizon of the triune God."[14] It is also where we need to experience the repercussions of our work, and where we will seek forgiveness for our sins and reconciliation within the communion of saints.

Notes

1. Peter Slade, *Open Friendship in a Closed Society: Mission Mississippi and a Theology of Friendship* (New York: Oxford University Press, 2009).
2. A number of scholars are asserting the importance of ethnographic research as an important methodology for the traditional subdisciplines of systematic and practical theology. See, *Ethnography as Christian Theology and Ethics*, ed. Aana Marie Vigen and Christian Scharen (New York: Continuum, 2011).
3. Loïc, J. D. Wacquant, *Body & Soul: Notebooks of an Apprentice Boxer* (New York: Oxford University Press, 2004), viii.
4. Slade, *Open Friendship*, 123.
5. Ligon Duncan, comment left on July 6, 2010, on Anthony Bradley, "Why Didn't They Tell Us?: The Racist & Pro-segregation Roots of the Formation of RTS, the PCA, and the Role of First Prez in Jackson, Miss in All of It," *The Institute*, July 2, 2010, http://bradley.chattablogs.com/archives/2010/07/why-didnt-they.html#comment-202563.
6. Michael Milton, "Acknowledge the Sin, Accentuate the Grace, Honor the Fathers: Why I love the PCA and RTS" blog post on *MichaelMilton.Org*, July 9, 2010, http://michaelmilton.org/2010/07/09/acknowledge-the-sin-accentuate-the-grace-honor-the-fathers-why-i-love-the-pca-and-rts/.

7. Later that week I had my meeting with Ligon Duncan. He was charming and informed me with a smile that no one in the congregation at the church had mentioned the book to him; he doubted many were even aware of its existence. We are now Facebook friends. On May 19, 2016, in a public discussion on Facebook about the history of First Presbyterian Church and race, Ligon Duncan (now the Chancellor of Reformed Theological Seminary) replied to my comments, "Your work is very important, and excellent, in this area and I deeply appreciate it. I appreciate it all the more since you didn't have access to all you wanted to see. And I have come to appreciate it still more as I have grown in my knowledge of the history of the events and era." https://www.facebook.com/jemar.tisby/posts/10208711979889612.

8. Mary McClintock Fulkerson, *Places of Redemption: Theology for a Worldly Church* (Oxford: Oxford University Press, 2007), 13.

9. Fulkerson, *Places of Redemption*, 22.

10. Slade, *Open Friendship*, vii.

11. This is an ethical concern of modern ethnography. Caroline Brettel, *When They Read What We Right: The Politics of Ethnography* (Westport, CT: Bergin & Garvey), 1993; Kristy Nabhan-Warren, "Embodied Research and Writing: A Case for Phenomenologically Oriented Religious Studies Ethnographies," *Journal of the American Academy of Religion* 79, no. 2 (June 2011): 383.

12. Miroslav Volf, *Exclusion and Embrace: A Theological Exploration of Identity, Otherness, and Reconciliation* (Nashville: Abingdon Press, 1996), 257.

13. Charles Marsh, "A Journey without Maps: Does Lived Theology Need a Method?" (paper presented at the Spring Institute for Lived Theology, University of Virginia, May 25, 2011), http://www.livedtheology.org/resources/a-journey-without-maps-does-lived-theology-need-a-method/.

14. "Introduction," this volume, 5, 7.

3

Doing Theological Ethics with Incompetent Christians

SOCIAL PROBLEMS AND RELIGIOUS CREATIVITY

Willis Jenkins

RELIGIOUS SOCIAL ETHICS commonly supposes that its task is to apply religious ideals to social problems. Authentic Christian engagement with society, in this view, starts from fundamental moral values, and then works toward concrete situations. Paul Ramsey, in *Basic Christian Ethics*, expressed the commonsense, intuitive impulse behind this assumption well: "before there can be a Christian social ethic, understanding of the fundamental moral perspective of the Christian must be deepened and clarified." So, first one must work out the moral meaning of Christianity, and then attempt to apply it in practice. As for where to find the moral meaning of Christianity, Ramsey was clear: "It would never occur to an unprejudiced mind ... to look for the meaning of Christian ethics anywhere else than in the biblical record and in the writings of men of the past whose thinking about morality has been profoundly disturbed and influenced by what they found there."[1]

An "unprejudiced mind" seems likely to be a disembodied fiction. In any case, it has indeed occurred to some to look for examples of Christian ethics in places beyond "the writings of men of the past" and the biblical record. Traci West's *Disruptive Christian Ethics* contests the assumption that moral communities await updated findings from academic moralists about Christian fundamentals before confronting their challenges. West is liberationist in method; which is to say, she is convinced of God's preference for the poor, and her thinking about morality is profoundly disturbed and influenced by what she finds in their struggles. West takes the stories and activism of poor African American women as first interpretation of social problems. Material struggles become theological sources, as she treats grassroots projects as sites where moral knowledge is cultivated. Using sociological and ethnographic methods to recover community-based responses to racism and poverty, she calls on ethicists to develop scriptural readings and conceptual resources that work with what agents are already doing, in order to make a difference to their struggles. In West's approach, social ethics is itself an embodied social practice that nurtures moral agents and builds shared values across boundaries of thought and borders of power.[2]

Between "basic" and "disruptive" modes of ethics lies a question about the moral significance of everyday life. West's approach is one part of a broad turn away from the philosophical idealism with which Ramsey thought all religious ethics should make common cause. Across theology, religious studies, and sociology of religion, theorists have been reversing the priority represented by Ramsey's commonsense approach: from embodied practice toward the interpretation of religious meanings. Liberationist epistemologies may have begun the shift, calling on theological scholars to work from participation in concrete political struggles. While often different in priority, turns toward narrative and virtue in religious ethics have put church practices at the center of the conversation. In sociology of religion, ethnographic approaches interpret the meaning of religion and offer attentive description of how it is embodied and experienced. Those various intellectual movements are not using material practices in the same ways, obviously, but they do share a broad turn toward everyday life. Scholars are interpreting religion not only as it is thought and written, but as it is cooked and served, planted and built, dressed and traveled.

I appreciate this turn toward the everyday; it has tutored my own attempt to do ethics on problems of sustainability and social justice. Working on problems like climate change, however, made me confront a vulnerability of the turn toward lived religious life: it seems to make ethics captive to incompetent performances. In the case of climate change, if there are no meaningful struggles against it, then religious social ethics might become complicit with catastrophe. In that case it might seem that Ramsey's method—rearticulating fundamental beliefs first in order to make actual behavior conform to the ideal—would be preferable. I want to resist that conclusion, but doing so requires some account of the possibility of doing theological ethics amid "incompetent" Christians. I will explain what I mean by further establishing the attractiveness of West's liberationist style of Christian social ethics, and then explaining the difficulty that problems like climate change pose for the entire family of methods informed by the turn to lived religion.

Lived Theology and Everyday Denialism

For theological ethics, the turn toward lived religion draws ethicists into closer contact with how the faith is enacted and inhabited and allows ethical interpretation to arise from how Christianity takes shape as a way of life. Yet it also renders ethics vulnerable to the incompetence of everyday Christianity. What should ethicists do when most ways of living Christianity seem ugly or violent? A common complaint made to theologians of an ecclesial bent, especially Stanley Hauerwas, is that putting church practice at the center of Christian ethics ends up validating or ignoring much of the bad behavior within Christian communities. Surely the lived reality of most churches fails to reflect what theology's ecclesial romance suggests we should find there. Ethics must retain ground to critique bad, harmful, or ugly practices, even when they can coherently present themselves as the practices of a community telling their story of God—as "church" practices.

That complaint can be answered by selecting better practices. With a prejudice toward struggles for freedom at margins of power, an ethicist might work from practices that bear transformative significance, even if they do not represent mainstream Christianity. They may not even represent the mainstream of a particular community. Traci West argues for ethics to work with particular edges of lived religion, and she wants ethicists to help those communities transform themselves.

For West, turning to religion as it is lived makes Christian ethics itself an organic practice, intentionally waged through community building. Doing Christian ethics this way is not a matter of articulating the moral genius of a great tradition, but rather a critical way of participating in what communities are doing in response to dehumanizing challenges. West contrasts her method with the legacy of Reinhold Niebuhr, whose analysis of prospects for racial justice amid the realities of power and pride can seem to presciently describe the civil rights strategies of the 1960s. It can look as if Niebuhr works out a theory later implemented by King, who translated it for a waiting community of action. Thinking of ethics that way, however, with Niebuhr as the genius behind King's thought, and King as the genius of a movement, "conceals the multiple actors and innovators in the moral dramas of history, and reinforces the supremacy of whites in our understanding of how moral knowledge is generated."[3] West observes a Harlem network of agents bubbling with social creativity, including some strategies similar to those Niebuhr was proposing as he wrote in his office, just blocks away. Had Niebuhr looked among those projects for hints about the meaning of Christianity in white racism, suggests West, some of his perceptions of sin and group power dynamics would have shifted. West's intention is not to deconstruct Niebuhr's theology (several points of which she appreciates). Her aim, rather, is to dismantle a model of ethicists as elite producers of guiding ideals, and set up her own practice of social ethics, which she understands as participation in projects with many kinds of collaborators.

The crucial first move is deciding where to participate. Which material struggles represent the sort of lived theology that an ethicist should want to deepen, defend, and empower? West's claims align with characteristic epistemological stances of liberation theology: that theological production should happen through the communities of those suffering the world's evil and struggling against it. Liberationist responses to poverty, for example, situate the role of professional theologians within the agency of poor communities reading scripture along with sociology, political theory, and economics in order to open ways of participating in God's liberation. Interpreting poverty therefore must happen within "church," in this sense: theological responses to poverty must arise from participation within practices of prophetic confrontation and alleviation of suffering that are the movement of God. Not every lived theology matters in the same way, nor are the approaches of every self-designated church equally interesting. On this account, ethicists must follow God's preference for the poor into practices where people are struggling for freedom. Christian ethics is indeed a secondary product of Christian community—but not every community counts as a church. Jon Sobrino completes that point with his dictum, updating Cyprian's "outside the church there is no salvation" to say: *"extra pauperes nulla salus."* Outside solidarity with the poor, there is no salvation, because ideas about salvation become theologically unimaginable outside the practices that carry their intelligibility.[4]

Here, then, is the liberationist answer to the complaint about turning toward unjust or corrupt religious practices: ethicists (perhaps unlike ethnographers and sociologists) must first search for struggles against injustice and domination in order to find the right sort of communities and practices. Not any lived religion will do; an initial sense of (what Ramsey might call) the moral meaning of Christianity and of its biblical record prejudices ethicists toward communities seeking to locate ways of freedom amid overwhelming challenges.

Now consider the problem of climate change, which presents a different kind of difficulty. What to do when there do not appear to be any meaningful practices with which to work? The complexity of climate change seems to overwhelm what paltry Christian responses exist (which amount mostly to a paper trail of official disapproval). The gap between the demands of the challenge and available practices seems to represent a larger problem than a pervasive failure to live the real meaning of Christianity (as a liberationist like Sobrino can claim in the face of global poverty); rather, it seems to represent a failure of practical imagination. Climate change overwhelms moral agency in a different way than economic domination; it overwhelms a community's sense that it *could* act meaningfully. The opacity and multiplicity of relations involved, the aggregation of nonintentional actions driving such perverse outcomes, the global and temporal extent of human powers—all this seems to overwhelm the possibility of meaningful practices.

Explicit Christian climate denialism grabs attention, but it is not nearly the real ethical problem. Theological communities who bet the integrity of their beliefs on the nonexistence of empirical events ridicule their own faith more than the science. (The fate of those communities is now pegged to the fate of North Atlantic fossil-fuel culture.) The real ethical problem is the implicit denialism of everyday life. Kari Norgaard's ethnography of non-response among well-informed and concerned Norwegians points to a more subtle social organization of denial that works to protect cultures from change.[5] The most damaging form of climate denial may be the token forms of concern that a high-carbon culture organizes for itself (change a lightbulb, buy a hybrid car, etc.). Such tokenism may not open possibilities of agency, but may in fact contribute to the defeat of agency, given that those actions hardly bear the realities of climate change. Perhaps the best a Christian climate ethic can do through a lived theology method is offer ethnographies of absent action.

Norgaard's work suggests one approach for doing lived theology in the absence of meaningful practices: ethnographies of absence could inform a theological account of denialism. Attending to the social organization of implicit denial within North Atlantic moral communities would amount to an ethnography of privilege that could at least summon people to develop their moral imagination differently. Christian communities who recognize how the coping and validating mechanisms of fossil-fuel culture undermine possibilities of faithfulness may be spurred to develop the sort of practical and theological imagination that better responds to reality. So one approach to doing lived theology in the absence of live practices is to offer ethnographies that explain the lack, in anticipation that the recognition may at least give rise to the sort of struggles for moral agency in which a theological ethicist could participate.

For lived theology in high-carbon cultures, the austerity of an ethnography-of-absence approach could be important for honestly reckoning with what suppresses faithful theological practice. My own approach takes a more ambivalent view of the hitherto inadequate array of responses to climate change.[6] Just because most Christian responses to climate change seem incapable of generating practical responses, that does not mean they are only token actions, implicitly denialist in function. In the face of a problem with unprecedented scales of power and unanticipated kinds of moral relation, theorists should not expect initial responses to bear responsibility for the whole of the challenge. What matters is whether they begin to make the repertory of faith learn how to bear responsibility for new realities.

For Christian ethics to work from lived responses to climate change and still hope to offer an adequate ethic, it must suppose that new possibilities of Christian life can be learned and invented through responses to social problems. Ethics needs to suppose that climate change can be an adaptive occasion, pressing communities for theological innovation that makes the moral repertory of Christian life competent enough to face new challenges. In this view, the task of ethics is to find, critique, and cultivate the trajectories of theological creativity through which a community is struggling to open possibilities of moral agency in the midst of problems that would overwhelm them. Taking that creativity as a way to work at once with and beyond lived Christianity, the ethicist need not recoil from the moral incompetence of Christian practices.

Creative theological thinking, observes Mary McClintock Fulkerson, arises from the scene of a wound; "is generated by a sometimes inchoate sense that something *must* be addressed."[7] In the case of climate change, the wound includes frustration at one's inability to respond. While Fulkerson is writing about how to describe a particular community, her charged sense of situation holds, I think, for the general condition of how social problems challenge Christian communities. Churches face a situation that carries an inchoate demand; it may be a wound so confounding that it eludes interpretation as a wound. Climate change seems to demand practices that will make communities more capable of interpreting the wounds they must acknowledge and address.

By focusing on the tensions between theological production (organic and systematic, explicit and implicit) and the demand of a problem, Christian ethics need not arrive to the scene of social problems with an already complete theory—(not even an account of what a decent practice will look like, as in liberationist responses to poverty). In fact, in this view, ethics begins in recognition of incompleteness—of something that compels a response not yet given. This production may not necessarily happen through self-critical reconsideration of a community's moral beliefs about the world. In fact, the least interesting part of a community's response is what its authorized spokespersons say that their beliefs mean for a problem. (For proof, see denominational statements on climate change.) The interesting moral production happens as a community's actual life changes: as European churches try to love their neighbors by purchasing carbon offsets grown by partner churches in East Africa; or as South American base communities rally in support of legal rights for nature; or as evangelical youth ministries incorporate birding into spiritual formation; or as Korean Presbyterians experiment with church-based sustainable agriculture. As communities cook and landscape, pray and preach differently, they invent new moral capacities from their repertory of faith, and so begin to make their way of life more accountable to the world's reality.

I do not wish to appear too irenic about these types of responses. Christian climate responses remain functionally incompetent to the problem they take themselves to address. The moment they become pious about those practices, they quickly become part of the repertoire of denialism rather than faithfulness—part of the way of death rather than life. I imagine a book written in the style of Charles Marsh's *God's Long Summer*, only now inquiring into the long summer of climate change action and inaction.[8] How do organic theologians invent possibilities of response to overwhelming problems and how do they suppress their demand, looking away from the wound?

Theocentric Pragmatism

This strategy supposes that Christian ethics should interpret difficult social problems in relation to communities already creating live strategies

of response. Rather than proposing an arrangement of symbols, met-
aphors, and beliefs that could lead to new kinds of action, a pragmatic
strategy supposes that the most important interpretive resources lie in the
strategies generated by communities trying to confront new social problems. What a community says it believes, and even what it already does,
matters less than the potential of the strategies it is organizing. Ethicists
can help realize that potential by cultivating and criticizing a community's
initial responses, working to make their trajectory more competent in facing their problems.

By now, my account may seem terribly instrumentalist toward the
beliefs of adherents. Its reliance on "adequate" and "fitting" responses
would surely incur the sarcastic dismissal of ecclesial theologians like
Hauerwas. Let me then offer a brief sketch of the cultural and theological
coherence of this view, and explain what it means for notions of "church."

This strategy of Christian ethics entails a pragmatist view of culture and
of the relation of theology and culture, yet also an important role for treat-
ing beliefs as in some ways transcendent of Christian practices. This third
point transgresses the usual allowance of pragmatist commitments and
raises questions about what counts as a "living theological community,"
so I will state the first two briefly and then turn to the role of theological
beliefs in a pragmatic strategy. I will demonstrate what I mean by appealing to two figures especially beloved in Lived Theology circles: Dietrich
Bonhoeffer and Martin Luther King, Jr.[9]

First, a pragmatic strategy of ethics understands moral culture in
terms of an embodied *habitus* (Pierre Bourdieu) or learned repertory (Ann
Swidler) by which persons interpret and meet everyday problems of their
world. Against a view in which culture shapes activity by ideal worldviews
organized by a governing logic or guiding set of values, a pragmatic view
supposes that cultures shape agents into patterns of action. Those patterns
of action carry ways of interpreting the world by interacting with it. They
are always under pressure to change as contexts change or new problems
arise. Actors create adaptive cultural change by arranging the various elements of a cultural repertory (symbols, ideas, practices, worldviews) in
support of some new pattern of action that seems to afford better interpretive interaction with contexts.[10]

Second, a pragmatic strategy understands the relation of theology and
culture in terms of a distinctive style of using available cultural repertories.
Theology is not, then, the articulation of a Christian sociality complete in
itself (John Milbank), nor explication of the countercultural worldview or

narrative that makes Christian identity (Stanley Hauerwas). It is rather, as Kathryn Tanner argues, a distinctive style of cultural use. Christian styles of cultural use are fabricated by both organic and professional theologians, and are marked by their peculiar, ironic function: theology refers all of cultural life to God in order to keep opening cultural space for persons to respond to God. Theology does not, then, arbitrate a certain kind of cultural flow (religious stuff) or defend the boundaries of a certain subculture; rather, it is a way of doing something with culture to open space for an odd way of being a material, encultured creature—a way of living life as response to God.[11]

My pragmatic view of Christian ethics suggests that this theological creativity will be particularly intense where the general task of responding to God occurs in relation to the demands of a particular social problem. The ferment should be still more intense when Christian responses to those demands reveal a failure to make any kind of answer to God. So Christian ethics can take the account of cultural creativity in Swidler and theological creativity in Tanner in order to expect strategic innovation in the gap between overwhelming social problems and a community's life. It can expect that climate change presses moral cultures to create new patterns of action, and work with Christian attempts to open within climate change a cultural space for the possibility of discipleship in a world of atmospheric human powers. The ethicist's task, here, is to help Christian social reform projects become more satisfactorily creative, working like a savvy reformer or community organizer.

Confronting social problems, this strategy supposes, is a way of learning theology from the world, for the meanings of religious traditions are renegotiated as the elements of their repertory are deployed to interpret and meet the world's needs. This seems close to the view of Cornel West, whose "prophetic pragmatism" summons skilled cultural actors to help communities on a "quest for wisdom that puts forth new interpretations of the world based on past traditions."[12] Organic intellectuals, in West's view, are especially important in helping communities find new capacities in their moral inheritances, inventing possibilities for practical cultural reforms that in turn enable communities to take responsibility for society's deepest and most difficult problems. "The most significant and successful organic intellectual in American history," says West, was King.[13]

However, what drove King's creativity was not only a readiness to learn from the inventiveness of reform communities around him (to wage ethics through community) but also a belief that contextual demands mediate transcendent responsibilities. That belief carries hope that imperfect responses can be transformed by the work of God. That hope exceeds the usual pragmatic frame, as already seen in Tanner's description of a Christian style as using culture for "responsibility to God." Responsibility names a pattern of interacting with the world as accountable to a God always beyond immanent goods, problems, and possibilities. That "beyond" is not superfluous to a community's way of life; rather, it sustains the gap that drives creativity and allows a community to hope in transformation beyond what they can accomplish. As H. Richard Niebuhr noted in *The Kingdom of God in America*, pragmatists cannot reduce transcendent faith to its instrumentalist function without undermining the work. The missional creativity depends on the community objectively holding the hope in a transformative God.[14] King's bricolage was prophetic because he understood the creativity of the movement to be interpreting and answering the demands of the situation as demands of God. "What sets [King] apart from exemplary organic intellectuals of the past such as W. E. B. DuBois or Frederick Douglas," writes Luther Ivory, is his "God-centeredness."

Because King learned God's purposes from "radical involvement" in social confrontations, writes Ivory, he "combined revolutionary consciousness with a radical pragmatism."[15] King sought not only to use the cultural flows around him in a particular way; he sought a particular pattern of action. The student sit-ins caught his attention because, by putting their bodies on the line in a drama of confrontation with social evil, they embodied Christ's style of acting. His pragmatism was not the realism or instrumentalism that would constrain ethics to immutable historical constraints of coercive powers, observes Ivory; it was a theocentric pragmatism that sought concrete, political opportunities for changing power in view of God's relation to history.

This remains pragmatist in that King held the wound of the world as the most apt site to find the creative action of God, and because he interpreted God's action through community strategies to bear and heal the world's wounds. Yet those pragmatic moments were sustained by a belief intentionally and self-consciously sustained: that a transcendent God was reshaping history. King could hope to overcome the incompetency of everyday Christianity because of his belief that embodied responses to a situation could be caught up into and transformed by God's drama with history. "Belief in Christ," in other words, is key to understanding King's social ethic, and it must be understood not as a cognitive idea about the transcendent divinity or as a homiletic motivator, but as a lived reading of the movement as participation in the incarnating God.

The point here is that, for a pragmatic strategy of Christian ethics to irenically engage the inadequate and incompetent responses to contemporary problems like climate change, it needs to rely on a community's beliefs to drive transformative ethical innovation. Focusing on the "lived" aspect of theology cannot become an excuse to overlook constructive tasks of "theology." If confessed beliefs play a role in driving the innovativions in action that make communities better than they are, then those communities may need help understanding how their beliefs can support new patterns of action. One way that happens is when theologians explain how patterns of action found outside communities of confessed belief already embody what Christian creativity should look like. So where do those beliefs come from?

Lived Theology Less Fascinated by Church

A pragmatic strategy of Christian ethics remains accountable to lived ecclesial practices without supposing that such practices must occur within churches. Frustrated that official churches often failed to recognize the theological demands of their contexts, King wondered about the integrity of churches that confessed themselves so, and was intrigued by the ecclesial reality of movements that did not understand themselves as a "church." He responded by generating a double sense of church: those communities gathered by shared beliefs about the story of Jesus may not be the same community where the reality of Jesus becomes incarnate. Yet the former maintain the interpretive lexicon for recognizing the latter by cultivating the narrative which tells the shape of Christ's becoming evident in the world, which may happen elsewhere. The confessing church's beliefs testify to its own absence of ecclesial practices—to its own nonexistence as a church.

Charles Marsh names that persistent "elsewhere" the "beloved community," which Christian social movements after King have sought wherever it might appear. "The church establishes the hidden meaning of beloved community even as beloved community makes visible that meaning in ways the church often may not." Theology sometimes helps believing churches recognize beloved communities as the actuality of their own real life, moving beyond the boundaries of the church by the movements of God's love. Thus Marsh points the church of believers to their doctrine of God to help them find their life outside their own bounds. When the church falters in its mission, it can be grateful that the Spirit brings forth the body of Christ elsewhere. If this elsewhere is alienated from the church, that is no reason to despise it. "The church should not be envious of her children," says Marsh, writing with Dietrich Bonhoeffer's meditation on good people of the world, "but should listen to them and should learn lessons . . . Christians should receive with gratitude the opportunity to participate in a common human struggle for a just world." If theologians understand that struggle not as the application of belief to reality, but as a demonstration of Christ's body—and so, as reality itself—then doing theology will mean starting from live pledges of hope for the world, no matter their relation to the official churches.[16]

Christian ethics thus meets the dilemma of overwhelming social problems with a paradox: the lived practices that make the meaning of the church can (and often do) occur outside churches. That view keeps Christian ethics accountable to concrete ecclesial practices while accounting for the boring, pitiable character of most churches. To say that Christian ethics explicates the implicit meaning of lived church practices is to say that Christian ethics is dependent on communities inventing ways by which creatures might bear responsibility for reality before God. These problem-focused communities of responsibility may not be faith communities. In fact, such missional projects often develop at and beyond the boundaries of visible churches, which they regularly criticize and cajole. Reform projects may reject conventional churches in frustration at their inert complacency, may confess on behalf of them, or may form in indifference to the churches and their beliefs.

The task of social ethics done in the style of "lived theology," then, is to find live reform projects, interpret how they bear responsibility for reality, and critically cultivate their trajectory of response. Christian ethics, I have argued, takes shape around creative responses to social problems that make evident the reality of Christ. It can be thought of as a "strategy of action," as a continual redeployment of a cultural repertory to open possibilities for taking responsibility. The creative drive of theological redeployments sources both from a gap between social problem and cultural capabilities, as well as from a surfeit of possibility in God's action for the world. The hope of that excess, that grace, is told in the narratives of belief-formed communities, even though the life of those communities often belies their official stories—especially when they become obsessed with the preciousness of their story-formed identities. Yet those stories still matter, for in them is a hope about the real life of the world that keeps showing up, in odd forms and places, as the real body of God.

Notes

1. Paul Ramsey, *Basic Christian Ethics* (Louisville, KY: Westminster John Knox Press, 1993), xxxiii.
2. Traci West, *Disruptive Christian Ethics: When Racism and Women's Lives Matter* (Louisville, KY: Westminster John Knox, 2006).
3. West, *Disruptive Christian Ethics*, 9.
4. Jon Sobrino, *No Salvation Outside the Poor* (Maryknoll, NY: Orbis, 2008).
5. Kari Norgaard, *Climate Change, Emotions, and Everyday Life* (Cambridge, MA: The MIT Press, 2011), 207.
6. See Willis Jenkins, *The Future of Ethics: Sustainability, Social Justice, and Religious Creativity* (Washington, DC: Georgetown Press, 2013).
7. Mary McClintock Fulkerson, *Places of Redemption: Theology for a Worldly Church* (New York: Oxford University Press, 2007), 13.
8. Charles Marsh, *God's Long Summer: Stories of Faith and Civil Rights* (Princeton, NJ: Princeton University Press, 1997). The stories recorded on Claasen's Carbon Sabbath blog began to tell some of those narratives.
9. This section draws from Chapter 2 of Jenkins, *The Future of Ethics*.
10. I have summarized the view in more meliorist terms that Bourdieu or Swidler seem to suggest. The pressure to change, and possibilities for change, are more muted in Bourdieu's account, and Swidler does not promise that the change is adaptive.
11. Kathryn Tanner, *Theories of Culture: A New Agenda for Theology* (Minneapolis: Fortress Press, 1997).
12. Cornel West, *The American Evasion of Philosophy: A Genealogy of Pragmatism* (Madison: University of Wisconsin Press, 1989). 230.
13. Cornel West, *The Cornel West Reader* (New York: Civitas Books, 1999), 426.
14. H. R. Niebuhr, *Kingdom of God in America* (Middletown, CT: Wesleyan University Press, 1988) 12.
15. *Toward a Theology of Radical Involvement: The Theological Legacy of Martin Luther King, Jr.* (Nashville: Abingdon, 1997), 111, 108.
16. Marsh, *The Beloved Community* (New York: Basic Books, 2006), 207–210.

4

Disfigurations of Christian Identity

PERFORMING IDENTITY AS THEOLOGICAL METHOD

Willie James Jennings

WHAT DID IT mean to think as a Christian in the New World? What did it mean to be taught Christian faith in that same New World? Christian theology entered the New World of North and South America *diseased in form* and *distorted in performance*. The strange career of Christian theology in the New World remains the untold story of Christian identity in America. That story is not located in the history of theological concepts spoken and written by various theologians in the New World. Nor is it found in the multiple schools of theology that emerged across the American intellectual landscape. It is a story of *placement inside of displacement and location inside of dislocating habits of mind* in the New World. Christian theology in the New World is also about Christian theology in the Old World, and they are bound together not simply as constellations of traveling ideas, but more decisively through the ground-clearing operations of settlers in the New World. This chapter outlines those ground-clearing operations, and in so doing narrates *the disfiguring of Christian identity inside theology in the New World*. This chapter also will point to the roots of what seems to me to be our moment of crisis in modern Christian theology.

That crisis is not in regard to its content, or its context, but rather its *identity-performing character*. What identity does Christian theology perform? This is an exceedingly complicated question for Christian intellectuals, because we have not attended to the *identity-housing capacities of Christian theology itself*. Christian theology and ethics at this moment is captured in an endless, even obsessive, presentation of the nature of theology as, for example, a kind of grammar, or forms of traditioned intellection, or constellations of practices woven inside a liturgical imagination, or reflection on the everyday activities of congregations as they negotiate and shape doctrinal beliefs, or the core gestures of indigenous logics aimed at emancipatory theological practice. I am not questioning these various ways of defining or presenting theology as much as I am interested in registering the *tragedy-inflicting conditions for identity formation that came to be embedded in Christian theology in the New World*. Those conditions are far more important for grasping the troubles that plague Christian theology than the enlightenment problematic or the poststructuralist dilemmas of modernist thought—and far more important for imagining the possibilities of theology for the future.

Those conditions were set in place by a moment of innovation, a collaboration unanticipated in the New World, but one that nonetheless has framed our reality. The collaboration I am referring to was the interplay of three crucial agents who together created or recreated much of life in the New World—which is our world. They were the merchant, the soldier, and the missionary. Of course, these were not the only agents in the New World of settler colonies. We could add the citizen, the statesman, or even the peasant, but these other agents derive their identities and operations in the New World from the ground-clearing work of the merchant, the solider, and the missionary. I am not going to rehearse the complex histories in multiple nations and at different times of these three agents. Nor am I going to lift up particular examples of the three in collaboration because that, in fact, is part of my work in progress. Rather, I will propose a paradigm that I hope may function as an analytic through which we might begin to see, in more detail, the conditions that plague theology.

I want to focus on the effects of the interplay of these three agents on the identity-performing character of theology. We have to understand the incredible power of their interaction, that is, their mutual indwelling. There is a technical theological term in Trinitarian thought that refers to the mutual indwelling of the three persons, Father, Son, and Spirit. It is *perichoresis* (in Latin the term is *circumincessio* or *circuminsessio*), a term that tries to capture the ways in which the divine relations of Father, Son, and Spirit constitute specific divine identity without individuation. The term also helps to frame a way we might grasp how the works or operations of the triune God in the economy of salvation are distinct but not divisible.[1] *Perichoresis* suggests operations that are distinct but not divisible, and an identity revealed only through the relations themselves. There is a mutual indwelling that developed between these three agents that set in place structuring processes out of which came a) our modes of relationality, b) the material content of our gestures of obedience, and c) the performances of identity within theological work.

My current writing projects take up these first two structuring processes, but in this chapter I want to focus on the third: the performances of identity within theological work. Those performances are fundamentally connected to modes of relationality and gestures of obedience, but here I want to tease out the historic activation of a particular constellation of identity performances that grew in theology at the emergence and flourishing of the colonial moment. Christian theology is yet caught in the forces unleashed by this activation. I do not mean that we see ourselves as merchants, soldiers, or missionaries. I mean that these forces set in place the ways we imagine ourselves to be doing creative activity. In proper theological language, they perform a created order, and we are yet caught up in seeking lifelong alignment with that order. Alignment is a key conceptual and architectural term I will use here in order to highlight *the spatial dimensions of identity performance.* Christian theology is in fact about spatial alignment, but Christian intellectuals have yet to grasp what that means and has meant for pedagogy, discursive practices, and the work of translation—not simply words and ideas but of desire, life, and worlds.[2]

It Begins with the Earth

It all begins with the land. Nothing is more important than the land. For those who risked everything to travel across unknown and unstable waters to places beyond their imaginations, this was their theme. Their risk met their hope once they arrived at the New Worlds of Africa, or the Americas, or the many islands that hung like jewels on the necklace of the earth. The colonialists came and found land, but not only land: they found breathtaking landscapes, terrain that seemed endless, overwhelming amounts of natural resources, incomprehensible varieties of plants and animals and peoples, and tongues as diverse as the snowflakes, similar but very different.[3]

If there was a shared spirit or a common virtue among these travelers, these explorers, it was their courage—courage that was no doubt mixed with desperation and the desire to survive, but courage nonetheless. We must never underestimate this single virtue. It takes courage to be a missionary. Yet alongside the courage of a missionary is the courage of a merchant, and alongside the courage of a merchant is the courage of a soldier. Our modern world comes to life inside that courage, because it is precisely that courage that binds spaces together. Geographies are connected through the bodies of these three agents. They will go where no one else has the courage to go, and each will present a way to be and to live in the New World. We should also add another energy that flows between these three agents: greed. We must also never underestimate this single energy. Greed is, of course, the desire to accumulate, but also the desire to gather together, to bring into the fold (as Pope Nicholas stated), and to make all things new through possession.[4] Courage and greed bookend our three agents: merchant, soldier, and missionary.

I would, however, like eventually to dissect the missionary figure and articulate two kinds of missionary. There is the missionary who is fully located between the merchant and the soldier—and then there is her or his echo, a missionary or a missionary presence that is an excess, an unassimilated fragment that haunts the missionary lodged between the other agents. This is a missionary against the missionary. Yet what is most crucial are the spatial transformations energized by the interplay of these three agents. I will consider two transformations: first pertaining to *how we relate* and second to *how we become (or develop)*.

The Transformation of Relationality
The Way of the Merchant

The land was taken. This is the first work of the merchant. The way of the merchant was to build on the separation of people from land, never questioning the forms of death that lay under the destruction of places, special and mundane, or connections of people to place, connections sacred and eternal. The merchant mode was quickly, and without regard for place, to imagine the possibilities of landownership. Those possibilities included forming ways of life that would revolve around individual property owner—first and foremost, white male property owner—and then all other visions of property ownership deriving from his body as owner. The merchant mode enforced the material reality of individualism. If you had the money in the New World, you could own the earth. This was an absurdity made truth. It did not matter what people existed there, what history shaped that space, what ancestral voices echoed through that land—you could nevertheless own it. So the merchant mode invited people to live oblivious to the deep histories and textures of specific places, of animals and plants and peoples. It meant to imagine the only logic of place—where one lives—as an economic logic. I do not mean that economics was or is the only consideration one has about habitation. I mean that through the merchant mode, we have come to accept the economic determination of space, imagining inside of that determination what we (I) may do with this (my) space. In this regard, the merchant mode profoundly disrupted assumptions of connectivity and relationality.

The merchant did, however, imagine a form of relationality and connectivity, and his vision for this was nothing less than missional. If we begin to ask what kind of relationality did the emerging global merchant establish, then we can begin to see the depths of *our* dilemma. The merchant sought to bring peoples into an ever-expanding network of exchange. The expansion of that network would be inward, down into the bodies of indigenous peoples, and outward, joining peoples across vast distances and times. The exchange network envisioned by the merchant would manipulate, supersede, and if necessary utterly destroy other forms of communal relation and other cultural logics of connection. Indeed, the merchant envisioned people joined simply by voluntary and involuntary processes of exchange.

Here, what took place on the continent of Africa is absolutely crucial for us. That space shows us the fundamental completion of the commodity chain, reaching down to black bodies and their transport and sale as goods and services. In this regard, racial identity emerged as a commodity form. The social operations on the African continent and on the slave ship exemplified a way of relating that not only signaled the transition from societies formed through kinship relations to contractual relations, individual choice and so forth, but also revealed the shrinking of our imaginative capacities for relating into primarily the possibilities of exchange. What are people for inside such a vision? People serve two purposes: they are nodes or sites for exchange (e.g., producers and/or consumers), or they are tools to be employed by others. Thus the imagined structure of relating has human utility as its basic impulse. The way of the merchant was to come to new places, encountering new peoples and asking the basic question, "what can I use these people for?" And then the merchant proposed answers that would become the operating assumption of human connection.

The Way of the Soldier

The *way of the soldier* follows from the way of the merchant. Space that is commodified and segmented is already bounded and territorialized space. The spatial fragmentation imagined by the merchant is made possible by the soldier. It is the soldier that pushes people into their boundaries and defends those boundaries. It is the soldier who eliminates dangerous difference in bounded and territorialized spaces. All peoples who came to the New World who wanted land agreed with the merchant mode and enacted the way of the soldier. The way of the soldier here is to imagine sequestered and protected spaces for me and my people. There is ironically an echo here of what was lost—that is, of people defined by specific places, by the deep ecologies of place. But the difference in this modern connection of peoples to particular places is its economic determination and its racial texture.

Relationships built inside networks of exchange are the imagined alternative to the relationality imagined in the mode of the soldier. We know that the soldier was crucial to establishing viable markets, by clearing the way through the execution or even the mere appearance of military power. Yet this close collaboration with the merchant is also important for understanding the reductive nature of the mode of soldier in imagining relationality. The merchant reduces people to utility; if they resist that utility, then they will be seen through the mode of the military, as either enemy or competitor. This certainly became the way of nation-states and corporations, but this is more than macro-processes of relating. The way of the soldier denies love of the other and the way of the merchant disciplines that love, binding it only to the other's utility.

What is crucial here is the spatial dynamics of these modes of relating. From the colonial moment forward, these modes of relating required the reconfiguration of place in order to ensure their life. They required the control of space and the ability to designate places as market zones or militarized zones. By that I mean these modes depended on the ability to control the spaces of our relating. The struggle was and is always over the spaces of our relating. Where do people interact, reach, and touch each other? This is the question the merchant and the soldier continually asked and ask themselves in order to discern where people are and how they might control their relating even more. Thus the merchant and the soldier have engaged in unrelenting mapping of space, not only where things and animals and people are, but where they should be located, and what should and should not take place in those spaces. Together they sought to anticipate and channel our intentions of relating toward the ends of the market and the ends of security, national and local. Here we have the transformation of relationality through *the capture and control of space* and *the intentionality of spatial design*. The missionary situated by and between merchant and soldier will not only accept this reformation of relationality, but will bring it into theology as a mode conducive to evangelization and salvation.

The Way of the Missionary

The missionary in the New World entered a realm of crisis. It was a crisis missionaries did not realize they had entered, but it was a crisis. They were now faced with the sheer epistemological density of the New World, coupled with unprecedented power to change that world. These new geographic realities penetrated Christian theology as they expanded the epistemic horizons of Old World Christians in the New World. The missionaries, who came to the New World, standing between merchant and solider, stepped into an intense reality of vulnerability. That vulnerability was good, but they did not sense it as good. It was a vulnerability based on the unknown and the uncharted. Clearly, incredible courage brought them to the New World, but as the historian/anthropologist Calvin Luther Martin put it, the missionaries were often overwhelmed by the strangeness of place.[5]

They saw the indigenous peoples on the horizon of anxiety. Missionaries imagined the demonic in the different and spiritual sickness in what was to them strange. The missionary struggled between loving the place of the native as he found it and experienced it *as native space,* or love of the native but hate of *native* space and desire for its absolute transformation, its absolute domestication. The body of the native and native space would be coordinated with the body of the missionary, and the place of the native would be made *missionary* space. Some pushed against this domestication, but far more yielded and collaborated with merchant and soldier in the transformation of space.[6]

The mode of the missionary in this regard was to be committed to the transformation of the alien into the familiar. Outside space was made to conform to the interior of the missionary, and to signifying his or her identity. Here with merchant and soldier, we have the material conditions necessary for domestication, assimilation, and the cultic gestures of the familiar that are then drawn into the mode of operation of the missionary. More importantly, the missionary is imprinted with a different kind of spatial reorientation. The body of the missionary reorients space before it is reoriented to space. The missionary aligns spatial transformation with his bodily presence and draws that transformation into imagined signs of salvation, rather than aligning his body toward native space.

Would bodily alignment, however, have been even conceivable for a missionary? Bodies reoriented to native space would in fact become a kind of native space, and such native space in the New World was imagined to be filled with demonic influence and shaped in cultural deficiency. Yet bodily alignment was a possibility, because we know of those missionaries who "went native," as the saying goes, who entered native space and joined that space. Unfortunately we do not have enough published narrative accounts of such people and events. We also know that bodily alignment was possible because transformation itself (spatial or otherwise) was never pure. There was always cultural mixture, always the cultural baroque and the interplay of multiple cultural logics and cultural fragments woven together to form *sui generis* social and cultural form.

Yet we know most definitively that bodily alignment was a possibility because it was deeply embedded in the most basic logic of Gentile Christian existence. The Israel that followed Jesus was drawn into a painful and thorny joining with Gentiles through which a new bodily alignment expanded holy space to now include Gentile space and the Gentile body. This expansion grew directly out of the incarnate life of God that, like a seed planted in creaturely soil, now grew beyond the imagined reach of the disciples. The struggle, the genuine and good struggle, was how a follower of Jesus was to align herself or himself to this new holy space, become one with that new space. Jewish and Gentile followers of Jesus alike were called to a new alignment that would again and again create a new collective body in Jesus. Of course, what concealed this deep logic of alignment was a history of its fundamental denial, a history poorly called supersessionism.

Missionaries were not in control of the transformation of space. They were, however, deeply embedded in its normalization. This is not to say that missionaries always agreed with the ways of the merchant and the soldier—they did not. Normalization penetrated the missionary, which not only removed the necessity of alignment to new spaces and new bodily practices in those spaces but also drew that removal into their theological imagination. This in turn would set in place a trajectory toward spatial absence in their theologies that would mirror the geographic oblivious-ness that would mark modern life. But how would the missionary come to imagine space? There would be a spatial dimension in theology in the New World, but that spatial dimension would be expressed in boundary thinking, an imagined inside and outside. Boundary thinking in theology is not new. The moment of innovation (if we wish to call it that) comes at the confluence of the privatization of space coupled with the desire to have space signify missionary identity. *The imagined inside and outside now turned on possession.* A possessive vision of holy space constituted by the body of the missionary emerged at this confluence and would be reflected in theological intellection itself. At one level, the effect of this vision would be to drain theological (intellectual) work of its relational character. But in order to grasp the full effect of this possessive vision we must turn to the second spatial transformation activated by merchant, soldier, and missionary.

The Transformation of Becoming
The Way of the Merchant

The merchant had a flexible and expansive imagination. He could easily imagine multiple kinds of exchange with multiple peoples, bringing to those processes of exchange clear commitment to connect peoples in ways that they had never been connected before. This was the true power of the colonial moment, a new vision of global connectivity. A powerful example of this was the slave ship, which was the pivotal site for the growth of global cosmopolitanism. There on the ship people from a vast array of places were joined in an ever-increasing network of ports, villages, and plantations, all of which reorientated their lives to new geographic des-tinations. It is precisely in the context of this kind of reorientation that a new crucial question emerged: *what may people become?* No one necessar-ily asked it but everyone was being drawn toward it, as well as toward the answer to that question.

What may people become? Answer: *People may become significant.* Here we have to return to the original semantic trajectory of the idea of signifi-cance bound to signification. People may enter a network of meaning in which they may locate themselves and their people in a universal narrative of global development, evolution, and influence. At one level, this meant announcing yourself, your humanity, through the modes of intelligence of the West, but at another level *becoming significant meant imagining yourself*

marked (recognized) on the global landscape. This marking did not necessarily mean distinction (especially not celebrity); rather it meant simply
being part of a civilizing project, being part of an imagined community of
development.

Fundamental to this new becoming was the transformation of
becoming *away from the land.* If to become an adult, a man or woman
must show their skills in hunting, fishing, and carrying forward the
old agrarian ways, but those old ways have been cut off or destroyed by
land loss, or rendered *inconsequential* to thriving, then where would they
go to calibrate their *becoming,* their entry into adulthood in ways that
affirm their existence and their future? How does one set aspirations,
life goals? To use more theological language, how might one understand
one's vocation, one's sense of calling, within the destiny of one's people?
Historically, with the emergence of the global merchant and the seizing
of land it was as though, for vast portions of the world's population, the
runway necessary for local identities to take flight and lead somewhere
was reduced to, at best, a fraction of the needed distance. In effect, local
identities became geographically adrift, no longer calibrated by life with
land and animals.

How might we calibrate identities if no longer by land and animal? On
the one side emerged a racial calculus built within a scale of whiteness to
blackness that collapsed identity onto the body and forced indigenes to
negotiate a vision of the self with its new racial symbiote. But on the other
hand, the merchant would show peoples how to create significant identities. *The merchant was the one who gave us the eyes to see what was significant.*
As we stated before, the merchant was about connecting things. If architecture from one place may be *approximated* in another, if European dress,
manner, mood, ritual, gesture, foods, and animals may be transposed to
new locales, then in the context of global markets, aesthetic judgments
and desire could be cultivated across vast stretches of space and time. The
merchant would introduce to peoples in, for example, Brazil, Virginia,
Peru, Hong Cong, Nova Scotia, London, Ghana, Kenya, and Capetown the
idea of a beautiful building, a luxurious dress or coat, a fine cigar, a wonderful bottle of rum, whiskey, or wine, or a fine pair of shoes, and connect
those objects to eloquent and beautiful speech, beautiful bodies, refined
manners, and distinctive style. More precisely, the merchant could introduce *through objects a constellation of judgments* that could be coordinated
with local judgments of the beautiful, the desirable, or the ugly and the
repulsive.

The merchant established a global structure of approximation for the market.

What was beautiful or ugly in one place may now be seen in the same duality in another place. What was desirable in one place may now be desirable in another place. *Most importantly, through the merchant people would learn that they could approximate life conjured by the desired object.* This is not first a matter of policy or law, though it could be, but rather this was the possibility of accepting images of the true, the good, and the beautiful and coordinating native images with transatlantic or globalizing images.[7] It was on this structure of approximation that nations would emerge and cultural nationalisms would come to consciousness; yet what is crucial for our purposes *is the embodiment of approximation through which one learned how to discern significance (especially through objects of consumption) and to align one's own body, mind, and soul to move toward becoming significant.* This *becoming significant* bound to the way of the merchant became the most historically expansive and powerful invitation yet seen—that any people can be on their way too.

The journey itself is a crucial matter. On that journey, peoples looked on their own cultures as merchants would look, asking what might be useful in the advance toward significance, and what might be inconsequential. Indeed, this looking sliced indigenous worlds, cutting between the culturally relevant and the cultural past. This merchant-inspired looking positioned peoples each inside their own cultural archive at the precise moment it created that archive, and invited them to bring forward their unique contribution to a global market, and therefore toward global significance. One's identity (as Ibo or Zulu or Apache or Yupik, Khosa, Lumbee, Ashanti and so forth) is *one's past* and inconsequential in and of itself. It is significant only to the extent that one asserts its *possible* global significance.

The assertion itself is also a crucial matter. That assertion would gesture masculinity. This is not to say that only men assert the significance of their people and their own significance on the world stage. *Rather, masculine identity within the logic of the merchant circled around ownership.* Landownership was one of the most powerful and attractive means through which one might perform significance and masculinity, that is, the *masculinity* of significance and the *significance* of masculinity. A man who owns (the land) announces his power to shape his own identity and destiny. Landownership in the New World became a powerful way of showing the new global trajectory of becoming. Peoples, like a man stepping forward on the world stage, may assert ownership of their worlds, their land, and their culture. Obviously, colonialist land acquisition and expansionism inspired this assertion, and in the light cast by the global struggle of the European man for preeminence, all peoples might also imagine their people becoming a significant player on the world stage, the many in the one gesture of assertion, that is, one significant man. The point not to be missed here is that local identities, gendered identities, and personal identity can all be captured inside this masculine quest.

This should not be read as exaggerated ambition; rather, this has to do with the forming of an image that would guide the drive "to make something of yourself," especially for the sake of your people. Such an image would school the countless immigrants coming to the New World in hopes of moving from a position of cultural and racial alienation to one of assimilation. The way of the merchant formed the fertile image of a white man who embodies self-sufficiency, control of his destiny, and is the creator of his world. Not any one man, but the embodiment of the masculine, this image was capable of covering the identity of a people and reaching down to cover individual bodies, male and female.

The Way of the Soldier

The soldier, however, is not primarily the tool of the merchant. The soldier is first a site of embodiment, a center for vicarious existence. The soldier is quintessentially the one for the many. Simply put, the way of the soldier was and is to perform collectivity. Through the body of a soldier flow the wishes and anxieties of family, people, culture, or a nation. That body presents a kind of baptism into a collective desire for securing the future of a people. We know that the baptism of the soldier into the collective identity of the nation-state is never completely stable, because it depends on the tacit assumption of a shared project of enhancing life and promoting a better future for a people. The way of the global merchant, however, often undermined that very assumption. For the global merchant, the only true site of military stability bound in complete alignment to a nation's wishes was and is with the machines of war, and not warriors themselves.

The warriors from the beginning of the colonial theater forward, however, performed the formation of bodies in space in ways that collaborated with the aspirations born of the merchant. The discipline of the body established by military training announced and translated *the becoming of a people* in immediately accessible ways to generations of immigrants. Such a formation is of course ancient, yet on colonial sites this ancient work of "making warrior-men" joined with the merchant's work of making significant men. Together these *identities in progress* also constituted *solidarity in the making*—solidarity that on the one side established an imagined fraternity of white men, and on the other side offered an open invitation to anyone to become a person of honor and recognition. The soldier's discipline inspired conformity—not bare conformity, but rather one bound to self-making. The soldier was one whose agency was secured by his own hands, and his example as a *man-in-the-making* had longitudinal effects on ecclesial and catechetical imaginations in the New World.[8]

The Way of the Missionary

If the missionary was deeply embedded in the normalization of the transformation of space, he was even more deeply embedded in the transformation of becoming. Here I want to underscore the mutual interpenetration of merchant, soldier, and missionary because it is precisely that *perichoresis* that will permeate their bodies and be drawn into theology itself. Together they will be caught up in the very processes of becoming they created, and together they will form a pedagogical field where language and landscape will be coordinated with built environments. The becoming of space and land will mirror their own quests to become significant. Spaces will be presented as sites of constant becoming that parallel processes of human becoming.[9] The development of space joins the development of the body. Indigenous peoples will be brought into this dual work of becoming through regimes of enunciation that embody the inseparable connection not only of language to empire but also of language and empire to habitation.

The way of the missionary has always carried unbelievable pedagogical potential. Yet its potential was from the beginning of the colonial moment coordinated between these two powerful realities of becoming—architectural and anthropological—which together produced a deeply deformed vision of making disciples in the New World, a distorted form that marks the Christianity we have inherited. That distorted form was executed through what I call a pedagogical imperialism. The missionary entered the New World imagining it shaped by fundamental social, cultural, and intellectual deficiency. Additionally, the vision of the culturally deficient and the vision of the demonic mutually informed one another. Christians entered the worlds of indigenous peoples in unrelenting evaluative mode, as eternal teachers with eternal students. We may call this cultural paternalism (as some historians have), but that term really does not get at the tragedy here. The tragedy here cannot be grasped by simply seeing this as a form of cultural paternalism. *This is a Christianity and Christian theology encased in evaluative mode.*

Whiteness was at play here. The possibilities of authentic Christian performance, authentic Christian life and knowledge, were gauged by the possibilities of being white, becoming white, and/or imitating whiteness. The scale implied by this gauging indicated an irreversible asymmetrical relation. Indigenous Christian life was never in the position of teacher, never in the position of really altering Western ways of life, never in the position of offering the Word of God to the missionary; the divine word could only go to work on those subject to the missionary. This asymmetrical theological relationship was coordinated with and nourished by the transformation of space into private property, and it rendered not only the Christians of the New World mute but also closed off the Christian church of the West to the expansion of its own Christian identity inside new places and newly encountered identities of God's creatures in the world.

My book, *The Christian Imagination*, notes some of the problems we are all familiar with that have been caused by this pedagogical imperialism. But, as I close, I want to press in on the problem of alignment, because it is precisely this problem that helps us see the identity-deforming and identity-mangling operation that is embedded in Christian theological intellection. Christian theology is aligned with the modalities of the merchant and the soldier, which means that it promotes an identity form that has at least three abiding characteristics: (1) it is dislocating; (2) it conceals the historical processes of becoming; and (3) it denies relationality and connectivity.

Pierrie Bourdieu, in *Pascalian Meditations,* writes of the scholastic disposition, that disposition inculcated in those who desire to inhabit the scholastic universe. Fundamental to this disposition is the forgetting of historical being, that is, the forgetting of the "historical conditions for the emergence of reason" or "the deliberate concealment of these conditions . . . [in order to] . . . legitimate the most unjustifiable of monopolies, the monopoly of the universal."[10] I take Bourdieu to be articulating a problem inside the larger problem of dislocation. Christian theology, for its part, dislocates intellectuals while at the same time drawing them toward a spatial desire to have their identities mirrored by place and space.[11] This dislocating affect is not forms of abstract thinking, or even dualistic disembodied ways of thinking. It is a way of theologizing that participates in modern spatial obliviousness and draws that spatial absence into blindness of space. This blindness attenuates our ability to discern the affects of real space and built environments on our bodies and the shape of our intellectual work. This spatial blindness cuts off our ability to recognize the historical trajectories of formation bound up in the intentions of geographic location and the architectural shape of habitation. So theological reflection as it has been presented to us is angled away from thinking location and its formative effects, and as a result Christian intellectuals operate with a very weak sense of positionality. By positionality I do not simply mean the different identity-spaces we occupy. Positionality is the crucial work of discernment of place and space, of conversations, discursive practices, and protocols. A healthy sense of positionality opens up the crucial work of negotiation through which theology could perform alignment.[12] Yet the dislocating affect mangled this skill in theological reflection, and drew it into the processes of becoming.

This dislocating habit of mind conceals the historical processes of becoming. Here we have to draw together class and gender analyses with architectural analysis in order to see how the creation of habitation is bound up with the creation of social form that guides visions of uplift. The stories of immigrant angst, assimilation, and survival, as well as the stories of nation-building and the rise of cultural nationalisms, are part and parcel with the stories of education, educational institutions, and especially theological education since the beginning of the colonial moment. The desire to become the self-sufficient man is a desire nurtured inside theological formation; it flows through the ecology of theological work in the academy. We could take, for example, the idea of intellectual rigor and how a rigorous mind is formed through battle, conflict, and debate that historically echoes multiple cultural forms of chivalric gestures and real-world battles, battlefield tactics, and the emergence of modern sport. Or we could take, for another example, the fetish shown in requiring the mastery of languages, especially European languages, for graduate education in the theological academy—a mastery that is less about the pedagogical usefulness of such languages, and more about the creation of a person who embodies languages that bespeak imperialist control of knowledge and knowledge production.

The third characteristic points to the painful loss of imaginative possibilities for identity formation within Christian theology. Those possibilities of joining, of merger, of alignment of body with space would have opened up the possibilities of thinking about orthodox practice embodied in native performance, and of native religious and cultural performance enacted in Christian form. Rather than these possibilities, Christian theology nurtured an unrelenting derogatory optic among indigenous peoples and the birth of a vision of *backwardness*, of a primitive character that must be erased. Thus alignment became the task of the indigene, the burden of the native to align herself with a faith that slowly drained the earth, animals, landscape, and places of their signifying power and turned it all into underdeveloped private property and underutilized foodstuffs. She would also be tied to a faith that invited peoples into obsessive evaluative gestures born of the missionaries. The theological imagination bequeathed to her and her kin was saddled with an obsession with discerning the orthodoxy/heterodoxy and orthopraxis/hetero-praxis of her own people.

Summary

When I began I mentioned that I wanted to split the missionary, that is, I wanted to bookmark at the very beginning of this chapter another kind of missionary, another kind of missionary presence that exists over against the missionary lodged between merchant and soldier. Christian theology is haunted by this other kind of missionary presence. We see fragments of it in those "MKs," those missionary kids who upon returning or "coming home" to the United States never feel at home, never feel at home in being white, or male, or female, or American evangelical, or Catholic. We can discern fragments of it in the quiet stories of those missionaries who got caught up in the local too deeply and lost themselves abroad. We also see it in the many students who study theology who feel that there is something deeply dehumanizing in the initiation to its study that is not explained by the unfamiliarity that they may have with philosophy, or the scholastic practices of reading and writing, or even academic ecologies. They see people who seem fabricated, yet perfectly aligned to a social form, whose way of talking aligns with the theology they articulate, which in turn aligns with particular class dispositions or distinctions which align with other matters like the examples, and anecdotes, and jokes they tell in class, and the student realizes that she enjoys no such alignment, and if there would be another kind of alignment, that would be the work of the people, people like her.

What would it mean for Christian theology to be a life form that generates a constellation of practices that invite people into multiple kinds of alignment, alignments that cover a lifetime and are never closed, never settled, but rather always show openness to the creation? It would mean that we seek to enter the trajectory of Gentile Christian existence not as an act of theological retrieval, but as the continuation of that unfinished project of the Spirit always working ahead of us. What would it mean to be in that fundamental posture of the *Gentile-become-Christian*, that is *one of wishing to learn*, one who will seek to perform Christian identity inside ways of life not naturally her own, first of Israel, then as those who will make disciples of other peoples? This is the missing element—a vision of Christian theology that is Ruth-like, one in which *we are required* by the very nature of faith (mixed with desire) to enter deeply into different ways of life and to perform Christianity within the cultural logics of peoples different from us.[13] This is precisely what the Gentile trajectory opened us toward—the performance of commitment to Jesus inside the cultural logics of people not our own.

Here is a vision of faith woven with desire as the inner logic driving theological work. Theology's "enactment," then, requires flexibility, adaptability, and translatability. Unfortunately, the colonial trajectory of Christianity robbed us of centuries of practice in doing this work of discipleship. Rather, this was the work of indigenous peoples having to accommodate their lives to a stable, often rigid, often unyielding, colonizing Christianity. Yet this alternative missionary mode remembers the invitation given by God to Peter—to desire new ways of life. This alternative missionary mode follows the Gentile gesture that is present in our very practices of reading scripture itself. Of course, the most powerful implication of our reading of scriptures *is concealed to us exactly in our reading of scripture*, because it sits on top of centuries of the negàtive effect of translation. *A translated bible meant a Christian life freed from the necessity of being translatable.* But that is another story.

Notes

1. Gregory of Nazianzus states, "No sooner do I conceive of the One than I am illuminated by the Splendor of the Three: no sooner do I distinguish Them than I am carried back to the One," in "Oration on Holy Baptism," Orations 60 and 61 in *NPNF*, 2nd series, bk 7, 375, cited in Otto Weber, *Foundations of Dogmatics*, vol. 1 (Grand Rapids, MI: Eerdmans, 1981), 390. Weber here is citing John Calvin's quotation of Nazianzus. See John Calvin, *The Institutes of the Christian Religion* (Grand Rapids, MI: Christian Classics Ethereal Library), I: 13, 17, p. 93. Weber states,

84

LIVED THEOLOGY

"This unity in triplicity, and triplicity in unity, can only be conceived of as living . . . Basically what is said here is that the triplicity never encroaches upon the unity of God, not even where Scripture speaks of an activity of one of God's modes of being alone, but also that this unity is not to be thought of in a rigid fashion. *This term belongs in a special way to the tools of interpretation*" (390, emphasis added).

2. Yi-Fu Tuan, "Body, Personal Relations, and Spatial Values," in *Space and Place: The Perspective of Experience* (Minneapolis: University of Minnesota Press, 1977), 34–50. Gaston Bachelard, "Intimate Immensity," in *The Poetics of Space* (Boston: Beacon Press, 1969), 183–210. Robert M. Fogelson, "The Sacred Skyline: The Battle Over Height Limits," in *Downtown: Its Rise and Fall, 1880–1950* (New Haven, CT: Yale University Press, 2001), 112–82.

3. Stephen Greenblatt, "Kidnapping Language," in *Marvelous Possessions: The Wonder of the New World* (Chicago: Chicago University Press, 1991), 86–118. Peter Hulme, "Tales of Distinction: European Ethnography and the Caribbean," in *Implicit Understandings: Observing, Reporting, and Reflecting on the Encounters Between Europeans and Other Peoples in the Early Modern Era*, ed. Stuart B. Schwartz (Cambridge, UK: Cambridge University Press, 1994), 157–97.

4. "Bull Romanus Pontifex, January 8, 1455," in *European Treaties Bearing on the History of the United States and Its Dependencies to 1648, vol. 1*, ed. Frances Gardiner Davenport (Washington, DC: Carnegie Institution of Washington, 1917), 20–21. Cited in Willie James Jennings, *The Christian Imagination: Theology and the Origins of Race* (New Haven, CT: Yale University Press, 2010), 26.

5. Calvin Luther Martin, *The Way of the Human Being* (New Haven, CT: Yale University Press, 1999), 26ff.

6. I know that such missionaries existed, yet stable and reliable documentation of their struggle is extremely difficult to gather together. In future work I hope to gather such testimony.

7. Monica L. Miller, "Crimes of Fashion: Dressing the Part from Slavery to Freedom," in *Slaves to Fashion: Black Dandyism and the Styling of Black Diasporic Identity* (Durham, NC: Duke University Press, 2009), 77–136.

8. Bernardo de Vargas Machuca, *The Indian Militia and Description of the Indies* (Durham: Duke University Press, 2008). This is a fascinating account famously known as the first warrior's manual against Amerindian guerilla warfare (original published in 1599) in which Captain Machuca considers not only military tactics but also issues of formation of solider and priest alike, as well as the kind of Christian character a soldier, especially a leader of soldiers must exhibit on the stage of war. See 30ff, 58ff.

9. A powerful account of a city becoming is the magisterial work of William Cronon, *Nature's Metropolis: Chicago and the Great West* (New York: Norton, 1991). This should be read in relation to the classic work of St. Clare Drake and Horace R. Clayton, *Black Metropolis: A Study of Negro Life in a Northern City* (Chicago: Chicago University Press, 1945), and more recently, Edward W. Wolner, *Henry Ives Cobb's Chicago: Architecture, Institutions, and the Making of a Modern Metropolis* (Chicago: Chicago University Press, 2011).

10. Pierre Bourdieu, *Pascalian Meditations* (Stanford, CA: Stanford University Press, 1997), 70.

11. In a forthcoming essay, I suggest that this should be one way to consider the assertion of tradition in theology as a form of spatial desire bound up with identity formation. See Willie James Jennings, "The Traditions of Race Men," in *South Atlantic Quarterly* 112, no. 4 (2013): 613–24.

12. Chela Sandoval, *Methodology of the Oppressed* (Minneapolis: University of Minnesota Press, 2000), 42.2.–63.4. Sandoval brilliantly notes the oppositional consciousness developed by Third-World feminist intellectuals who have had to negotiate the multiple forms of racial and gender dislocation at work in the prevailing discursive operations of various disciplines intended to offer resources for political emancipatory work.

13. Of course, the historical point here is not how different was Ruth's way of life from Israel (though she clearly announces a difference), but rather, how different are our lives from Israel?

PART TWO

Lived Theology as Style

5

Daring to Write Theology
without Footnotes

Susan R. Holman

IN 2005, THE Project on Lived Theology (PLT) at the University of Virginia, directed by religion professor Charles Marsh with funding from the Lilly Endowment, brought together seven writers from across the academic spectrum and representing a number of different religious traditions for the first "Virginia Seminar," a multi-year working group to explore together what it meant to write about "lived theology." Specifically, we were funded in order to develop publishable, book-length narratives that would reflect on our various individual perspectives, bringing and applying our personal voices and perspectives to our respective areas of expertise.

We first met in the beauty of spring in Charlottesville, some of us already old friends, others—like me—making our first visit to the land of Thomas Jefferson and a stranger to everyone in the group. Each of us arrived at the Bonhoeffer House (Charles Marsh's home) that first evening with the book idea that was our ticket to this opportunity. Some of these ideas were little more than a cloud cartoon hovering at the edge of the imagination, bolstered at best by the printed outline we distributed during our initial discussion. The Seminar's purpose was to nurture and foster these ideas into a book over as many annual gatherings as the Lilly Endowment and wizardry of UVA's grant administration would permit. During that first three-day seminar, we laughed about books, sat spellbound in a roundtable discussion with a real live Manhattan-and-London book agent, and worked hard at constructive collegial critique. By the time we headed home, we realized that we not only could trust one another but also were having a great deal of fun together. It was Charles's dream to hold the second meeting in New Orleans, but Hurricane Katrina got there first. And so we met in Manhattan instead, each year after that first spring, trekking the neon city through rain, snow, and taxicabs across a paradox of two realities: the wood-polished elegance of the Harvard Club on West 44th Street and the simple, joy-filled, no-frills welcome of City Seminary in Harlem, seventy-five blocks uptown. We crossed these borderlands by subway and on foot, talking endlessly and avidly (mostly) of books. And indeed, when the first seminar grant ran dry, we had each (mostly) produced a book, a direct and gratifying consequence of these amazing conversations.

Our significant output was due in part, I suspect, to the fact that we were not "just another writing group." There was at our core something that held us together like jambalaya with risotto: a commitment to what we had come to call "lived theology." But what did this mean for our very different approaches to writing, and what might others learn from our encounters together? In this chapter, I would like to reflect on one of the questions that we all brought with us to that first spring evening at the Bonhoeffer House: what does it mean to *write* lived theology?

Well, we might say, first of all, it means writing about something that is *lived*, whatever that means. And indeed, we were inspired by the activities and connections with the Seminar's "home" organization, the PLT and its associated graduate students and faculty at the University of Virginia, with their focus across a broad spectrum of theologically informed *action* for social justice. But where does the more solitary act of *writing* fit into this mix?

As I wrestled with this question during the years we met—and then watched it take shape with a new group of scholars and writers in the second funded Virginia Seminar, a few years later—there seemed to me three parts to how I might answer this question. The first was what "writing lived theology" meant in our obvious efforts to write *about* lived theology. The second was what I came to experience of writing *as* lived theology. And finally, less distinct than these two ideas but holding them together, I found myself stockpiling a trove of eclectic wisdom—random utterances that someone had made over dinner or deep in the heat of a chapter critique—wise scraps that seemed worth passing on to others engaged in similar efforts. Whatever one aims for in community dialogue about "lived theology," every group will have its own spirit. The points here refer to very specific examples from participants in the Virginia Seminars between

2005 and 2013, and may say more about our peculiar dynamics than about lived theology itself. But writers around the world, I suspect, share many of these oddities, and may find our experience a prompt for their own creative development and design.

Writing about Lived Theology

Writing *about* lived theology was what we came together expecting to do. It is what we had been doing—in some cases for many years. But in the seminar context, we found ourselves asking new questions. In particular, a key debate that shaped our discussions across every meeting was that of genre: how does writing about lived theology vary according to the genre or type of writing that one is called to do? What would be the particular challenges—and perhaps related opportunities—for each of the different "genres" represented by the writers in the group?

We were all academic scholars of one sort or another, from disciplines that included religion, history, and English. The writing we had done before the Seminar fell into four basic types: (1) academic scholarly writing; (2) memoir/biography; (3) what might be called inspirational, moral, or didactic instruction in or for organized religion; and (4) popular trade writing. What were the challenges we faced in writing about "lived theology" in each of these categories?

Academic Writing

Most of us had established our credentials as writers in our field largely through traditional academic or scholarly writing, but this genre "writ large" in our lives for some more than others. In the later, second Virginia Seminar, the obvious academic writers included Shannon Gayk, who writes about medieval religious expression,[1] and Amy Laura Hall, through her books on Kierkegaard and *Conceiving Parenthood*.[2] In the first Seminar, I may have been the one who wrestled most with the challenge of combining "lived theology" with my very academic writing style—perhaps along with Chuck Mathewes, whose passion for academic writing was matched only by his passion for finding excellence in the perfect fountain pen in downtown Manhattan. Carlos Eire was also very familiar with this struggle—until he won the National Book Award for *Waiting for Snow in Havana*, his first book without footnotes.[3] Some of our earlier books had combined lived theology and academic "objectivity" more intentionally than others; for example, Jennifer McBride's *The Church for the World*[4] and Russell Jeung's *Faithful Generations*, on new Asian American churches.[5] Whatever it is that academic writing means and requires of us as scholars, it seems to me that we who write it are faced with four key challenges when it comes to shaping it into a narrative of lived theology.

The first challenge is very basic: how to turn "academese" into accessible ordinary English with an engaging narrative. Graduate school tends to brainwash us into thinking that academic sentences reflect the highest intelligence when they are as convoluted as possible. Rather, be clear. Second, academics live with certain ghosts who populate our unspoken audience. We may subconsciously target our book to an agenda that feels far more urgent than the need for clarity or personal narrative. We often write because we need tenure, or to "prove" our academic career. Third, we may assume a style that works for others is wrong for us. We may particularly fear crossing over into that taboo area of the subjective voice and personal narrative. Am I afraid to use the words "I" and "me"? Do I quail at the thought of even voicing a personal unfootnoted experience or opinion? And fourth, we may—often with (we think) good reason—fear that if our book aims at something as mundane as "practical relevance," it will compromise our chances for grant funding. Even in religious studies, some academic grant committees may have a reputation for frowning on projects that are less than "pure" scholarship. Thus the contested distance, in some Ivy League institutions, between the divinity school and the academic department that is most intent on building expertise in "the study of religion."

Memoir and Biography

Second, what are the challenges for those who write memoir and biography? Does lived theology mean simply including details about some spiritual aspects in a lived life? Of course it needs more than that, but how do we push deeper? In our first seminar, four of the seven members of the group had written at least one memoir or biography, so this was a major topic for discussion at every meeting. Charles Marsh, for example, had published his own memoir, *The Last Days: A Son's Story of Sin and Segregation at the Dawn of a New South*,[6] and was hard at work on a new Bonhoeffer biography as the first seminar grant ended.[7] In the second Seminar, participants who had published in this genre included Valerie Cooper, with her book on Maria Stewart, and Vanessa Ochs's memoir, *Words on Fire*. I personally find biography very appealing, and the group inspired me to begin work on a project about one small narrative in my own family history, a story about a nineteenth-century public health doctor whose career dragged him through an international political scandal and into experiences with contagion, sick sailors, insanity, the New England poorhouse, and small-town murder. This project careened through more twists and turns than I imagined possible during that first Seminar conversation; it ultimately took shape not as memoir, but as a chapter in a book related to the history of public health and what it means for global health and human rights concerns today.[8] Yet even this would have been impossible without first daring to voice the kernel of an idea across our bagels-and-napkins-strewn table during one late-afternoon conversation. Our many talks about memoir helped me anticipate what can be difficult when we seek to bring lived theology to this type of writing.

For example, memoir and certain kinds of religious biography, intimate and up-close by nature, may seem antithetical to our ideals for academic writing. They face us with different challenges as we must continuously pause and ponder, "How do I step back in order to most effectively shape this overall narrative?" And even if the story we tell is not one from our personal history, our choice to write a biography, being as it is about a particular person, inevitably touches on our personal inclinations for relationships. It may tap our most deeply submerged views, biases, and motives for writing. How do we get in touch with those views and biases, given that they will inevitably influence the narrative? And what is the "lived theology" of such writing? Whose is the theological voice? The thread of theology can take many different patterns. How will we weave it?

Inspirational, Moral, or Didactic Narrative

Third, what are the challenges for those projects that more intentionally target a faith-based reader and setting? Writings that are inspirational, moral, or didactic, about or for organized religion, typically include books we love to hate—often for good reason. And depending on the topic and fame (or infamy) of the author, these are sometimes the books most likely to sell even when they are very badly written.

As far as I can tell, no one in the seminar had their heart set on churning out a syrupy or trashy pulpit potboiler. And yet, each of us was driven in our writing by some degree of personal faith and theology. Inspiration and moral lessons likely drive at least part of our projects and motives, as these aspects are inevitably a piece of our background, our ideas, the things we hold to be important. How were we to shape features in our narratives that might contain echoes of—or be frankly and explicitly—inspirational, moral, or didactic narrative about or for organized religion? Where does one draw the line between a work of art that reflects one's whole integrity—including our views on the world—and risking a reputation for "sermonizing" or writing "Gospel Lite"? How does one avoid a book that is little more than a string of interesting stories or, on the other hand, avoid too much use of a prescriptive voice? I do not think any of us seriously risked crossing this line, but for some participants in the Seminar, especially those who were ordained clergy, this specter loomed more darkly than it did for the rest of us. In the first seminar, for example, we shared the experience of Charles Marsh's *Wayward Christian Soldiers: Freeing the Gospel from Political Captivity*, which he himself admitted first took shape as a "jeremiad" against a particular perspective.[9] For other ordained Seminar members, like Mark Gornik and Sam Lloyd (able to be with the group only briefly), such writing drew on fieldwork and life lived in the sanctuary moments. Together, we wrestled over keeping at bay the demons of such genre, while honestly working toward a narrative that would be excellent in all that we held to be true. I think not only of Mark Gornik's stories about all-night prayer meetings in New York City[10] but also Vanessa Ochs's shaping of creative feminist narrative both before and after her rabbinic ordination, in both memoir and wry inspiration.[11] The takeaway message is that this genre, like the others, offers us an opportunity for new ideas and exciting original insights. For is not lived theology the very essence and heart of all good preaching?

Popular Trade Writing

Finally, what are the challenges for those who write "popular" or trade books? Trade books sell, and all writers want to publish and have many good, thoughtful, paying readers. As a "critically acclaimed" cultural critic, what would David Dark say about the lived theology in his *Sacredness of Questioning Everything*?[12] And what about poetry—and god forbid, maybe even fiction—as it relates to religion in trade writing? In the first seminar, those we viewed as successful trade writers included Carlos Eire, Patricia Hampl, Alan Jacobs, and Charles Marsh. But Carlos often reminded us that "popular" writing can bear a high cost in the academy. Faculty scholars who succeed with trade books may be treated by their peers as less than serious about what they do; he advised perhaps waiting until tenure before taking such a risk. I once read that murder mysteries used to be the only popular genre that British academics considered acceptable for scholars to write—if only because university professors all read them whenever they got sick! While none of our Virginia Seminar books were murder mysteries, only the English professors in the group seemed to feel safe with a reputation for acclaimed trade books; the rest of us approached the issue with fear and trembling. To its credit, Oxford University Press has made deliberate efforts to court and publish manuscripts that combine good academic writing with aspects of popular trade narrative, in part distilling this classic anxiety. Even so, freedom to write safely in this genre does not guarantee you will want to keep it up; Alan Jacobs began one meeting, soon after publication of *The Narnian*,[13] by exclaiming, "I will never *ever ever* write another word about C.S. Lewis!"

I offer here no easy answers for the challenges that face writers in these four particular groups of writing. Even within a similar genre and discipline, each of us will need to wrestle with particular answers and opportunities that vary depending on our projects and our own personal voice. The type of writing we choose will depend on who we are. Honoring our gifts as writers engages us in a sacred dynamic of accountability to all the forms and genres of writing, both as craft and as art.

Writing as Lived Theology

It is all too easy to think of lived theology as something we write *about,* as the living of theology "out there," in direct personal engagement in history or in our everyday religious expression, work in our worship space, teaching, social action, and activism. This was how I had envisioned it during the time I was writing my dissertation about faith-based responses to poverty, hunger, and disease in early Christian sermons from the fourth century, describing a theology in action to invite reader response.[14] But when Charles Marsh invited me to think about my own personal experiences, and to bring first-person voice to the project, his invitation made me aware of a sort of split-identity issue in my writing that had been there for a long time—one that would continue to dog me throughout the work I wanted to do for the Seminar. Others in the academy may face a similar dilemma, one that I ultimately was able to shape into what became my Virginia Seminar book, *God Knows There's Need: Christian Responses to Poverty.*[15]

The tension is common to those of us who both specialize in the study of religion and also self-identify as people of a particular religious faith or philosophy. On the one hand, we own our belief systems and are willing to honestly admit that we belong to a particular faith group. On the other hand, we have also committed to practice scholarship with the integrity that requires a particular type of detached objectivity and distance in any discussion from the use of personal voice. This separation may not be an iron curtain, but it is one where we are quite clear to ourselves about what is what and how to keep them separate. Charles was inviting me to consider a book that consisted of both, in dialogue together.

I take theology very seriously, and I have long been deeply formed by it. And as my faith relates to ethics and political action on social justice and human rights, naturally it will have a bearing on my research and writing, even in the carefully "objective" scholarly work I do for the academy. But as they concern my personal acts of worship in relation to deity, and my spiritual identity as a religious person, my faith-based thoughts, perceptions, and experiences are more private. The existence of these separate, if psychically integrated, "spaces" in my life have always caused me to think very carefully about how I choose to use the "personal voice" in writing for my academic peers, and beyond annual Christmas letters to friends, I have never felt any particular "call" to what might be labeled "devotional" writing. The invitation to write a more personalized book forced me to reflect: what aspect of personal voice has its best fit in public space? What personal experiences "work" in such writing as I might develop through this intriguing (and tempting) invitation? And how does one take such risks?

My writing style was further shaped by the fact that I began what might be called my "professional" career writing in the sciences, which was not at all a natural preference. Writing health science began as a tool for survival, starting in college, when my parents were determined I should major in something likely to result in a "real job." My first successful book was a nutrition textbook for nursing students. I wrote it during time off from my first "real job," an intense clinical teaching role that was entirely unsuited to my temperament and, even though I cared deeply about the concept and moral ideals of public health, was tearing me apart inside. I had always loved to write. So when I left clinical nutrition to go back to school for graduate studies in religion, I found work in medical writing, and it was good. Privately, I continued the writing I had always loved, in poetry, journaling, some fiction, and reflection. The result was a strong sense of split between my private and public identity—both as a person of faith, and as a writer.

Faced with the invitation to join the Virginia Seminar, could I weather the bridge that would bring these narrative islands together? Did I dare?

I was also a bit flummoxed by the idea of "lived theology," because it seemed to be the stage for outgoing social activists rather than people like me, who are more naturally solitary. My acute and regular need for predictable solitude to write, think, and process the world (including my social friendships in it) affects how I work, teach, and inevitably how I might be said to practice "lived theology." Thus writing, even as it related to my responses to social justice and poverty issues, became for me a way of *living* theology, a way to embrace theological action in itself. For those of us who believe in prayer, writing as lived theology is perhaps like prayer in its capacity to pursue effective expression that, we believe, might actually make a difference in this world, even if it is one that we hardly begin to perceive or understand. In other words, lived theology is so much bigger than what we *do*; it goes to the theological foundations of what we *are* as beings made by God—to *be*.

Even within its Christian variants, some religious traditions seem to be better than others at affirming this value of *being* independent of social or religious *action*. Over the years, I have found writers from early Christianity and modern Orthodox Christianity most helpful in expressing lived theology as it relates to writing and being. Gregory of Nazianzus, for example, was intentional about both theological expression and writing, and both in the context of living faithfully. He was deeply reflective, for example, in all of his preaching, and yet his spectacular refusal to serve as bishop in two very different appointments—one in backwater Sasima and the other in glittering Constantinople—created a huge mess for his life, one that he spilled much ink to complain about. His theological treatises are the foundation of traditional Trinitarian doctrine today, while his writing about himself is full of details, specifics on friendships and family dysfunctions, and objections to circumstances. In his old age he wrote hundreds of poems, many or even most of them still untranslated; those that have been translated are often marked by a haunting beauty. As deeply as he valued monastic reflection, he also valued his friends and his various communities. His last will and testament, which we have in translation, is an expression of his lived theology in relationship to community.[16]

In the Orthodox Christian tradition, true "theology" is about *life*, about living and breathing prayer rather than intellectual expression. Theology is relational by definition. Evagrios of Pontus, for example, taught that,

"If you are a theologian, you will pray truly. And if you pray truly, you are a theologian" (*Prayer*, 60). One of my favorite modern Orthodox writers is the late Father Dumitru Staniloae, a Romanian priest who spent long years in prison under communism. In his life work on Orthodox dogmatic theology, he wrote:

> Theology will be effective if it stands always before God and helps the faithful to do the same in their every act: to see God through the formulae of the past, to express [God] through the explanations of the present, to hope and to call for the advancement towards full union with [God] in the life to come.[17]

Thus for me, at least, writing was itself a lived theology even as I worked on my book for the seminar. Even solitary writing is certainly both physical and social, engaging conversation partners even during its long, agonizing process of creation. Writing as lived theology is both practice and full of practical challenges—including the challenge of how to make a living while you write!

For example, I largely opted out of the traditional teaching route, and chose instead to combine research and scholarship with more conventional employment as a writer and editor in academic medicine and health. In most cases, this meant that I could not consider applying for year-long research or travel grants to write (even though I was qualified) because I did not have the kind of job where sabbatical was an option; I need to remain employed simply to survive. I have been blessed with work opportunities; I do not complain. But lacking that "dream job"—the role of a permanent, full-time academic senior research scholar, where I can write what I like and engage in the academy as a mentor but with minimal teaching responsibilities—I need to live within the limits that will put food on the table. And so, in 2004, when Charles's invitation to apply for a seminar grant arrived in its Fedex envelope from Virginia, I barely skimmed the details for a couple of weeks, figuring that I was probably not eligible and did not want to be disappointed. Happily, he sent a little reminder, and I realized that this grant opportunity was possible even for me.

On Process and Dare: What Made it Work

Both writing lived theology and writing *as* lived theology reflect a particular way of being. But there is a third ingredient that kept us all going and made it work for the seminar: this was the mundane, practical task of meeting, sharing drafts, and taking action on how we wanted to turn our ideas into books. We met for 2 three-day sessions in the first year, with email conversations to encourage one another to put flesh on the bones of our initial rough outlines. For most of us, I think the final book was radically different from our early drafts, thanks to the group feedback and conversations. Outlines are crucial, especially in the early stage, when you are not ready to write in full sentences yet. But prepare to throw them out once the book starts to take life.

Some of us had an agent or a publisher from the start; I was one of those who had neither. Cynthia Read at Oxford University Press was interested but needed a manuscript to market the book internally. I know what it's like to be possessed with a pen, in frenetic stream-of-consciousness creative writing, but in the academy I am fond of carefully argued ideas richly supported with footnotes. I write slowly, with every chapter going through seven or eight major revisions. And so the book developed slowly, and the contract came late. And yet the market was not my greatest challenge in writing this book; the hardest task was to find the right tone, the right mix of personal and scholarly voice. When *God Knows There's Need* finally came out, my *doktormutter*, a wise and deeply spiritual woman, said to me, "*This* is the book you have always wanted to write. Not everyone has that opportunity."

Writing to find your voice for the first time in a new genre means taking risks. For example, I chose to permit a couple of drafts to be shared with two academic colleagues (outside the Seminar) who clearly found my narrative more "personal" than they were particularly comfortable with. Their honesty was hard, but happily both remain friends and their advice certainly saved me from mortification. The best advice I received on how to write in this personal voice came from another Seminar participant, the writer Patricia Hampl, who told me during one session: write as one standing beside your reader, pointing *together* at something you can both see. That way, the personal voice is not "look at me!" but rather, "look at that!"

Other seminar manuscripts also changed, sometimes radically, at each meeting. We talked in great detail about several books that I still hope to see in print from members of the group someday. These constant shifts and transitions encouraged us to bring up other ideas that we might not have mentioned in a more formal context, our candor shaped by developing trust and friendship from the years of exchange. I suspect that a number of the books we produced would not exist—and none of them would be as vibrant with potential for "lived" theology—without the landscape that was for us the Virginia Seminar.

In conclusion, I would offer an invitation to any writers who are embarking on a similar journey: an invitation to dare what we dared—and survived. Dare to be subjective—and outside the box—as long as you're honest. Dare to use plain English—including the first-person perspective. Dare to tell stories. Dare to cross genres, or even mix them up if it makes your creative writing more effective. Dare to abandon footnotes—or even merge them into reader-friendly comments. Dare to let one another read what might indeed be truly awful. Dare to want sales and marketing—and help make it work. Dare to follow your heart in your first draft, putting the inner critic on hold for the third, or even fourth, draft. Dare to endure several rounds of edits before you seek a publisher. Dare to continue academic writing—if it works and is your calling. Dare to delight in theology written—and lived.

Notes

1. See, e.g., Shannon Gayk, *Image, Text, and Religious Reform in Fifteenth-Century England* (New York: Cambridge University Press, 2010).
2. Amy Laura Hall, *Conceiving Parenthood: American Protestantism and the Spirit of Reproduction* (Grand Rapids, MI: Eerdmans, 2007).
3. Carlos Eire, *Waiting for Snow in Havana: Confessions of a Cuban Boy* (New York: Free Press, 2003).
4. Jennifer McBride, *The Church for the World: A Theology of Public Witness* (New York: Oxford University Press, 2011).
5. Russell Jeung, *Faithful Generations: Race and New Asian American Churches* (Piscataway, NJ: Rutgers University Press, 2004).
6. Charles Marsh, *The Last Days: A Son's Story of Sin and Segregation at the Dawn of a New South* (New York: Basic Books, 2002).
7. Charles Marsh, *Strange Glory: A Life of Dietrich Bonhoeffer* (New York: Knopf, 2014).
8. Susan R. Holman, *Beholden: Religion, Global Health, and Human Rights* (New York: Oxford University Press, 2015), 45–81.
9. Charles Marsh, *Wayward Christian Soldiers: Freeing the Gospel From Political Captivity* (New York: Oxford University Press, 2007), 3.
10. Mark R. Gornik, *Word Made Global: Stories of African Christianity in New York City* (Grand Rapids, MI: Eerdmans, 2011).
11. See, e.g., Vanessa Ochs, *Words on Fire: One Woman's Journey into the Sacred* (San Diego: Harcourt Brace Jovanovich, 1990); *Sarah Laughed: Modern Lessons from the*

Wisdom and Stories of Biblical Women (New York: McGraw-Hill, 2004); *Inventing Jewish Ritual* (Philadelphia: Jewish Publication Society, 2007); for her reflections on ordination, see Vanessa Ochs, "Free Range Rabbi," *Huffington Post*, February 21, 2013, http://www.huffingtonpost.com/vanessa-l-ochs/free-range-rabbi_b_2716209.html.

12. David Dark, *The Sacredness of Questioning Everything* (Grand Rapids, MI: Zondervan, 2009).

13. Alan Jacobs, *The Narnian: The Life and Imagination of C. S. Lewis* (New York: HarperCollins, 2005).

14. Susan R. Holman, *The Hungry are Dying: Beggars and Bishops in Roman Cappadocia* (New York: Oxford University Press, 2001).

15. Susan R. Holman, *God Knows there's Need: Christian Responses to Poverty* (New York: Oxford University Press, 2009).

16. For more on Gregory's life, see, e.g., John McGuckin (himself an Orthodox priest, highly respected scholar, and poet), *St. Gregory of Nazianzus: An Intellectual Biography* (Crestwood, NY: St. Vladimir's Seminary Press, 2001).

17. Dumitru Staniloae, *Orthodox Dogmatic Theology [1]: The Experience of God* (Brookline, MA: Holy Cross Orthodox Press, 1998), 93.

6

Crossing and Experimentation

PAULI MURRAY'S ACTIVISM AS CHRISTIAN PRACTICE AND LIVED THEOLOGY

Sarah Azaransky

LIVED THEOLOGY CONTENDS that the "patterns and practices of lived communities offer rich and generative material for theological inquiry."[1] Integral to the Project on Lived Theology's work is recovering the voices of lesser-known, but nonetheless prophetic, figures who work to build just and compassionate communities. Pauli Murray is such a figure. This chapter demonstrates how Murray's mature theology linked Christian faith and democratic action—a primary interest of the Project on Lived Theology. It also examines Murray's earlier activism as a source for her disciplined reflection on God and God's relation to the world. I aim to show how the Project on Lived Theology's commitments and convictions prompt a series of theological, historiographical, and methodological questions, such as: what counts as theological reflection? Can movement work be theological data? What kind of hermeneutic do we need to read practices as theological texts?

Pauli Murray (1910–1985) was a lawyer, professor, Episcopal priest, and a significant figure at the intersection of the civil rights and women's movements who made substantial contributions to American democratic and religious life. In 2012, the Episcopal Church admitted Murray to the pantheon of "Holy Women, Holy Men: Celebrating the Saints" in honor of her efforts toward "the universal cause of freedom." For those of us interested in Murray's theological perspective, it makes sense to look at her work in seminary and at her sermons, when she was actively and self-consciously engaged in theological reflection.

Murray developed her mature theological voice at New York's General Theological Seminary (GTS) in the 1970s and during her work as a priest in the 1970s and 1980s. Murray began at GTS in the midst of debates about women's ordination and, when she entered seminary, it was not clear that women would be ordained. What led Murray to ordination? She said that she felt called because, "the particular profession to which I had devoted the larger section of my life, law, was—that we had reached a point where law could not give us the answers ... that all the problems of human rights, that basically these were moral and spiritual problems."[2] Her seminary papers and sermons reflected theological trends of that moment, including earnest term papers about Tillich and sermons that quoted Rosemary Ruether, Letty Russell, and William Stringfellow.

Murray's writing and preaching from the 1970s and 1980s made innovative theological arguments and addressed moral and spiritual problems that plagued the nation. For example, she engaged critically with black theology: she recognized why it was necessary, but also pushed it toward a broader theological agenda. In 1975 she affirmed that, "the difficult theological questions being asked in the racial ghettoes are quite different from those being raised in white middle-class suburbia. Blacks are seeking ... a meaningful theology of hope in the *here* and *now* in the midst of racial oppression."[3] Yet, Murray was not convinced by black theology's emphasis on blackness, in James Cone's work in particular. When Cone explained the need for a specifically *"Black theology*, a theology whose sole purpose is to apply the freeing power of the Gospel to black people under white oppression,"[4] Murray heard a false dualism between black and white, neither of which was an adequate category to describe complex experiences she felt are implicated in class, gender, and other power relations.

Murray preferred Deotis Roberts's work, for he argued that black theology should be premised on liberation *and* reconciliation. Yet she resisted Roberts's concept of the Black Messiah. While Murray cheered a Christology that would make Christ meaningful to black people, she worried that Roberts's assumption that the Messiah is male indicated "a preoccupation with black liberation which tends to narrow his focus and suggests an insensitivity to the oppression of women, who, after all constitute one half of the black community."[5] In a paper she wrote for a seminar she took with Roberts, Murray wondered, "Is Dr. Roberts prepared to suggest that a 'female Christ' would be valid as a symbol for women fighting to affirm their personhood? And if a woman is also black, what images or symbols of Christ would have meaning for her?"[6]

Murray went on to suggest that black theology would benefit immeasurably from a dialogue with feminist theology. Murray's call for black male and white feminist theologians to be in conversation emerged from decades of work at the intersection of the civil rights and women's movements when Murray had insisted that coalitions were crucial for the left to realize its political goals. She predicted that "a dialogue between the two would serve as a continual reminder of our common humanity and solidarity in the 'groaning toward freedom.' "[7] Indeed, in her seminary thesis, Murray argued that black (male) theology and (white) feminist theology were natural allies. Until each realized the strengths of the other, the theological significance of African American women's experiences would go untheorized. Murray's thesis, then, is an early articulation of black feminist and proto-womanist theology. Anthony Pinn has noted that including Murray complicates womanist genealogy in an interesting way, because she was a black, feminist figure who aligns herself more with Roberts's theological project than with Cone's.[8] Murray is an important figure in the history of American liberationist theologies and she "offers invaluable insights into ways of refining theological conversation so as to keep it viable and vital."[9]

Murray's sermons also deserve scholarly attention. To demonstrate the connection between theology and social action, she often employed American history as a way to think through theological categories, such as soteriology, anthropology, and Christology. In a 1978 sermon in which she argued that salvation will be a social event, rather than experienced on an individual level, she compared the contemporary plight of migrant workers with African Americans who fled the South:

> The risks endured by tens of thousands who have ... perished of thirst in the Arizona desert should recall us to our own racial history of little more than a century ago—the history of runaway black slaves in the United States seeking freedom in Canada. Human need and the urge for freedom know no national boundaries.[10]

She concluded simply, "we are all involved with one another, and salvation is more than an individual matter; it involves the whole world."[11]

Murray celebrated her first Eucharist at the Chapel of the Cross in Chapel Hill, North Carolina, where black and white members of her extended family had once attended. In 1977, Murray preached to an integrated congregation about *two* American revolutions. She called the events from 1789 through 1976 efforts to complete the first American Revolution and January 1, 1977, the date of the first woman's official ordination in the Episcopal Church, as a signal for the visible beginning of the second American Revolution. The second revolution, preached Murray, should carry on the work of the first, the healing and reconciliation of people alienated from each other by race, sex preference, political differences, and economic status.

Murray offered herself as a sign of these first and second revolutions—an African American woman with multiple ancestries who celebrated her first Eucharist at the church where her grandmother was baptized into freedom in Christ but recorded by church records as enslaved. Presenting herself as evidence that reconciliation is possible, Murray preached:

> It was my destiny to be the descendent of slaveowners as well as slaves, to be of mixed ancestry, to be biologically and psychologically integrated in a world where the separation of the races was upheld by the Supreme Court of the United States as the fundamental law of the Southland. My entire life's quest has led me ultimately to Christ in whom there is no East or West, no North or South, no Black or White . . . There is only Christ, the Spirit of love and rec-onciliation, the Healer of deep pychic [sic] wounds, drawing us all closer to that Goal of perfection which links us to God our creator and to eternity.[12]

Well before recent theological interest on hybridity, Murray affirmed that her identity exceeded available classifications.[13] This sermon also con-tinued, in another way, the work of her MDiv thesis: she affirmed that theology is contextual, that a person's disciplined reflections on God and God's relation to the world are influenced by who she is, by how she is a product of intersecting histories.

Now I turn to earlier moments in Murray's work as an additional source for her theological perspective. In the spirit of how Lived Theology concentrates on practices, I will analyze her 1940 arrest in Virginia for sitting in the front of an interstate bus as theological practice. To do so, I will describe her arrest and its historical context. Then, I will explore interpretative tools and frameworks that can help us to identify Murray's own theological perspective.

At the time of her arrest, Murray was living in New York. Murray had left Durham in the late 1920s for New York City, where she attended

Hunter College. She graduated in 1933, at the height of the Depression. As she bounced from job to job, she came of age politically in the midst of socialist politics, on the tail end of Harlem's Renaissance, and through community work with pacifist groups. In these years, Murray was developing the habit of confronting Jim Crow. In 1938 she waged a public campaign to gain admissions to UNC's grad school, which was then still segregated. In the springs of '43 and '44 she organized sit-ins of segregated DC lunch counters. This activism put Murray at the forefront of developing nonviolent direct action tactics to confront white racism.

In her autobiography, she described her bus arrest. In March 1940, Pauli Murray and her friend Adelene MacBean departed New York City on a bus for Durham, North Carolina, to visit Murray's family for the Easter holiday. After Murray and MacBean transferred busses in Petersburg, Virginia, the driver asked them to move to the back of the bus. When the pair refused, they were arrested for disorderly conduct and creating a public disturbance. Murray remembered saying to the driver as she left the bus, " 'You haven't learned a thing in two thousand years.' I could not forget that it was Easter Even."[14] Murray would later write to a friend, "We did not plan our arrest intentionally. The situation developed and, having developed, we applied what we knew of Satyagraha on the spot,"[15] including by petitioning the warden for courteous treatment.

Her autobiography minimizes two significant aspects of her arrest, however. The first is her omission of the context of her and MacBean's visit to Durham. MacBean was more than likely Murray's romantic partner, whom Murray was bringing home to meet Murray's family. Murray did not identify publicly as a woman who loved other women, and the categories of lesbian or transgender person were not then widely available. Yet, we know something of Murray's sexual and gender identities because Murray herself saved journals, medical records, and memos to doctors. Her archives indicate that in the 1930s she was enthralled by emerging scholarship about sexuality and hoped that it would provide categories to describe her own experiences as a male-identified woman who loved other women. At the time, there were two normative explanations for same-sex love and attraction: it was a pathology, or it was what was then called "hermaphrodism."[16] Wanting to avoid the mental illness explanation, Murray experimented with cross-dressing, tried hormonal therapy, and petitioned doctors to perform exploratory surgery to find the latent male organs that she was convinced she had.

Historian Glenda Gilmore has discovered a fascinating subtext to the Petersburg episode. In May 1940, two months after Murray's arrest, the Urban League's *Opportunity Magazine* published a story about a young black couple who were arrested while integrating an interstate bus. The story drew from an eyewitness account of a white passenger who was traveling from Washington to Durham in late March 1940 and described the pair as a "light-colored but not very good looking" young woman and a "young man ... of slight build ... and sensitive in voice and manner."[17] The story reported that the young man presented himself as "Oliver Fleming." In all likelihood the couple was Murray and MacBean. The eyewitness recognized Murray as she had wished to be understood—that is, as male. The irony, in this case, is that she was at the same time engaged in activism that challenged Jim Crow. Murray's choice to dress as a man for the trip indicates that the bus protest was likely not planned. As Gilmore points out, Murray would have been aware of the risks of being arrested under the Mann Act if she and MacBean had been caught posing as a heterosexual couple.[18]

The second, less sensational, but just as historically significant aspect of her arrest is Murray's part in a growing black activist network that studied the Indian independence movement and Gandhi's use of nonviolence. In fact, Murray lived for a time at the Harlem Ashram, a multiracial and experimental Christian commune with the purpose, according to an Ashram brochure, of "bringing the reality of the Kingdom of God on earth through inner responsiveness to God, through creative living in a deeply sharing community, [and] through meeting injustice and conflict through the power of realistic love in action."[19]

The Harlem Ashram's interest in Gandhi exemplified how two groups of Americans—black internationalists and mostly white pacifists—were engaging with Gandhi's ideas. For the first group, black internationalism posited a new way of thinking about black Americans as part of a global majority of peoples of color, whose identity was forged, in part, through resistance to colonial and imperial oppression. Gandhi's efforts in South Africa and as the leader of the Indian independence movement had a special claim on the African American democratic imagination. In Gandhi, black intellectuals saw the paradigm of a person of color who was leading a well-organized and insistent campaign against British imperialism.[20] American pacifists, for their part, saw in Gandhi how a particular religious outlook fueled a political movement.[21] Harlem Ashram members, including internationally-minded blacks, black pacifists, and white pacifists, studied Gandhi's writings and met with Indian scholars at Columbia University who were writing the first critical academic assessments of his work.

The Ashram became, then, an important location for ongoing discussions among a committed group of American Gandhians, including James Farmer and Murray, who both lived at the Ashram for a time, and Bayard Rustin, who visited often. Here are roots of an interreligious and international encounter: Murray and others understood their confrontations of American racial injustice as part of a global resistance movement; and they engaged in comparative religious study that encouraged them to think about their own tradition in a new light, and that generated revolutionary practices that would transform American democracy. Though the Ashram disbanded in 1947, we can trace important and innovative experiments with nonviolent direct action in the 1940s to Ashram members: sit-ins in Chicago and Washington, DC, a multicity march to protest the poll tax, and the Journey of Reconciliation—all precursors to the sit-ins, marches, and freedom rides of the later civil rights movement.

Having examined her bus arrest in some detail, I now return to my initial query: might we consider Murray's activism as a source for her disciplined reflection on God and God's relation to the world? The same question, in other words, may be posed as follows: what does getting arrested on a bus while she was perhaps dressed as a man, in the wake of studying Gandhian tactics, have to do with outlining Murray's theology? This points to historiographical and methodological questions about how we identify what constitutes her theological perspective. These questions are at the heart of Lived Theology's convictions that practices matter, and that important theological lessons are to be learned when we investigate the connection between faith and social action.

Ought we read Murray's arrest theologically? And if so, how do we do so accurately? Mary Fulkerson's innovative work on the role of ethnography in Christian theology is a place to start. In *Places of Redemption*, Fulkerson demonstrates that for theologians to reflect on "tradition," we must necessarily interpret bodily practices, that is, we need to know how to decipher messages that are bodily performances.[22] In the 1940s, Murray *wrote* about Christian nonviolence, but she also practiced it with her body.[23] When sitting in the front section of a bus, Murray used her body as a means to protest segregation and as a way of meeting injustice with Christian love in action.

The Harlem Ashram, where Murray studied and practiced nonviolent tactics, endeavored to develop Christian practices that could change social realities. Its professed mission of "bringing the Kingdom of God on earth through inner responsiveness to God" is directly in line with how contemporary American theologians have characterized Christian practice. For instance, Craig Dykstra and Dorothy Bass have described that Christian practice is "how a way of life that is deeply responsive to God's grace takes actual shape among human beings."[24] According to Dykstra and Bass, "Christian practices thus involve a profound awareness, a deep knowing: they are activities imbued with the knowledge of God and creation."[25] Christians connected to the Harlem Ashram were self-consciously trying to develop kinds of Christian practices that would reflect God's kingdom as these activists confronted white racism and Jim Crow. Murray's activism was a kind of Christian practice when she used her body in these incipient nonviolent protests in order to bring the kingdom to earth.

How can we consider, at the same time, Murray's gender and sexual presentations and identities? In a 1977 letter to friends, Murray talked about her vision for her ministry, that "we bring our total selves to God, our sexuality, our joyousness, our foolishness, etc. etc. I'm out to make Christianity a joyful thing."[26] How can those of us who work on Murray bring her whole self to assessing her theological voice? It may be useful to look at how contemporary theologian Patrick Cheng uses queer theory in his own constructive work. Cheng argues that theology done in a queer way is self-consciously transgressive, as it seeks to unearth silenced voices or hidden perspectives. As a primary theological source, experience necessitates drawing on queer experiences, and thus entails recognizing how God acts within the specific context of LGBT lives.[27] For example, Murray's embodiedness, which resisted available gender and sexual categories, may be a source for understanding how she was thinking about God and God's action in the world.

If we do indeed consider Murray's experience as an expression of embodied theology, it is crucial that we put her racialized, sexualized, and gendered body into historical context. Murray was in the vanguard of African Americans who experimented with nonviolent direct action; Murray's activism took on special significance because she was an African American woman. In 1940, Murray's forays into nonviolent activism challenged her "deeply ingrained sense of respectability" and "made her fearful of engaging in behavior that not only put one's physical well being on the line, but might embarrass or cause stress for her family."[28] Respectability refers to historical practices of middle-class black women appropriating Victorian conventions of morality as a way of distancing themselves from the prevalent racialized myth that African American women were hypersexual. Historian Hazel Carby has charted how black women who were part of the Great Migration "generated a series of moral panics. One serious consequence was that the behavior of black female migrants was characterized as sexual degenerate and, therefore, socially dangerous."[29] As a woman who has migrated north in the late 1920s, Murray's behavior as an independent, college-educated, and unmarried woman already posed a social danger. Caught between racist myths of black hypersexuality and distorted sexuality that maintained the subordination of all women, black women were already seen as deviant by the dominant society.[30]

For Murray to employ her body, which was racialized and sexualized in a particular way, to confront Jim Crow was to risk her own sense of middle-class respectability. To do so when she was dressed as a man was to compound the risk of physical harm. Womanist ethicist Katie Cannon points out how even today, the sexual agency of black women who love other women is further circumscribed, for "lesbian sexuality becomes a kind of deviant sexuality existing within an already deviant sexuality (that belongs to all black women)."[31] To heed Cheng and consider Murray's experience, we need, therefore, to attend to its historical specificity. As we do so, Murray's experiences may indeed reveal how God acts in the context of LGBT lives. Murray's experience may also contribute to Cannon's efforts to "excavate" and "recover" stories of African American women "in order to craft stories that reveal hidden meanings of complicated, survival strategies."[32] Murray's and others' stories may provide, then, "counter-hegemonic strategies that debunk and unmask normalizing structures of compulsive heterosexual acceptability" in the Church and larger society.[33]

When Murray admonished the bus driver that he hadn't learned a thing in two thousand years, she compared Jim Crow to Roman occupation. This is a Christian claim. Is it complicated by her subsequent reference to Satyagraha and what we know of her broader attempt to create a Christian response to racial injustice? As we are tracing her Christian theological voice, how do we account for the influences of her study of Indian religions? John Thatamanil's work on comparative theology, in which he engages closely with postcolonial theory, may help us to identify what is at stake here. Thatamanil has written, "Christian reflection has, from its inception, been situated in a world of difference. Indeed, it would be possible to craft a history of Christian thought and practice written as

a series of interactions with and transmutations of movements and traditions that Christians have come to demarcate as non-Christian."[34] Using
Thatamanil, we may begin to account for Murray's study of Indian religions as shaping her Christian theological voice, because religious identities are always, on Thatamanil's account, "hybrid and polyphonic."[35]

In the Harlem Ashram's study of and experiments with Satyagraha, it
becomes a category that is both external and internal to Christianity.[36] As
external, Satyagraha constitutes a particular matrix of religious, political,
and practical commitments that were employed in the Indian independence movement. When Ashram members read about Gandhi's organizing efforts and quizzed Indian scholars, the African American activists did
not yet know what the outcome of the Indian freedom movement would
be. For them, Satyagraha was a foreign and historically situated tactic that
may or may not be applicable in the American context. In their efforts to
inaugurate the Christian kingdom by, in part, experimenting with their
own Satyagrahas, Harlem Ashram members rendered Satyagraha an
internal category. They employed it as a tactic to confront white racism as
part of a larger Christian theological goal to reorganize society so that it
better reflects God's intentions. The Harlem Ashram's use of Satyagraha
produced a paradox that was not a contradiction: by respecting the historical, political, and religious contexts that produced Satyagraha, Ashramites
were able to experiment with it in their own situation.

Recent work in theology about ethnography, queer theology, and comparative theology, then, provide tools to interpret how Murray getting
arrested on a bus when she was perhaps dressed as a man and employed
Satyagraha is related to her Christian theological perspective. Her bodily
practices are indeed a source for her reflections on God and God's relation
to the world. Yet Lived Theology's focus on patterns and practices of *communities* should prompt us to consider how Murray is part of social, intellectual, and religious networks. In other words, when I am investigating
Murray's theology, I should not just be investigating Murray. I ought to
consider also how Murray's ideas emerged in the midst of an intellectual
and activist movement. Murray's theological pedigree is not only interesting because we can trace it through Roberts rather than through Cone
but also because we can trace it back to a formidable group of theological thinkers and activists in the 1930s and 1940s, including Farmer and
Rustin, and also Howard Thurman, Benjamin Mays, Mordecai Johnson,
Dorothy Height, and others. Many in this group—and they did work
together and in overlapping associations—ventured abroad for potential

resources, looking even in other religious traditions, to develop ethical and political methods for Christians to transform the American political order. This group worked at the fertile intersections of worldwide resistance movements, American racial politics, and interreligious exchanges that crossed literal borders and disciplinary boundaries.

To include Murray's 1940s activism as part of her theological perspective, we must undertake the kinds of disciplinary and intellectual boundary-crossing that these folks were doing. Lived Theology affirms the theological necessity of boundary crossing, for charting the patterns and practices of lived communities requires a number of methods, disciplinary approaches, and a generous intellectual disposition. It may be that boundary crossing is, in fact, a theologian's vocation, for "crossing boundaries means living in a new kind of space, but more importantly it means proving that boundaries are not so much barriers as invitations to insight."[37] Murray's writing, preaching, and activism have shown us how to live in a new kind of space and invite us—indeed require us—to cross boundaries if we are to follow where she leads.

Notes

1. Project on Lived Theology, "Overview of the Project," available at http://livedtheology.org/overview.html.
2. Genna Rae McNeill, "Interview with Pauli Murray," Southern Oral History Program University of North Carolina at Chapel Hill (February 13, 1976), 89.
3. Murray, "Black Theology: Heresy, Syncretism, or Prophecy?" April 16, 1975, in Pauli Murray Papers (Box 23; Folder 472), 7; emphasis in original, MC 412 on file at the Schlesinger Library of the Radcliffe Institute for Advanced Study, Harvard University; hereafter cited as "PM Papers."
4. James Cone, *Black Theology and Black Power* (San Francisco: Harper, 1989), 31, author's emphasis.
5. Pauli Murray, "J. Deotis Roberts on Black Theology: A Comparative View," November 20, 1975, PM Papers (Box 23; Folder 474), 19–20.
6. Murray, "J. Deotis Roberts on Black Theology: A Comparative View," 11.
7. Murray, "J. Deotis Roberts on Black Theology: A Comparative View," 21.
8. Anthony B. Pinn, ed., *"America's Problem Child:" An Outline of Pauli Murray's Religious Life and Theology* (Eugene, OR: Pickwick Publishers, 2008), 88–91.
9. Pinn, *"America's Problem Child:" An Outline of Pauli Murray's Religious Life and Theology*, 82.
10. Pauli Murray, "What Shall I Do To Inherit Eternal Life?" undated, PM Papers (Box 64; Folder 1101), 9.
11. Murray, "What Shall I Do To Inherit Eternal Life?" 8.

12. Pauli Murray, "Healing and Reconciliation," in *Pauli Murray: Selected Sermons and Writings*, ed. Anthony B. Pinn (Maryknoll, NY: Orbis Press, 2006), 87.

13. Two representative examples of theological attention to hybridity are Brian Bantum, *Redeeming Mulatto: A Theology of Race and Christian Hybridity* (Waco, TX: Baylor University Press, 2010); and Patrick Cheng, *From Sin to Amazing Grace: Discovering the Queer Christ* (New York: Seabury Books, 2012).

14. Pauli Murray, *Song in a Weary Throat: An American Pilgrimage* (New York: Harper & Row, 1987), 142.

15. Murray, *Song in a Weary Throat*, 144.

16. Joanne Meyerowitz, "Sex Change and the Popular Press: Historical Notes on Transsexuality in the United States, 1930–1955," *GLQ* 4, no. 2 (1998): 164; Henry L. Minton, "Femininity in Men and Masculinity in Women: American Psychiatry and Psychology Portray Homosexuality in the 1930s," *Journal of Homosexuality* 13, no. 1 (1986): 7.

17. Glenda Gilmore, *Defying Dixie: The Radical Roots of Civil Rights, 1919–1950* (New York: Norton), 323.

18. The Mann Act, better known as the "White-Slave Traffic Act," was passed in 1910 in an effort to prevent interstate travel of prostitutes. The Act's prohibition against "sexual immorality" meant that the Act was often used to criminalize consensual sexual behavior, including between same-sex couples.

19. "The Harlem Ashram," brochure dated 1944 (?) in Fellowship of Reconciliation Records, D13, Section II, A-3, (Box 13, Folder: Harlem Ashram), Swarthmore College Peace Collection.

20. Nico Slate, *Colored Cosmopolitanism: The Shared Struggle for Freedom in the United States and India* (Cambridge, MA: Harvard University Press, 2012), 107.

21. Joseph Kip Kosek, *Acts of Conscience: Christian Nonviolence and Modern American Democracy* (New York: Columbia University Press, 2009), 87.

22. Mary Fulkerson, *Places of Redemption: Theology for a Worldly Church* (New York: Oxford University Press, 2007), 42, 43.

23. Pauli Murray and Henry Babcock, "An Alternative Weapon," *South Today* (Winter 1942–1943): 53–57.

24. Craig Dykstra and Dorothy C. Bass, "A Theological Understanding of Christian Practices," in *Practicing Theology: Beliefs and Practices in Christian Life*, ed. Miroslav Volf and Dorothy C. Bass (Grand Rapids, MI: Eerdmans, 2002), 15.

25. Dykstra and Bass, "A Theological Understanding of Christian Practices," 24.

26. Pauli Murray, "Dear Jim and Mary," February 4, 1977, PM Papers (Box 63; Folder 1078), 2.

27. Patrick S. Cheng, *Radical Love: An Introduction to Queer Theology* (New York: Seabury Books, 2011), 18.

28. Doreen Drury, "Experimentation on the Male Side: Race, Class, Gender, and Sexuality in Pauli Murray's Quest for Love and Identity" (PhD dissertation, Boston College, 2000), 228.

29. Hazel V. Carby, "Policing the Black Woman's Body in an Urban Context," *Critical Inquiry* 18, no. 4 (Summer, 1992): 739.

30. Katie G. Cannon, "Sexing Black Women: Liberation from the Prisonhouse of Anatomical Authority," in *Loving the Body: Black Religious Studies and the Erotic*, ed. Anthony B. Pinn and Dwight N. Hopkins (New York: Palgrave, 2004), 13.

31. Cannon, "Sexing Black Women: Liberation from the Prisonhouse of Anatomical Authority," 14.

32. Cannon, "Sexing Black Women: Liberation from the Prisonhouse of Anatomical Authority," 19.

33. Cannon, "Sexing Black Women: Liberation from the Prisonhouse of Anatomical Authority," 19.

34. John Thatamanil, "Comparative Theology after 'Religion,'" in *Planetary Loves: Spivak, Postcoloniality, and Theology*, ed. Stephen D. Moore and Mayra Rivera (New York: Fortress University Press, 2011), 238.

35. Thatamanil, "Comparative Theology after 'Religion,'" 252.

36. To think through Ashramites engagement with Satyagraha, I relied on Paulo Gonçalves's discussion of how the concept of "religion" has led to representations of "autonomous worlds of praxis and discourse" that overlook the hybridity and plurivocity that is necessarily constitutive of tradition, in Paulo Gonçalves, "Religious 'Worlds' and their Alien Invaders," in *Difference in Philosophy of Religion*, ed. Philip Goodchild (Burlington, VT: Ashgate, 2003), 115–134.

37. Jill Raitt, "The Vocation of The Theologian: Crossing Boundaries," *CTSA Proceedings* 58 (2003): 22.

7

Ethnography in Theology

A WORK IN PROCESS

Mary McClintock Fulkerson

SO WHAT WOULD count as "theological" in a Christian community? Is it the scripture reading? The sermon? Recital of creeds? Singing of hymns— that is, if they are orthodox? Is the chatter at church suppers or the work to clean the yards "theological"? Or does "theological" only refer to certain things said in sanctuary space? If so, where does that leave those who live on the streets—whose major vocation is survival? And what have the color of bodies and the status accorded different bodies in our cultures to do with "theology"? Unfortunately, many expert definitions of "theological" do not offer ways to read these other spaces, practices, and material realities. Or, they construe the dilemmas raised by these other spaces and lives as secondary issues, not primary to normative theology. That's the way I thought about theology—that it was a certain kind of language and articulated Christian beliefs, and I (unconsciously assumed) that it was associated with sacred space. That's the way I thought, at least until I decided to do ethnographic work—to "study" an interracial church, which I believed was a sign of God's liberative presence. And I discovered that attention to lived faith requires "lived theology."

In what follows, I will explore some of the issues that emerged from my participant observation in Good Samaritan United Methodist Church (UMC), an interracial church that included people with disabilities. First, there is the issue of why theologians need ethnography, and how ethnography opens to view the need for other frames—so wonderfully developed by Manuel Vasquez's work, which foregrounds the crucial role of (non-reductive) materiality in religion.[1] Second, there is the issue of the importance of understanding such explorations as "theological" inquiry, and its benefits. Thirdly, there are the challenges generated by ethnographic research for many traditional modes of theological reflection. And finally, I conclude with the naming of a few of the issues that I have not yet resolved.

The Need for Ethnography

While typically, systematics or the "traditional" creeds have dominated what counts as theology, for quite some time now criticisms of the theory-practice model in theology, a model implicit in such definitions, have floated around. Charles Taylor exposed the inadequacy of the causal force of rules relative to practice. David Kelsey long ago suggested that a mobile is a much more accurate image for theological reflection than a foundation that then leads to an interpretation of situations. Liberation theology exposed the contextual, power-laden character of any "starting place" and proposed the notion of a hermeneutical spiral, rather than a circle or unidirectional causal impact of text or belief and action. However, such shifts are still primarily hermeneutical. Ethnographic study, of course, will complicate such approaches enormously. To its credit, though, liberation theology did generate the need for attention to popular faith culture, which is what shifted my focus.

Out of my commitment to feminist theology, my first book was an attempt to interpret non-feminist women in different social locations through the lens of feminist theology. Judging their "beliefs"—including their dislike of the term "feminist"—to be inadequate indicators of their creative practice of faith, I used poststructuralism to destabilize fixed meaning, and culture theory and communications theory to flesh out the "agency" of non-feminists: namely, poor Appalachian Pentecostal women and white middle-class Presbyterian women's organizations. A cultural anthropologist who read my book, *Changing the Subject,* recommended ethnographic study via participant observation, noting that it would allow for much richer accounts of a community, as its living complex dynamics would become more available. Taking a course on ethnography was, then, my introduction to a kind of exploration that opened my theological world—and continues to—in ways I could never have imagined. So, I went from using poststructuralism and culture theory, which tend to read practices as "texts," to a new awareness of the need to move beyond that, as Vasquez's work makes clear.[2] With ethnographic study, the possibilities for moving outside of the textualizing of Christian faith emerge.

My first sense of this need happened with the discovery that most members of the UM church I "studied" did not do "orthodox" theological-speak. I tended to silence many of them when I asked for theological reasons or explanations for their commendable and unusual multiracial community. What I gradually came to understand is that the criterion of orthodoxy is not only inadequate, it is dehumanizing. If correct belief, whether liberal or conservative, is the prerequisite for Christian faithfulness, it will exclude most of humanity—many of whom were never given access to such beliefs and many of whom could not have understood them even if they had been catechized in Chalcedonian or Niceno-Constantinopolitan creeds.

In short, the claim that ethnography is needed in theology is deeply important and timely, as well as provocative. It is deeply important for many reasons. Common sense tells us that attention to lived faith, or the lived situations of human beings everywhere, should be basic to Christian faith. Before splitting into a speculative science (with the university), "knowledge of God" or *theologia*, in its best classic sense, has always entailed formation.[3] While there was no one use of the term "theology" in early Christianity,[4] from the beginning Christians adapted the basic centuries-old Greek sense that faith was a *paideia*, i.e., a "knowledge of God" that entailed formation of persons' souls.[5] Indeed, theology at its most profound has always been "practical" in some sense. And since formation and lived "knowledge" of God necessarily require assessment of one's situation and the parameters of faithful response, "practical" entails conviction, reflection, and much more; "souls" is problematically associated with a mind/body dichotomy. While "practical theology" has come to mean different things—from the lived faith of believers, to a curricular area, a method, and an academic discipline[6]—its ideal use, as *"theologia,"* invokes this general overarching sense of reflective, formative, lived "knowledge" of God, and "lived knowledge" is precisely what ethnographic study is filling out.[7]

In short, what is the point of religious faith if it is not about, or relevant to, life in all its complexity? How can theology matter if it is not able to take seriously all the difference, ambiguity, beauty, horror, and tragedy of created life? And while the notion of *theologia* continues to be relevant, classically many of its contextual specifics were not fully acknowledged—given ancient anthropology, with its patriarchal and inadequately sexual, carnal, and psychological assumptions. Contemporary Christian theology must have some grasp of these complex and messy realities, and participant observation is a marvelous way to initiate access to them. To put this more explicitly, a theological rationale for ethnographic work is the incarnational nature of Christianity. While differently narrated over the centuries, such a defining theme as incarnation at its very minimum affirms the immanence of the Divine—an immanence that requires the honoring of the finitely good creation in all its ambiguity, brokenness, and potential redemption. There is no other place to look for God than as mediated through the messy place that is the world.

What is Theological Ethnography?

So, given that theology needs attention to lived faith, what kind of analysis is ethnography? Some would worry that it is a risky appropriation of "social sciences" and endangers theology with the stain of "the world," as opposed to valorizing the church's take on and distinction from "the world." While I did not take on that debate, I did assume that the very use of ethnographical inquiry is, as the postmodern cultural anthropologists argued, a value-laden endeavor, and there are no *absolute* distinctions between so-called "Christian/church" takes and "worldly" takes on lived faith (and a defense of mine comes later). Refusing "blueprint theology," or the imposition of forms of belief and practice that may be at odds with a living situation, theologian Nicholas Healy rightly argues for theological ethnographic accounts of communities.[8]

A quite relevant book, *Ethnography as Christian Theology & Ethics,* makes just this argument, but without grounding it in a doctrine, like the Trinity, as does Healy. Ethnography is not simply a precursor to theological/ethical reflection, nor is it simply for "thick description." Rather, its very practice is "theological." The primary editors of *Ethnography as Christian Theology & Ethics,* Chris Scharen and Ana Vigen, argue that the use of ethnography is theological; it "can serve as an intervention that calls into question antagonistic 'Church or theology vs. world' kinds of thinking . . . exploring 'worldly theology' through the use of ethnography invites scholars and others to see how intertwined faith, theology, church, culture, and the larger societies are." Indeed, they insist, "no one domain ever truly exists in a 'pure' or isolated state." And theology, cultures, sciences, history, etc. are "all in a dynamic spiral—informing, revising, reinforcing, critiquing, and responding to one another."[9] They also present ethnographic study as a form of "witness." Refusing to take the social location of the "expert," they rightly suggest that we think of ourselves as "participant witnesses" rather than "participant observer," and "ethnographic witnessing on the part of both ethnographer and collaborator/informant can take on a normative quality in the sense that witnessing to human struggles can implicitly or explicitly carry an imperative to transform suffering into healing and well-being."[10]

Such an interpretation, of course, is relatively new and will likely generate more debate. However, by interpreting the practices of ethnography as "theological," these worldly realities, in all their complexity, difference, and messiness, are thereby granted status as places where the divine presence can and must be discerned and are seen as central to "real" theology. What is more, the role of the theologian—that is, his or her social location—begins to matter. (More about that later.)

So how is the resulting account based upon participant observation theological? The first seven chapters of *Places of Redemption* are descriptions. However, they are not intended as some kind of objective, empirical analysis. Any and all descriptions entail some degree of valuational character—whether from the explicit moral, valuational judgments that x is preferable to or better than y, to the more subtle valuational judgments regarding what needs to be attended to or what is important to describe. Non-theological approaches tend to think that theology is a completely and problematically uncritical form of valuational discourse, but I do not think that is completely fair. Unacknowledged valuational commitments are operative in all sorts of academic reasoning. A secular feminist theorist, for example, invokes values and theories that are intended to complicate power because they enhance or improve an analysis relative to oppression and liberation. That secular feminist does not have to justify those given and assumed values or goods (except, perhaps, to a social scientist). Academic theology illustrates this blindness to values in another way, when a contrast is assumed between what is called "contextual" theology and the kind of theology that is proposed as if it came from nowhere. The latter privileges certain kinds of subjects—white male, and supposedly rational—without acknowledging that a subject position is operative.

My favorite example of the *acknowledged* and *valuational* character of ethnography is found not only in the postmodern view that the cultural anthropologist brings her or his contextual lens and produces an ethnographic account rather than discovers the empirical truth, but also in the claim that ethnographic *description itself* is basically allegorical. James Clifford argued in *Writing Culture* (a significant milestone in cultural anthropology) that ethnography is "a performance emplotted by powerful stories . . . (which) simultaneously describe real cultural events and make additional, moral, ideological, and even cosmological statements. Ethnographic writing is allegorical at the level both of its content (what it says about cultures and their histories) and of its form (what is implied by its mode of textualization)," and "recognition of allegory inescapably poses the political and ethical dimensions of ethnographic writing."[11] Ethnographic accounts "can never be limited to a project of scientific description so long as the guiding task of the work is to make the (often strange) behavior of a different way of life humanly comprehensible. To say that exotic behavior and symbols make sense either in 'human' or 'cultural' terms is to supply the same sorts of allegorical added meanings that appear in older narratives that say actions are 'spiritually' significant."[12] Thus allegory "prompts us to say of any cultural description not 'this represents, or symbolizes, that' but rather, 'this is a (morally charged) *story* about that.' "[13] In other words, ethnographic accounts inevitably have transcendental meanings—not that are simply "added to some original, simple account," but rather as "the conditions of its meaningfulness." Clifford's primary example is the work of Marjorie Shostak on Nisa, a !Kung woman, and the story of giving birth; this story evokes a distinctive cultural form of labor, but it compels because it also registers as a common human, female experience.[14]

So given this acknowledgement by cultural anthropology, what constitutes the more explicitly normative approach of theology? Here is my version. My study of and account of the church is articulated around particular valuations, most of which are only implicitly theological until the last chapter. I began with the claim that an incarnational God would invite attention to more of reality, rather than less. Thus my move beyond belief and my choice of theoretical lenses (such as place theory, Paul Connerton's account of incorporative practices, etc.) is motivated by a conviction that is implicitly "theological," but this move could have simply resulted from a desire like Vasquez's to flesh out a material theory of religion. Further development of my valuational logic resonates with Kathy Tanner's observation that typically it is only disruptions or crises that generate explicit theological reflection.[15] Normally, we live our lives out of deeply embedded, pre-reflective "habituations," not as the conscious "application of rules/doctrines." To defend my logic at this point, I invoked Charles Winquest's claim that creative thinking is generated by a wound. Now by that I do not mean to exclude everyday believers, where something similar happens, but in this case I want to highlight this point with respect to my own analysis as a professional theologian. We can understand "wound" rather broadly: what was perceived by Bonhoeffer as the sell-out of the German church, the perceived threat of under-rating the divinity in the life of Jesus, or the too-long ignoring of the role of bodily habituation, carnality, and aversion are a few examples.

Thus rather than simply writing about a community—that is, valuing it—I discerned a particular set of *wounds* in the community, wounds around the continuing harms perpetrated against minority populations, particularly people of color and people with disabilities. Given the clear faith commitment in the church to welcoming outsiders, loving the neighbor, and being interracial and so forth, the discernment of harm is connected to practices that *fail* to support a "place to appear" for these persons; the discernment of the good is connected to practices that enhance places to appear for previously marginalized folks. My use of images from Hannah Arendt is not intended to "reduce" theological analysis to some secular account of reality, but to employ a more flexible image for harm and redress than I find in a typical theological repertoire.[16]

In short, my ethnographic narrative develops and "maps out a terrain of *needed and actualized transformation*" as a story of obliviousness, aversiveness, and other forms of ostensibly unintentional harms that endure and forms of constructive alteration of these harms.[17]

Of course the narrative changes for different groups. A primary harm displayed in whites' practices is deeply embodied habituations of obliviousness/color-blindness or aversion or both, displayed as what I term the "ownership of space." For (primarily) African Americans, that harm is deeply embodied habituations of hypervigilance and sometimes self-loathing. For the "normate" population, harm is aversiveness to certain kinds of bodies, and for those categorized as "disabled," mentally or otherwise, the harm caused by that aversivness is being treated as less than fully human. This is, again, a valuational reading with the potential for connections with more formal reflections of faith—as in, how "the diminishing of fearful obliviousness and protective vigilance through enhancement of places to appear can conceivably be a narrative about the presence of God."[18] As I said, more explicit reading of this narrative of harms and transformation in theological terms occurs in Chapter 8 of *Places of Redemption*. There I use a theonomous anthropology, categories of idolatry, and the social brokenness entailed by this understanding of sin to interpret the "places to appear" as redemptive changes. (More about that later.)

New Realities Appear

Now of course ethnography is not all that is going on here. As a result of interviewing, observing, and participating in worship, Sunday school, and other events, realities emerged that led me to find *new frames* for interpreting the place. Questions about the legitimacy of these frames is, of course, an important issue for discussion. Positively, however, one of the contributions of ethnography may be seen as the eruption of new elements/dimensions of a place.

Three examples follow.

First, the presence in church of people with disabilities, many of whom did not have language. Of course I could not interview them in a traditional sense, so I needed new lenses. One of the most significant new realities for me occurred through my experience of folks from the group homes. What I first ignored as bizarre physical movements and noises had to be redefined. These behaviors were not simply disruptions; nor were they just secondary parts of a context that did not need to be on a theologian's screen. Research shows that these movements and noises were *communications*—at least for those who took them seriously and worked with them. Theology needs to attend to *nonsymbolic communication*.[19]

Another example comes from a special-needs service when Bob, a participant from the group home who did have language, came to the front and spoke in images of heaven and God and angels, saying "and laying on your back, the clouds above roll by." Bob's associative thinking about heaven is not peculiar to him.[20] The role of affective association—the refractory character of all signifying—adds important complications to any interpretation. "Resonances," an acoustical term, suggests that sympathetic vibration is part of all communication, i.e., indirect connections between things said, events, and experiences. As Michael Holquist puts it, communication is "strewn with previous claims that slow up, distort, refract the intention of the word."[21] This is not just about Bob, but invokes an element of any place that makes Christian (or any) discourse inevitably mean different things to different people. Furthermore, it reminds us of the affective character of communication—preaching or otherwise.

The point is that this is not simply an "ethics" issue; rather, it challenges dominant assumptions in theology. The notion that there must be correct beliefs and also that there must be a logical coherence between these beliefs—between traditional loci—entailed in classic definitions of theology as systematics would clearly rule out some of the passionate expressions of the folks who came to this church. Ethnography itself, then, did not define these complicating features of the place, but it did generate a sense that I needed other categoreal frames to have a fuller sense of the elements that made up this "situation"—in this case the non-cognitive, aural, physical forms of human experience and communication. Lived theology is thus attending to the more complex ways that sense and order can be made out of human lives. While this is not to valorize anything humans do, it is, in short, an honoring of the complexity of the finitely good creature as imago Dei.

A second example comes from the complaint of a group of white members to their pastor that "the church is getting too black." Even though they were a consciously multiracial church, these folks complained after a black Liberian preacher substituted for their white pastor one Sunday. While Vasquez's work on bodies would have been helpful here, it was only later, after the church shrank and was folded into an African American United Methodist church in the area, that such observations generated for me the need for a new frame.[22] The disconnect between language about how color-blind they were, and some of the reactions of whites to different events—such as black bodies in leadership positions—led me to appropriate sociologist Paul Connerton's analysis of the bodily proprieties that come with social identity. Tradition, as he argues, is not simply practices of inscription (memories that can be saved) but also incorporative practices, bodily habits that communicate in the performance.[23] Like Vasquez, Connerton's work "questions the currently dominant idea that literary texts may be taken as a metaphor for social practices generally."[24] It is typical of much focus on bodies in recent writing to understand them as "expressing" meanings, an approach that Connerton would identify as a practice of inscription. Instead, with Vasquez, he insists that bodies do their own communicative work in the performance. They cannot be understood as simply expressing, or acting out, the meanings of the explicit "tradition" or commitments of a community. What is really challenging is his claim that incorporative practices are as crucial to social memory as are the typical practices of inscription (written, linguistic memory). Thus, for Good Samaritan, this means that their traditions were not simply United Methodist, or whatever other denomination shaped them. Their traditions were not simply biblical or doctrinal or liturgical. They were also racialized, normate, gendered, and other cultural habituations that operated as bodily incorporate practices. Lived theology is about bodies.

A third example where ethnographic work generates new categories is the complicating of situation and context. Problematic theological assumptions about situation and context include the view of context as a blank space where biblical teaching is applied, and the inadequate valorizations of certain Christian practices that ignore the complexity of context. Bernd Wannenwetsch claims that "(i)t is *in worship itself* that the ethical in-forming of human acting and judging comes about."[25] According to Stanley Hauerwas, sacraments "are the essential rituals of our politics"; "liturgy *is* social action."[26] There is, however, a need to flesh out "place," not simply as the empty space where something might happen, or the frame of a normative ritual, but as the territory of meaning constructed from the physical and the residual, a gathering of elements that is never ordered or unified in one simple way.

In order to avoid the simplistic church versus world thinking, *or* the fact that theology does not typically offer categories for the complex ways places of faith are shaped by affect, physical realities, and residuals, I used postmodern place theory, which I will not elaborate here. Minimally, to define a community as place disrupts accounts of context that ignore the synchronic, with its physical, affective, residual, and complex circulating of meaning via resonances, and how the synchronic intersects with the diachronic, ordered around practices. As such, place refuses to allow the diachronic (or temporal, or historical) as simply inherited written tradition, or as virtue theory practices, for these are accounts that ignore the power dynamics and bodily character of practices. There is no Eucharist where the marked/unmarked character of bodies does not matter.

With place theory, categories for discernment—that is, for the "ordering" of the physical, affective elements of place—include narrative, but a helpful way to think of this ordering comes in part from literary theorist Stanley Fish. To think about the way a particular community discerns, attends to, or notices a reality or problem, it helps to think of "stipulations of relevance" as that which link a theological community's belief-full knowing to a new problematic. What makes a community *notice* something, stipulations of relevance are any number of possible dispositions in the communal repertoire that allow a developing situation—a "wound"—to appear significant. Understanding change in this way means that the discourse of faith is never simply a language world, nor is it an insulated world. There is always an "outside" creating what it means to be Christian at any particular time.[27] What is supposedly the "inside," that is, the convictions that help create stipulations of relevance, according to postmodern place theory, is complex. Since convictions are not simply cognitive, they entail affective associations and fears. Nor are they "all held at the same level or operative at the same time." While there were overlapping themes in this church community that constituted convergences (with centripetal or unifying force), they did not always function in the same way: themes of welcome, conviction, and God-dependence had different associations for different groups. Factoring in other levels of social reality helped constitute centrifugal forces that pulled people apart.[28] Sometimes traditions about Jesus matter most, sometimes convictions about proper bodies for leadership. Convictions are "nested," which is to say that they do not all hold the same importance or matter equally at the same time.[29] And usually—no surprise—they are multiple and contradictory.

Challenges to Standard Theology

Issues that have surfaced as challenges to "theology": the standard litmus test for faith in congregations cannot be doctrinal orthodoxy; nor can it be reduced to articulated beliefs; nor can they be found as ordered in a consistent or logical way; nor do they necessarily have systematic connections. So, I raise three questions: what does it mean to trace theological reasoning in a community? What genres might be most helpful? What are other significant challenges to the definitions of theology?

First, let us briefly consider a way to imagine the tracing of theological reasoning. We obviously need to reject a view of doctrine that functions something like what Stanley Fish means by "theory," i.e., a formalizable rule, which "can be programmed on a computer and, therefore, can be followed by anyone who has been equipped with explicit (noncircular) definitions and equally explicit directions for carrying out a procedure." Such a view represents "an effort to govern practice . . . to guide practice from a position above or outside it."[30] This is not to do away with coherent thinking, such as that one's Christology must have some connection to one's soteriology. It does, however, complicate our defining of that connection.

The systematic character of theological reasoning is historic, but not adequate in and of itself. Genres of reflection that have developed in the history of *theologia*—doctrine, dogma, creeds, confessions, systematics—are by no means consistently defined. Sometimes "doctrine" has been distinguished from "dogma," when the latter is treated as required belief. Widely used creeds such as the Apostles', the Nicene, and the Athanasian are distinguished from the confessions of particular denominations.[31] Systematics has sometimes been identified with a particular genre of work produced by academic theologians, but is increasingly understood more broadly. We can assume there is sometimes overlap between other genres and systematics to refer to the search for theological coherence in the broadest sense. Dietrich Ritschl's *The Logic of Theology* offers one example of the fact that theologians have employed images that go beyond the more simplistic versions. It is possible, then, to construe a theo-logic that might be similar to the valuational narrative I have employed.

But there is also sometimes a disconnect between stated beliefs and practices. This is not simply reducible to hypocrisy or deception, or self-deception or deception of the other. Nor is it to deny that there may be "theological reasoning" there. *It is, however, to demand other genres.* Not just systematic thinking, or even thinking that might look like logical connections between beliefs. Narrative has been an important genre for theology for quite some time. What about genres for survival, resilience, regret, relationships, resistance? Mourning, prayer, and testimony are important. And what about the genres that help us to recognize the non-cognitive elements crucial to lived faith—what is their role? What are other forms of wisdom and other forms of communication that matter? The importance of oral cultures, of inevitable conflict between a variety of practices and beliefs, for example, and the normative lens for "disconnect or conflict" all need more attention. And, of course, as I have argued, bodies communicate. How can we think of this as a theological genre, rather than as a secondary site to the important stuff?

Finally, the standard way of understanding the *work of the theologian* is implicitly challenged by all these issues. How might other approaches than texts-about-texts be useful or even necessary? Wesley Kort's *Bound to Differ: The Dynamics of Theological Discourse* is a significant exposure of the limits of this long-standing habit of defining theology in relation to texts by other "theologians" and the problems raised by such textual self-enclosure.[32] In his ethnographic work in Northern Uganda, Todd Whitmore, an author in Scharen and Vigen's book, critiques theologians' obsession with texts, noting that Western theologians would most likely attend to African practices by reading texts by African authors or Europeans on Africa.[33] The sources for theological reflection must be broader than texts about texts. This shift needs to break the pattern of "Augustine said ... " as an adequate justification for contemporary discernments, just as the pattern of "The Bible says ..." has been broken.

The social location of theology as the production of knowledge—certifying discourse—also needs serious attention. The images that suggest this knowledge production occurs "nowhere"—whether in the "ivory tower" or whatever else—require critical analysis. There are material relations that construct the ivory tower. I am not rejecting the importance of discernment of general patterns over and above the specifics of everyday life, discernment that requires research of all sorts. I am, however, questioning the idea that contexts do not entail blindnesses, interest, and power dimensions that need attention. "Academics" is a context. (As "certifying discourse" theology is produced by the professional managerial class.[34]) I also think Scharen and Vigen have a deeply theological point related to this: the participation of theologians in other contexts—that is, social locations that are strange in many ways (class, race, geographic factors, cultural factors, etc.)—is crucial for our healthy development. Not only must we participate in other (foreign) contexts, we must be changed by this participation. With ethnographic work, we are not simply reporting what is "out there," and we are not simply bringing gifts to others. We are and need to be "receiving from others"—especially others who are not writers of books. This is not to say we should not write books; rather, it is to demand a better balance between kinds of knowledges. Of course there is a danger in this, but how to define it? How to avoid a kind of tourism? That is an important issue for further reflection. Having experience, of any sort, is no guarantee of wisdom. However, the *failure* to encounter, explore, and be challenged by realities that expose the messy, risky, dangerous, horrific, and wonderful elements of our world is a highly problematic way to avoid, or protect ourselves from, tourism. Our production of theology, then, is as much "lived theology," constituted by the messiness of life, as is the lived faith and theology of those we consider ordinary believers. And both are places where the Divine may be discerned.

Remaining Challenges

There are, of course, many other important issues to pursue, but I will close with three. First of all, the role of my own social location in the production of this account. While I did have experiences that deeply altered my academic sense of the world, there is more going on in my book than ethnography, even as ethnography admits a necessarily biased account of encounters between the participant "witness" and members of the community. Not only did I not get community response to my final book, but I eventually developed new frames (bodily proprieties, etc.) that were certainly not directly reflective of the community members' comments and testimonies to me. On the one hand, an important trajectory of ethnographic work calls for shared input—even shared research—into the production of a written account. On the other hand, the production of critical categories, such as those expanding aversiveness to pre-reflective bodily habituations, may not be easily approved by a community—and I am reluctant to rule out such lenses. There is no easy answer here.

A second trajectory needing further exploration comes from my "theonomous" reading of a place—in other words, how the Divine is entailed in an account of this community or any situation. This is obviously a crucial element of ethnography as theology. I draw upon E. Farley's work to allow for an account of faith as lived experience that is not the so-called reduction of faith to human experience. This account, rather, is based on the assumption that God is not an object of knowledge, but is only available as *mediated*. If God is only available via a textual tradition, that makes God "thinkable," and Farley rejects that approach. "Only if God in some way comes forth (actively, redemptively) can we proceed to assess and reinterpret our textual legacy, and only from that coming forth do we have grounds for appraising the ways we bespeak God and God's activity."

To fill out "mediation," Farley uses Edmond Husserl's notion of appresentation to indicate that an act of meaning always entails unpresented but entailed elements via the object of discernment, just as the perception of an object such as a tree only involves one side of that tree, but the perceiver indirectly "attends to" and apprehends the back of the tree, as well as its interior and the underground roots that cannot be seen.[35] Analogously, we do not "perceive" God in any direct or ordinary way, yet there is some kind of apprehending that is mediated. Farley uses an altered notion of appresentation to indicate that when we experience (individually, intersubjectively, and socially) the diminishing of sin and the *enhancement of freedom for and courage for the world, in short, when we are founded in that which is our true telos,* God is in a sense *appresented.*[36] In other words, from a Christian perspective, the reality of the sacred is indicated (indirectly), with the enhancement of the capacity to honor self and other (as finitely good), and to move out of the need to vilify the other, or participate in other forms of diminishment, otherwise known as a theonomous account of sin as idolatry—absolutizing that which is not truly "God"—with its secondary oppressive effects.

There may be numerous questions and further issues about ways of accounting for the entailment of the Divine in certain kinds of human practice, but I have found this account of mediation enormously helpful in the approach of lived theology, an approach that calls us to take so seriously the actual practices of lived faith, rather than to create a kind of dualism between something designated as the sacred and something else as human experience. This employment of Farley's account raises the crucial question of how God's "mode of presence" is understood by a theological ethnography. An account that assumed God is present in the ideational mode, or revealed ideas, would, of course, differ quite a bit.[37] But this is definitely a project for further exploration.

Finally, an issue for development concerns the degree to which ethnographic discernment and the need to generate new categories can challenge traditional and founding themes in theological worldview. As noted, my interpretation assumes a *theonomous* account of human being, i.e., that the root of broken human relations—(sin, etc).—is found in forms of substitution for dependence upon that which is truly God. This rooting of human brokenness in idolatry is, of course, a very "traditional" claim. However, given the social and institutional aspects of sin (what Farley calls "processes of subjugation") and their effect on culture, such that some individuals and communities grow up diminished by racist and sexist residuals, for example, is the notion of idolatry as root sin inadequate? Do we need more categories to identify the multiple, overlapping effects of social residuals with particular cultures, and individual agency? Also, given the importance of honoring people with disabilities, is idolatry still overdoing the focus on reflective capacities?

Where, then, do the boundaries lie in the generative and critical forming of theological claims through the processes of ethnographic work? What is the final authorizing factor? Is it an appeal to "the tradition," or might it be a concrete witness with compelling and widespread implications? The relation of theology and ethnography are and continue to be a work in progress, and that I end with questions is quite fitting for a theology of lived faith. Indeed, any attempt to portray real closure in our reflective musings on the faith would be at odds with the open-endedness of our lives and God's creative and redemptive activity in the world.

Notes

1. Vasquez makes the point that his materialist theory is "non-reductive." Manuel A. Vasquez, *More Than Belief: A Materialist Theory of Religion* (New York: Oxford University Press, 2011), 6.

2. Vasquez writes, "The insight that language is not the only form of material agency is crucial in my call for scholars to avoid semiotic reductionism and to engage in a holistic exploration of the diversity of practices that constitute religion as a constructed yet lived reality. In this approach, signification, representation, and hermeneutics would be clusters of practices in a shifting interplay with other forms of material activity" (*More than Belief,* 84).

3. Edward Farley, *Theologia: The Fragmentation and Unity of Theological Education* (Philadelphia: Fortress Press, 1983.) The process of critical and constructive thinking developed in part through its shifting relation to the *paideia* character of *theologia.* An important split between views of theology as a practical "knowledge" and a speculative discipline occurred with the fourteenth-century debate between Thomas Aquinas and such thinkers as Bonaventura. Given such interests as Thomas's focus on faith and reason, the development of theology as a speculative science aimed at the contemplation of God became a dominant model for theology for some. Monasteries became the primary locus for theology as an endeavor or practice of spirituality and mysticism, independent universities the place for theology as a science.

4. See Yves M. J. Congar, O.P., *A History of Theology,* trans. Hunter Guthrie, S. J. (Garden City, NY: Doubleday, 1968), 25–36.

5. Ellen Charry describes historic Christian teachings as "aretegenic," by which she means "the virtue-shaping function of the divine pedagogy of theological treatises." Ellen Charry, *By the Renewing of Your Minds: The Pastoral Function of Christian Doctrine* (New York: Oxford University Press, 1997), 19.

6. See Bonnie Miller-McLemore, "Practical Theology" *Encyclopedia of Religion in America,* ed. Charles H. Lippy and Peter W. Williams (Washington, DC: Congressional Quarterly Press, 2010), 1739–43.

7. A now classic account of the development of theology and its founding in this transformative knowledge, later termed *theologia,* is found in Edward Farley's *Theologia: The Fragmentation and Unity of Theological Education* (Philadelphia: Fortress Press, 1983). Defining various modes of divine "disclosure" is too big a topic to explore here.

8. Nicholas M. Healy, *Church, World and the Christian Life: Practical-Prophetic Ecclesiology* (Cambridge, UK: Cambridge University Press, 2000), 21, 38.

9. Christian Scharen and Aana Marie Vigen, eds., *Ethnography as Christian Theology and Ethics* (New York: Continuum, 2011), 67.

10. Scharen and Vigen, *Ethnography as Christian Theology and Ethics,* 73. Critics, of course, include John Milbank, who suspects the use of social science as a

functional employment of knowledge that entails a metaphysic of sorts that excludes the transcendent, a reduction of religion to an element of the larger culture and society; the assumption is that Christian theological vision entails its own "sociology." See Sharen and Vigen's critique of Milbank, *Ethnography as Christian Theology and Ethics*, 47–57.

11. James Clifford, "On Ethnographic Allegory," in *Writing Culture: The Poetics and Politics of Ethnography*, ed. James Clifford and George E. Marcus (Berkeley: University of California Press, 1986), 98–121.

12. Clifford, "On Ethnographic Allegory," 101.

13. Clifford, "On Ethnographic Allegory," 100.

14. Clifford, "On Ethnographic Allegory," 99.

15. Kathryn Tanner, "Theological Reflection and Christian Practices," in *Practicing Theology: Beliefs and Practices in Christian Life* (Grand Rapids, MI: Eerdmans, 2002), 228–43.

16. I appropriate Kimberley Curtis's interpretation of Arendt's images for "places to appear." See Curtis, *Our Sense of the Real: Aesthetic Experience and Arendtian Politics* (Ithaca, NY: Cornell University Press, 1999), 14.

17. Mary McClintock Fulkerson. *Places of Redemption: Theology for a Worldy Church* (Oxford: Oxford University Press, 2007), 236.

18. Fulkerson. *Places of Redemption: Theology for a Worldy Church*.

19. Symbolic modes of communication rely on forms that represent . . . something else, such as the word *shoe*, spoen or signed, referring to the shoe that you put on this morning . . . Combining the words *my* and *new* with the spoen or signed word *shoe* requires understanding of the formal rules of language." Educators have discovered other modes of communication—bodily, vocal affective, etc.— used by persons with disabilities. Ellin Siegel and Amy Wetherby, "Enhancing Nonsymbolic Communication," in *Instruction of Students with Severe Disabilities*, 5th ed., ed. Martha E. Snell and Fredda Brown (Upper Saddle River, NJ: Prentice-Hall, 2000), 409.

20. In the service Bob spoke in images of heaven and God and angels, saying "and laying on your back, the clouds above roll by."

21. Michael Holquist, ed., *The Dialogic Imagination: Four Essays by M. M. Bakhtin* (Austin: University of Texas Press, 1981), 432.

22. See Vasquez, Part I, "Embodiement," op.cit., 21–208.

23. Paul Connerton, *How Societies Remember* (Cambridge, UK: Cambridge University Press, 1989). His focus is to move away from the hermeneutical view that takes inscription "as its privileged object." So his focus is on non-inscribed practices, or performance—which "cannot be thought without a concept of habit; and habit cannot be thought without a notion of bodily automatisms" (4–5).

24. Editor's comment on book cover, Vasquez, op.cit.

25. According to Bernd Wannenwetsch, "the formative happening takes place in the context of a human *receptivity which can also be described as acting and judging*. So

the acting and judging of human beings is only an outgrowth of worship, a pos-
sibility which *then* arises of responding in daily life to the acting and judging of
God which has been experienced. It is *in worship itself* that the ethical in-forming
of human acting and judging comes about." Bernd Wannenwetsch, *Political
Worship: Ethics for Christian Citizens*, trans. Margaret Kohl (Oxford: Oxford
University Press, 2004).

26. Stanley Hauerwas, *The Peaceable Kingdom: A Primer in Christian Ethics* (Notre
    Dame, IN: University of Notre Dame Press, 1983), 108.

27. This is meant in the sense that any structuralism (like Saussure's) is inevitably
    destabilized by poststructuralism.

28. *Places of Redemption*, 35f.

29. Stanley Fish, "Change," *South Atlantic Quarterly* 86, no. 4 (Fall 1987): 429.

30. Stanley Fish, "Consequences," *Pragmatism and Literary Theory* 11, no. 3 (March
    1985): 435, 437.

31. One definition of "dogmatic theology" draws upon historian Jaroslav Pelikan's
    definition of dogma as "the normative statements of Christian belief adopted
    by various ecclesiastical authorities and enforced as the official teaching of the
    church." Quoted in Leonard J. Biallas, "Dogmatic Theology," in *A New Handbook
    of Christian Theology*, ed. Donald W. Musser & Joseph L. Price (Nashville,
    TN: Abingdon Press, 1992), 127–30. Systematic theology is "the intellectual
    discipline that seeks to express the content of a religious faith as a coherent
    body of propositions." John Macquarrie, *A New Handbook*, 469–474. A liberation
    approach would identify doctrines as the display of "symbols, as key areas or loci
    around which Christian communities construct their beliefs, spiritualities, prac-
    tices, and relations to the world and other religions. (Often found in scriptural
    narratives, these) symbols can be understood as 'doctrines,' especially when they
    are further developed conceptually and then related one to another to form a
    kind of basic grammar for Christian communities ... doctrines are ... elabo-
    rated forms of symbolic knowledge; symbols and doctrines together constitute a
    type of practical wisdom in and for living Christian faith in the world. As a practi-
    cal wisdom theology enters into something like the fulfillment of the symbolic
    function ... (it) becomes the creation of spaces for Christian practice. This cre-
    ation brings together analysis of social situations, biblical interpretations, fash-
    ioning of new meandings and practices, and forms of spirituality." Rebecca S.
    Chopp and Mark Lewis Taylor, "Introduction: Crisis, Hope, and Contemporary
    Theology," in *Reconstructing Christian Theology* (Minneapolis: Fortress/Augsburg
    Press, 1994), 14–15, 1–24.

32. Welsey A. Kort, *Bound to Differ: The Dynamics of Theological Discourse* (University
    Park: Pennsylvania State University Press, 1992).

33. Todd Whitmore, "Whiteness Made Visible: A Theo-Critical Ethnography in
    Acoliland" in Scharen and Vigen, *Ethnography as Christian Theology and Ethics*,
    op.cit., 184–206.

34. "(S)alaried mental workers who do not own the means of production and whose major function in the social division of labor may be described broadly as the reproduction of capitalist culture and capitalist class relations." Barbara and John Ehrenreich, "The Professional-Managerial Class," in *Between Labor and Capital*, ed. Pat Walker (Montreal: Black Rose Books, 1978), 5–45. The point here has to do with the function of our actual jobs as salaried persons in institutions, since many of us think we are resisting capitalism via our writing.

35. For this argument see Edward Farley, *Ecclesial Man: A Social Phenomenology of Faith and Reality* (Philadelphia: Fortree Press, 1975).

36. Farley, *Divine Empathy: A Theology of God* (Minneapolis: Augsburg/Fortress, 1996).

37. For samples of different modes of divine presence, including the ideational, see David H. Kelsey, *Proving Doctrine: The Uses of Scripture in Modern Theology* (Harrisburg, Pa.: Trinity Press International, 1999).

8

Descending into the Ordinary

LIVED THEOLOGY, WAR, AND THE MORAL
AGENCY OF CIVILIANS

John Kiess

IN THIS CHAPTER, I will explore the import of lived theology for Christian
ethics, specifically, for moral reflection upon the problem of war. What difference might a methodological shift to the realm of the everyday make for
how we understand and morally judge the complexities of contemporary
war? How might attention to the theological grammar of lived experience
in particular expand our notion of moral agency and improve peacebuilding strategies in war-torn societies?

Debate about war among Christian ethicists typically focuses on the
moral justifiability of the use of force: while pacifists traditionally reject
the use of force as a means for resolving conflict, just war theorists seek
to restrain the use of force both leading up to and during war. For much
of the twentieth century, this debate focused primarily on interstate wars,
in which the relevant moral actors were political and military representatives of the state, and the relevant moral decisions concerned the state's
resort to war and its specific military campaigns. Over the past several
decades, however, trends in warfare have dramatically shifted.[1] The majority of recent wars have been intrastate (or civil) wars. Such wars have been
characterized by the rise of nonstate military actors, the use of alternative
funding sources such as the illegal exploitation of natural resources, massive internal displacement, and elusive and short-lived peace settlements.
In the interstate wars of the past, the majority of casualties were combatants; in more recent wars, most of the casualties have been civilians.[2]

While many of these civilians have been victims of indiscriminate military attacks, most have been victims of the indirect costs of war: the malnutrition and disease that results from the interruption of state services, destruction of public infrastructure, and the abandonment of traditional forms of subsistence.[3] In a global economy that has challenged the state's traditional monopoly of force and created new linkages between armed conflict, livelihood, and civilian vulnerability, the complexities of modern war raise ethical questions that reach far beyond the battlefield. These questions concern the everyday lives of civilians and what strategies will best enable them to endure the deep impact of war.

There is a need for research methods that will help Christian ethicists better account for the civilian experience in war. Accounting for such experience requires what Veena Das calls "a descent into the ordinary," or a methodological move to the domain of the everyday, where one seeks to attend to what is shown as much as what is said, and where one can dwell in time long enough to see suffering become the very means through which agency is recovered.[4] In what follows, I explore how lived theology might be understood as just such a method, a way of descending into the ordinary whereby attention to the theological grammar of lived experience can illumine overlooked civilian voices and agencies.

I will do so through the lens of the war in the Democratic Republic of the Congo, where my recent research and fieldwork has concentrated.[5] In studies of Congo, civilians are routinely discussed in the reductive terms of voicelessness, bare life, and victimhood. I have found that attention to the lived theologies of Congolese civilians offers a different picture: the possibility of voice beyond speech, the endurance of human particularity in the midst of dislocation, and the resurrection of agency in places of devastation. I argue that the acknowledgment of such voice, identity, and agency is essential to addressing key shortcomings in recent peacebuilding strategies in Congo. Such acknowledgement also helps to identify key gaps in recent Christian debate on war, revealing regions of the contemporary landscape of conflict where the Christian imagination is being embodied in fresh ways.

Three Scenes from the War in the Congo

To help illustrate the ways that attention to lived theologies complicates conventional accounts of war and the place of civilians in it, let me begin by presenting three scenes from the Congo.

The first takes place in the eastern city of Bukavu in the year 2000. The Rally for Congolese Democracy (RCD), a regional rebel group, had occupied the city since 1998 and attempted to exercise political authority by claiming the state prerogatives of taxation, trade, and protection.[6] This attempt did not go unchallenged, and the Catholic Church in Bukavu, led by its archbishop, Emmanuel Kataliko, spearheaded the opposition. On Christmas Eve in 1999, Archbishop Kataliko preached an electrifying sermon denouncing the RCD's many abuses, from excessive taxation and illegal exploitation of resources to the killing of activists and attacks against churches.[7] His sermon inspired a city-wide strike, as Catholic and Protestant churches, joined by Muslims and other members of society, closed schools and clinics, along with markets and transportation, bringing the life of the city to a halt.[8] The RCD responded by exiling Kataliko to another province, which prompted another round of strikes and an international campaign for his return. Kataliko did eventually return, seven months later, to throngs gathered at the cathedral, where he presided over a public Eucharist attended by forty thousand people. But he was soon forced into exile again, where he died of an apparent heart attack (although many Congolese continue to suspect foul play).

Kataliko's body was received in Bukavu on October 8, 2000. A procession began at the airport and moved toward the city center. In the archdiocese's video footage of the event, thousands of Bukavu residents can be seen lining the streets.[9] In the crowds one can observe a range of activity: some church groups have gathered to offer hymns of thanksgiving, while other residents are more visibly grief-stricken, calling out to their leader and striking their chests in lament. Some stretch out their arms, others bow their heads, some kneel, while others lock together, shoulder to shoulder.

At about the midpoint of the procession, the rebel-appointed governor of South Kivu, Norbert Basengezi Katintima, attempts to address the crowd. His guards fire warning shots into the air and the mourners scatter.[10] Some throw themselves behind walls and fences while others drop to the ground. One can see several women huddled together, the brilliance of their yellow and blue floral-patterned dresses covered in mud. When the gunshots finally stop, a silence spreads out across the streets. Some of the mourners slowly begin to stand up. A crowd moves back towards the truck carrying Kataliko's body. The wheels begin to turn again. The hymns begin again. The mourners continue their procession, and take the body of their fallen leader to the cathedral for burial.

The second scene takes place in a refugee camp in the town of Irangi in 1996. Marie Béatrice Umutesi was one of the million Hutu refugees who had poured into Zaire/Congo in the aftermath of the Rwandan genocide, creating one of the worst humanitarian catastrophes in recent memory, resulting in the death of a thousand people a week from cholera alone.[11] While many of these refugees were former genocide perpetrators and ex-*Interahamwe* (the government-supported Hutu paramilitary group), the vast majority were not. As the armed genocide perpetrators continued to launch attacks into Rwanda and the weak Congolese state did nothing to stop them, the Rwandan government decided to end the situation by shelling the camps, prompting a mass repatriation to Rwanda. But because many of the *Interahamwe* were using refugees as shields, Umutesi was forced to flee further west.

In her memoir, Umutesi provides the harrowing account of her year-long flight through the jungles of Congo, fleeing both the genocide perpetrators and the Rwandan army.[12] She fled from camp to camp before she arrived at a town called Irangi. She describes her arrival:

Irangi, where we stayed for about two weeks, is on the stretch of paved road between Bukavu and Kisangani, about ninety-two kilometers from Bukavu ... The refugees had put up their blindés all around a former hotel. It soon became a camp that was really a prison. In the event of a rebel attack we had little chance of escaping. There was only one exit and a few well-armed Tiri guarded it. Those who tried to leave were robbed of all their belongings, molested, and even killed.[13]

And yet, she writes, "In the prison of Irangi I rediscovered prayer."[14] She recounts how a woman named Immaculée, whom she befriended during her journey, helped her: "It was thanks to Immaculée that I again found the words that had been lost for so long."[15] With Immaculée's assistance, she relearned "the Lord's Payer, the Creed, the Gloria and other prayers that I had forgotten."[16] Later, "my daughters taught me religious songs that I sang often, even on the road or when I was fetching water. The songs that I loved the most were: Nyir'ibambe ndaje unyakire (Lord I come to you, welcome me) and Ni wowe rutare rwanjye (You are my rock)."[17] Umutesi writes, "After praying I felt restored. Thanks to my faith, I was able to bear the daily humiliations, deprivation, sickness, and misery better."[18] She goes on, "the most important thing that Immaculée taught me, which continued to help me even when we were no longer together, is to accept God in everyday life. To accept him like a loving father, who comes to our aid every time we call on him, even for the smallest things in life. This faith would be my greatest support during the year spent in the equatorial forests of Zaire."[19]

The third scene takes place in the town of Nyankunde, located in the northeastern province of Ituri, where I conducted fieldwork in 2009. Nyankunde was one of the hardest-hit towns during the war, destroyed in 2002 as a result of a major attack that killed over 1,200 people and displaced the entire population. The town remained empty until a small group of residents decided to return two years later. With militias continuing to roam only about ten miles outside the town, the area was highly unstable, policed only by a small UN peacekeeping force. Returning to Nyankunde meant exposure to further looting and attack, but for one of the residents, a Christian doctor named Mike Upio, returning was a moral imperative. Having worked for Médecins sans Frontières (Doctors without Borders), Dr. Upio was well aware that the death toll of the war was now approaching several million; he also knew that most of these deaths were not from direct fighting, but from easily treatable diseases and other medical conditions.[20] In returning to Nyankude, Dr. Upio was returning to the primary front of the war; he was returning to prevent this civilian toll from rising.

During one of my stays in Nyankunde, Dr. Upio invited me into the operating suite of the hospital, which he had been rebuilding one ward at a time for several years. A woman had arrived for a C-section, a straightforward procedure that has been unavailable in many rural areas, resulting in countless birth-related deaths. In the operating room, Dr. Upio began by making several incisions, and then he pulled the webbing of the woman's skin apart, delivering the limp body of a baby. He handed the child to a nurse, who gently rapped its back, and peals of newborn wailing filled the room. Dr. Upio then turned back to the woman and began to deliver a second child from her womb. When the nurse rapped this child's back, there was no movement. After repeated attempts to initiate breathing, the nurse stopped and put the child down. Later Dr. Upio said me, "The mother walked 20km last night to get here. I don't know if the second child was ever alive. But the first is alive, and the mother is alive."[21]

Three scenes from the war in the Congo, three scenes in lived theology. How might attention to such scenes challenge the way civilian life in Congo is conventionally narrated? And how might such attention change the way Christian ethicists think about the role of civilians in war more broadly?

Rethinking Civilian Life during the War in the Congo

Voicelessness

Perhaps the most pervasive descriptive trope that accompanies accounts of civilian life during the war in Congo is that of voicelessness. Evelyn Gordon, writing in *Commentary* magazine, provides a representative example of this when she observes: "the world rarely hears about Congo— because groups such as Amnesty [International] and Human Rights Watch have left the victims largely voiceless, preferring instead to focus on far less serious abuses in developed countries, where gathering information is easier."[22] Gordon expresses two common assumptions: that those in Congo are voiceless; and that they can only achieve voice through the speech of Western advocacy groups. French anthropologist Didier Fassin describes how second-generation humanitarianism (associated with the rise of such groups as Médecins sans Frontières and Médecins du Monde) differs from first-wave humanitarianism on precisely this score: whereas the International Committee of the Red Cross made a policy of not testifying on behalf of the victims they assisted, MSF and other groups deliberately speak out as witnesses to injustice.[23] The role of the witness shifts from the person who experiences suffering to the person who tries to alleviate it. This suffering is then translated into more familiar Western idioms, such as Conrad's "heart of darkness," Hobbes's state of nature, the clinical language of trauma, or the legal language of crimes against humanity.[24] Regardless of the idiom, the assumption is that the victims have been deprived of voice, and the humanitarian must supply it.

Such a narrative is difficult to resist if we confine ourselves to reports of slaughter, rape, abduction, and displacement. Yet by descending into the ordinary and attending to the way civilians negotiate violence in everyday life, we begin to hear overlooked voices. Returning to the scene in Bukavu, one is particularly struck by the outspoken voice of Archbishop Kataliko. The pulpit of the Catholic Church offered a powerful forum not only for highlighting injustices, but for offering a theological vision of solidarity in suffering and the power of life over death. Such a vision provided civilians with a framework for understanding their suffering and galvanized them into collective action. Contrary to the Hobbesian assumption that the collapse of the state entails the collapse of all forms of civic order, numerous churches endured during the war and supplied many of the services formerly provided by the state. In Bukavu, the Catholic Church in particular continued to operate schools, hospitals, counseling centers, and relief efforts.[25] Through these institutions and its ongoing life of worship, the Church helped to sustain a fragile common world in which disruptive speech could circulate and overflow into the streets.

Speech, however, was not the only register in which civilians made their voices heard. In the procession from the airport to the city center, the most eloquent testimony was offered not in the form of words, but in the mourners' bodily gestures: their physical presence in the streets, their unrestrained cries and laments, and their willingness to expose themselves to the violence of the RCD so that Kataliko could be buried. Through these and other gestures, they bodied forth their voice and witnessed to a number of crucial claims.[26] On the one hand, their unflinching determination to extend full burial rites to Kataliko made a claim about the value and dignity of human life. Ordinarily, burial goes without saying; it is one of those rituals that human beings offer one another without justification. It is only when burial is denied, as it was in countless cases during the war in the Congo, that we discover its essential role in human community, upholding the unspoken boundary between persons and things. To deprive a victim burial not only offends the dignity of the victim, but it also deprives a community of the opportunity to acknowledge publicly the value of all human life. It cheapens perceptions of human worth. In risking their lives to bury Kataliko, the mourners interrupted this process. They showed that Kataliko's life was worth dying for, which in turn communicated the value of all the lives gathered in the streets. In this respect, the burial of Kataliko, much like Antigone's burial of Polyneices, was not merely a protest of an unjust law or form of rule, but more fundamentally, and more constructively, an attempt to restore the moral order of things. It reestablished one of the basic unspoken boundaries upon which the everyday life of a city depends. It was not simply an act of private, religious devotion, but a public, civic act, helping to reweave the torn fabric of the ordinary, suggesting something about the ambiguous boundaries between church and city, and the worldly character of the church.[27]

Responding to the occupation of another city, St. Augustine wrote about how burial is not only a confirmation of the value of human life, but an expression of the hope for bodily resurrection. Care for the dead body was, for Augustine, unintelligible apart from the expectation that all flesh "shall be given back and made whole in a moment of time."[28] Kataliko himself often spoke of the power of the resurrection in his letters from exile, writing:

> The faith that we share in this message of Christ's resurrection must comfort us in the difficult times in which we are living. In the faith of Christ, death no longer has the last word. If life is stronger, we must continue to believe in the inviolability of human life. If our hope in the resurrection is stronger, let us persevere, faithful in distress and strong in our witness 'because hope never fails' (Rom. 5:5).[29]

The way the assembled mourners cared for Kataliko's body constitutes a fitting bodily response to his message, witnessing to this same hope for resurrection while making manifest the implications of such hope for the present. Going on with the procession in the face of violence displayed the future victory over death now, opening a way of being in the world beyond the fear of death. Kataliko recognized that the RCD's attempt to exercise sovereignty over the life of the city was grounded in the brute assertion of power over life and death. In proclaiming Christ's victory over death, Kataliko was declaring the release of Bukavu residents from the power of the RCD. Free from the fear of death, they were free of the RCD. The uninterrupted mourning of Bukavu Christians visibly displayed this release and manifested a way of being in the world over which no human power is sovereign.

Bare Life

If attention to lived theology helps us to acknowledge the voices of those assumed to be voiceless, illumining ways civilians help to sustain order in the midst of war, such attention also helps to challenge a related description, that of "bare life."

Philosopher Georgio Agamben is the most recent in a long line of thinkers who distinguish between two forms of life: the bare, biological life that human beings share with animal and vegetative life; and the qualified, biographical life that makes human life distinctively human.[30] For Agamben, following Aristotle, it is language that distinguishes human beings from other animals, and thus the loss of language entails the loss of the human.[31] Stripped of citizenship and the conditions necessary for speech and action, the refugee presents the quintessential figure of bare life. The assumption here, as in many accounts of refugees, is that once a refugee crosses a national boundary, he or she loses the qualitative markings of culture and history, and is reduced to the biological sameness that all living things share.[32] Agamben goes on to argue that rather than question the way states reduce citizens to this condition, humanitarian organizations become their unwitting accomplices by relating to refugees solely on the basis of their biological needs. Agamben writes, "The 'imploring eyes' of the Rwandan child, whose photograph is shown to obtain money but who 'is now becoming more and more difficult to find alive,' may well be the most telling contemporary cipher of the bare life that humanitarian organizations, in perfect symmetry with state power, need."[33] Thus while humanitarian organizations seek to keep refugees alive, they help perpetuate a condition in which refugees find themselves more vulnerable than ever. Constructed as "bare life," they fall into a category of existence that can be assaulted with impunity because their lives no longer register as fully human.

Agamben's understanding of bare life has been influential among Christian ethicists, shaping how a number of thinkers approach refugees and state exclusion.[34] If we return to the scene of Marie Béatrice Umutesi in the camp in Irangi, however, we find some compelling reasons for questioning Agamben's analysis. Umutesi's experience of exile is not some neutral, "bare" experience universally shared by all refugees. Her experience continues to be shaped by enduring aspects of her identity. First and foremost, her experience of exile is gendered at every point, as she has to escape the sexual advances of male predators repeatedly throughout her journey. Her experience is also deeply marked by ethnic identity, as her shared Hutu affiliation with genocide perpetrators makes her the target of relentless attacks by the Rwandan army. But it is her Catholic identity that challenges Agamben's account most profoundly. Her practice of prayer and song, and the way this fosters a sense of precarious community among her fellow travellers and a visceral sense of God's presence even in the stifling conditions of the camp, directly challenges the assumption that she has lost speech. More fundamentally, it challenges the idea that biological and biographical life can be easily disentangled. In prayer, body and biography, biological and qualified life, mutually intersect and articulate one another. Umutesi's posture of prayer witnesses to an ongoing relationship with God, suggesting that the human is ultimately not grounded through membership in a state, but rather in the self's relation to God. Such a posture suggests that dehumanization in Agamben's totalizing sense is not actually within the power of the state; no place is God-forsaken, and thus no place gives us privileged access into a bare life distinguishable from our biographical journey into God. The endurance of such identity makes the duty of care to refugees no less urgent, but it makes the fulfillment of such a duty contingent upon the prior acknowledgment of the enduring identity of refugees—in Umutesi's case, her identity as a woman, a Hutu, and a Catholic. To look for lived theologies in contexts of war is not only to look for voice beyond speech, but particularity beyond bare life.

Victimhood

These points about enduring voice and identity connect to a third point about agency. Descriptions that emphasize voicelessness and bare life often end up reducing civilians to victimhood. The reports of Human Rights Watch and other groups are filled with vivid accounts of Congolese towns destroyed, people displaced, and the rights of individuals trampled upon.[35] While these accounts rightly focus on what civilians suffer, they rarely go on to explore how civilians live with and respond to such suffering. As Liisa Malkki observes, "understanding displacement as a human tragedy and looking no further can mean that one gains no insight at all into the lived meanings that displacement and exile can have for specific people."[36] Echoing this, Veena Das suggests that instead of taking suffering as a given, it is important to trace the ways that signs of injury are inhabited, reinhabited, and worked through, becoming in some cases the very basis upon which agency is recovered.

To appreciate this agency, however, requires the crucial element of time. Das observes the tendency among journalists and scholars to narrate major acts of political violence as moments of radical rupture distinct from the everyday. For Das, however, the boundaries between the event and the everyday are not so distinct. Exceptional events exert intense and lasting pressure upon everyday institutions such as marriage, family, and work, often times threatening them with ruin. Yet by descending to the everyday, one can appreciate the way that men and women slowly weave these ruins into a new ordinary, transforming their suffering into a form of agency. Over time one discovers how "evidently small things," such as the healing of a broken relationship, become an appropriate and fitting way to deal with the consequences of seemingly great things.[37]

Returning to our third scene, the town of Nyankunde, the temptation is to isolate the 2002 attack and emphasize its destructive impact. It resulted in the death of over a thousand people, uprooted families, destroyed farms, and left homes, schools, churches, and a large hospital in ruins, cutting the town off from an international network of volunteers and donors. It so disrupted ordinary life that the town will never be the same again. But the return of Dr. Upio and the other residents shows how this violence was not simply a fate they passively suffered. A hospital that was once staffed by Western missionaries who treated common maladies is now a hospital staffed by Congolese who are mitigating the indirect costs of war. Instead of relying upon food supplies from humanitarian organizations, residents are replanting and harvesting their own farms. In reopening their markets and schools, they are offering youth constructive alternatives to the war economy. While cities are overcrowded and other villages remain empty, Nyankunde has become a place in which civilians are leading rebuilding efforts and imagining a Congo without war.

In reflecting on his decision to return and rebuild the hospital, Dr. Upio said, "Our mission is to preach the gospel and heal people. That is what Jesus did. Jesus suffered with people and he healed them. I saw that was our mission too. I saw that you have to suffer with the people if you want to heal them."[38] This points to the deeper theological grammar of this mode of repair, a way of understanding redemption that does not rest in the consolation of otherworldly visions of harmony, but lingers among the ruins in a posture of wounded healing. In the operating room of the Nyankunde hospital, Dr. Upio bodies forth a cross-grained love, and helps his community give birth to new beginnings.

Lessons for Moral Debate about War in Christian Ethics

I now want to return to the question raised earlier about how attention to lived theologies might reshape debate about war in Christian ethics. I mentioned at the outset of the essay how just war and pacifist approaches to war tend to focus on the moral justifiability of the use of force, which in turn limits their focus to state and rebel actors. As a descent into the ordinary, I take lived theology to represent an opportunity to explore the morality of war from the local perspective of civilians. This involves considering not only the traditional question of whether one should lend material assistance to combatants but also how civilians should navigate war's impact upon everyday life, including the challenges posed by rebel occupation and the need to develop alternative livelihood strategies. Such attention by no means supplants moral reflection on the use of force, but it helps to ground such reflection in a deeper understanding of the lives and communities that are affected by conflict.

In this way, a lived theology method offers a different way of arriving at moral judgments about war and peacebuilding.[39] If most moral reflection on armed conflict involves the ethicist applying a pre-existing moral tradition to a given context, a lived theology approach begins from the premise that local Christians themselves are already engaged in the work of theologically understanding and morally responding to their context. Acknowledging such judgments is an essential preliminary step to the formation of additional judgments, as it draws upon the local wisdom of those intimately acquainted with the conflict and builds upon efforts that are already underway. This then helps to illumine the way that broader national or international peacebuilding strategies might be strengthened.

I want to offer three specific ways that the lived theologies discussed above might improve existing peacebuilding strategies in Congo and, by extension, open fresh ground in the debate on war in Christian ethics.

Since 1999, Congo has been home to the world's largest peacekeeping mission, the United Nations Organization Mission in the DRC (known by its French acronym MONUC). MONUC was deployed to oversee the implementation of a comprehensive peace agreement between the major state and rebel participants in the war. The peace agreement, however, did not address the grievances of local militias in Eastern Congo, who have remained active in the region and continue to commit numerous human rights violations. Séverine Autesserre has argued that one of the major reasons that peacebuilding in Congo has had such a mixed record of success is that MONUC has focused on various statebuilding measures (national elections, integration of rebels into the military, etc.) to the neglect of local sources of violence.[40] In the process, it has alienated important stakeholders in the civilian community whose buy-in is crucial for the success of its mission. MONUC has neglected local partnerships, Autesserre argues, because it has assumed that the war destroyed most forms of civil order and that such order could only be repaired through top-down statebuilding.

But as we saw in the case of the Catholic Church in Bukavu, civil order did not simply erode under rebel occupation. Instead, there was a more complex relationship between rebels and civilians: occupying forces came to depend upon civilians for social services, which placed civilians in an unlikely position of strength, as they were able to concert action and leverage these services against the occupying forces. We saw the power of Kataliko's theological imagination in concerting such action, and the way religious liturgies such as burial helped to maintain not only a sense of solidarity among church members but also the deeper moral boundaries that ground perceptions of human worth. All of this reminds us that civilian agency precariously endures in war, and future peacekeeping missions will need to balance their emphasis upon statebuilding with strategic local partnerships that assist civilians in meeting livelihood needs and maintaining their civic institutions. In Christian ethics, this represents an underexplored point of potential consensus between just war theorists and pacifists. The prospect of such strategic peacebuilding partnerships invites just war theorists to think more deeply about the moral agency of non-combatants and pacifists to supplement their thinking about nonviolent alternatives to war with nonviolent strategies in the midst of war.[41]

In addition to highlighting the role of civilian agency, we have seen that attention to lived theologies also exposes the shortcomings of approaching refugees as bare life. Rather than a condition of undifferentiated sameness, Umutesi's experience of dislocation bore the specific traces of her identity as a woman, Hutu, and a Catholic. Appreciating this helps to reveal why both humanitarian and political responses to the refugee crisis in Congo in 1994–1996 were so inadequate. By providing aid to refugees regardless of their identity (in Agamben's terms, as bare life), humanitarian workers in eastern Congo inadvertently supported former genocide perpetrators and ex-*Interahamwe* who were actively re-arming and planning reprisal attacks against Rwanda. These armed elements also attacked local Congolese who had family ties to Rwandan Tutsis, exacerbating existing tensions and destabilizing an already fragile region. In neglecting differences among the refugees, humanitarian agencies also failed to meet the needs of women in particular, who had no access to basic hygiene supplies and were exposed to widespread sexual violence. These failures carried over into political responses to the crisis. The Congolese government was in no position to naturalize one million refugees in 1994, and yet political conditions in Rwanda discouraged a voluntary repatriation. There were widespread reports of government-sponsored, anti-Hutu violence and few opportunities for integration into the pro-Tutsi government. There was also the prospect of criminal trials without guarantees of due process. Luke Bretherton is right in suggesting that what refugees need most is a home, but this begs the question of which home is most appropriate given the identities of the refugees and, in the case of repatriation, the kind of reforms that are necessary to facilitate a voluntary, peaceful return.[42] Instead of creating such conditions, the Rwandan government sponsored a rebel movement in Congo with the intention of destroying the camps and forcing the refugees to return. This plan backfired, as nearly two hundred thousand refugees ended up fleeing further west. The rebels pursued them and committed countless atrocities, while thousands of others died from starvation. Meanwhile, two decades later, many of the armed refugees continue to roam eastern Congo, and the citizenship status of thousands of refugees remains unresolved.

Both humanitarian and government agencies ignore the particular identity of refugees at their own peril, as this leads not only to an inability to meet their temporary needs but also to reach effective conclusions to refugee crises. Christian ethicists routinely think of peace settlements in terms of the incentives they offer state and rebel actors to end their struggles, but such considerations should be expanded to include the kind of concessions and incentives that are required for refugees to return home as well. Doing so would require seeing refugees themselves as political agents, with as much at stake in a peace settlement as combatants; it would require re-envisioning formal peace processes with such agency in mind.

This point about integrating refugee perspectives into peace processes connects to a final lesson about transitional justice. As Congo emerges from nearly two decades of violence, much recent attention has turned to how the country will deal with the legacy of the past. The UN's recent *Mapping Report* made several recommendations, including war crimes trials, reform of the judiciary, and a possible truth commission.[43] The Congolese government has referred several high-profile cases to the International Criminal Court, resulting in two convictions to date. Debate in Christian ethics also revolves around the relative merits of tribunals and truth commissions, typically considered through the lens of one's conception of the relation between God's justice and mercy or individual responsibility and collective guilt.[44] Such national and international mechanisms for dealing with the past are critically important for ending cultures of impunity and providing public forums for victims to express their voices. But their role in helping communities heal should not be overstated. Attention to lived theologies points to another register of healing, the realm of the everyday. In Nyankunde, we saw how violence disrupted the very shape of the ordinary, seeping into institutions such as schools, churches, and hospitals. These represent ruptures that larger-scale mechanisms are not equipped to address. They require the patient, long-term work of residents returning to reweave these ruins into a new ordinary. Such repair does not replace these other mechanisms, but it balances their emphasis on public testimony with a focus on the largely unspoken boundaries, routines, and practices that give words their life and communities their sense of continuity in time. It leads to a heightened appreciation of how the seemingly mundane work of returning to a village and rebuilding a hospital can be an essential part of building a peace that endures.

Conclusion

In this chapter I have tried to consider how attention to lived theologies helps to challenge the way civilians are conventionally depicted in contexts of war, and to demonstrate how such attention might improve existing peacebuilding strategies and open new trajectories in Christian debate on war. If most accounts of Congolese civilians emphasize voicelessness, bare life, and victimhood, lived theology's descent into the ordinary reveals voice beyond speech, human particularity beyond bare life, and agency beyond victimhood. It helps to uncover overlooked interfaces in the contemporary landscape of war, and marshal underutilized resources in addressing the challenges of these conflicts.

Paying attention to lived theologies in places such as Congo, however, is more than a methodological shift or alternative research sensibility. In settings where assumptions about voicelessness and victimhood often enable deeper assumptions about the limits of the human, it becomes an essential moral sensibility. Attending to lived theologies is not about gaining new knowledge; it is about responding to a claim for recognition. It is about acknowledgment. A failure to acknowledge, a failure to hear the voice of lived theology in places of dislocation is, to borrow the words of Das, not a failure of the intellect; it is a failure of the spirit.[45]

Notes

1. Lotta Themnér and Peter Wallensteen, "Armed Conflicts, 1946–2011," *Journal of Peace Research* 49, no. 4 (2012): 565–75.
2. P. W. Singer, *Children at War* (Berkeley: University of California Press, 2006), 4.
3. On the indirect effects of war, see Human Security Centre, *Human Security Report 2005: War and Peace in the 21st Century* (New York: Oxford University Press, 2006), 124–43.

4. Veena Das, *Life and Words: Violence and the Descent into the Ordinary* (Berkeley: University of California Press, 2007).

5. This chapter draws upon six months of fieldwork conducted in 2008–2009 in the provinces of Ituri, North Kivu, and South Kivu, as well as sermons, letters, memoirs, and follow-up correspondence with informants. All translations are my own, except where noted. I provide a fuller account of the role of lived theology in the war in the Congo in "When War is Our Daily Bread: Congo, Theology, and the Ethics of Contemporary Conflict" (PhD diss., Duke University, 2011).

6. See D. M. Tull, "A Reconfiguration of Political Order? The State of the State in North Kivu (DR Congo)," *African Affairs* 102 (2003): 429–46.

7. Emmanuel Kataliko, "Console, Console My People: Hope Never Disappoints," (December 24, 1999), reprinted in Archdiocese of Bukavu, *Les Lettres et Messages de Monseigneur Emmanuel Kataliko.*

8. Gérard Prunier, "The Catholic Church and the Kivu Conflict," *Journal of Religion in Africa* 31, no. 2 (May 2001): 139–62.

9. Archdiocese of Bukavu, *Monseigneur Kataliko: Martyr de la Paix* (2000).

10. BBC News, "Bishop's Burial Highlights Congo's Crisis," October 13, 2000. See also African News, "Activists Severely Beaten; Conditions Deteriorate Following Robinson's Visit" (October 11, 2000).

11. For more on the refugee crisis, see David Rieff, *A Bed for the Night: Humanitarianism in Crisis* (New York: Simon & Schuster, 2002), 155–93; Jason Stearns, *Dancing in the Glory of Monsters: The Collapse of the Congo and the Great War of Africa* (New York: Public Affairs, 2011), 33–44; Gérard Prunier, *Africa's World War: Congo, the Rwandan Genocide, and the Making of a Continental Catastrophe* (Oxford: Oxford University Press, 2009), 37–72.

12. Marie Béatrice Umutesi, *Fuir ou Mourir au Zaire* (Paris: L'Harmattan, 2000). Quotations are from the English translation, *Surviving the Slaughter*, trans. Julia Emerson (Madison: University of Wisconsin Press, 2004).

13. Umutesi, *Surviving the Slaughter*, 116.

14. Umutesi, *Surviving the Slaughter*, 117.

15. Umutesi, *Surviving the Slaughter*, 118.

16. Umutesi, *Surviving the Slaughter*, 118.

17. Umutesi, *Surviving the Slaughter*, 214.

18. Umutesi, *Surviving the Slaughter*, 214.

19. Umutesi, *Surviving the Slaughter*, 118.

20. The International Rescue Committee estimates that 5.4 million people have died during the Congo war, making it the deadliest conflict since WWII. See Benjamin Coghlan et al., "Mortality in the Democratic Republic of Congo: A Nationwide Survey," *The Lancet* 367 (2006): 44–51.

21. Interview with the author, Nyankunde, September 15, 2009.

22. Evelyn Gordon, "The Voiceless Victims," *Commentary* (February, 14, 2010).

23. Didier Fassin, "Humanitarianism as a Politics of Life," *Public Culture* 19, no. 3 (2007): 499–520. He expands upon this analysis in Fassin and Richard Rechtman, *The Empire of Trauma: An Inquiry into the Condition of Victimhood* (Princeton, NJ: Princeton University Press, 2009); and Fassin, *Humanitarian Reason: A Moral History of the Present* (Berkeley: University of California Press, 2011).

24. On the uses of Conrad, see Kevin C. Dunn, *Imagining the Congo* (New York: Palgrave MacMillan, 2003), 1–20. On the uses of Hobbes, see Séverine Autesserre, "Hobbes and the Congo: Frames, Local Violence, and International Intervention," *International Organization* 63 (Spring 2009): 249–80. For an example of the language of trauma and crimes against humanity, see Human Rights Watch, *Soldiers Who Rape, Commanders Who Condone: Sexual Violence and Military Reform in the Democratic Republic of Congo* (New York: Human Rights Watch, 2009), 16–30.

25. Prunier writes, "In such a situation, in spite of its internal squabbles, the Church is more than ever seen as a social guarantor of last resort as well as the only moral and intellectual authority remaining" ("Catholic Church and the Kivu Conflict," 160). See also Laura Elizabeth Seay, "Social Services, Civil Society & the Catholic Church in the Kivus," in "Authority at Twilight: Civil Society, Social Services, and the State in the Eastern Democratic Republic of Congo" (PhD diss., University of Texas at Austin, May 2009).

26. I borrow the phrase "body forth" from Das's discussion of Wittgenstein in *Life and Words*: "What is fascinating for me is that in drawing the scene of the pathos of pain, Wittgenstein creates language as the bodying forth of words" (40). My thanks also to Brian Goldstone for valuable conversation on this theme.

27. On the worldly character of the church, see Mary McClintock Fulkerson, *Places of Redemption* (Oxford: Oxford University Press, 2007).

28. *De Civitate Dei* I.12.

29. Emmanuel Kataliko, "We are Risen with the Lord," April 20, 2000.

30. Georgio Agamben, *Homo Sacer: Sovereign Power and Bare Life* (Stanford, CA: Stanford University Press, 1998). Agamben traces this distinction back to Plato and Aristotle: "The Greeks had no single term to express what we mean by the word 'life.' They used two terms that, although traceable to a common etymological root, are semantically and morphologically distinct: *zoē*, which expressed the simple fact of living common to all living beings (animals, men, or gods), and *bios*, which indicated the form or way of living proper to an individual or a group" (1).

31. He is building upon Aristotle's twofold observation that "man is by nature a political animal" and "man is the only animal whom [nature] has endowed with the gift of speech" (*Politics* I.2).

32. For a critical analysis of this assumption, see Liisa H. Malkki, *Purity and Exile: Violence, Memory, and National Cosmology among Hutu Refugees in Tanzania* (Chicago: University of Chicago Press, 1995), 11–17.

33. Agamben, *Homo Sacer*, 133–4.
34. See Luke Bretherton, "The Duty of Care to Refugees, Christian Cosmopolitanism, and the Hallowing of Bare Life," *Studies in Christian Ethics* 19, no. 1 (2006): 39–61; D. Stephen Long and Geoffrey Holdsclaw, "Is Anything Worth Dying For? Martyrdom, Exteriority, and Politics after Bare Life," *Witness of the Body*, ed. Michael L. Budde and Karen Scott (Grand Rapids, MI: Eerdmans, 2011), 171–89; and Colby Dickinson, *Agamben and Theology* (London: T&T Clark, 2011). As Bretherton notes, John Milbank considers the ways in which Jesus himself can be seen as a figure of bare life. See his "Atonement: Christ the Exception," in *Being Reconciled* (London: Routledge, 2003), 94–104.
35. See, for example, Human Rights Watch, "Ituri: 'Covered in Blood'; Ethnically Targeted Violence in Northeastern DR Congo" (New York: Human Rights Watch, 2003); and UN Office for the High Commissioner of Human Rights, *Mapping Report on the Democratic Republic of the Congo, 1993–2003* (August 2010).
36. Malkki, *Purity and Exile*, 16.
37. This is how Stanley Cavell summarizes the import of Das's project in his foreword to *Life and Words*, xiv.
38. Interview with the author, Nyankunde, February 17, 2009.
39. Here I am drawing upon Luke Bretherton's helpful formulation of the role of ethnography in Christian theology in his essay, "Coming to Judgment: Methodological Reflections on the Relationship Between Ecclesiology, Ethnography, and Political Theory," *Modern Theology* 28, no. 2 (April 2012): 167–96. Bretherton writes, "Recourse to ethnographic methods is not simply in order to describe practices and interpret their meanings. Rather, on my account, theology is a constructive judgment that can utilize ethnographic modes of attention as ways of engaging not in abstract judgments but listening up close and participating so as to make judgments based on practical reason. Such judgments are in the service of better, that is to say more faithful, action" (190).
40. Séverine Autesserre, *The Trouble with the Congo: Local Violence and the Failure of International Peacebuilding* (Cambridge, UK: Cambridge University Press, 2010).
41. For one account that pursues these possibilities, see Gerald W. Schlabach, ed. *Just Policing, Not War* (Collegeville, MN: Liturgical Press, 2007).
42. Bretherton, "The Duty of Care to Refugees," 42, 49.
43. See "Transitional Justice Options for the DRC," in *Mapping Report on the Democratic Republic of the Congo*, 444–99.
44. For a defense of war crimes tribunals, see James Turner Johnson, "War Crimes and Reconciliation after Conflict," in *Morality and Contemporary Warfare* (New Haven, CT: Yale University Press, 1999), 191–218; Oliver O'Donovan, "Can War Crimes Trials Be Morally Satisfying?" in *The Just War Revisited* (Cambridge, UK: Cambridge University Press, 2003), 109–23; and Mark J. Allman and Tobias L. Winright, *After the Smoke Clears: The Just War Tradition and Post War Justice* (Maryknoll, NY: Orbis Books, 2010). On truth commissions, see Joseph

Liechty and David Tombs, ed. *Explorations in Reconciliation: New Directions in Theology* (Aldershot, UK: Ashgate, 2006); and Desmond Tutu, *No Future Without Forgiveness* (New York: Doubleday, 1999). For a mediating position, see Daniel Philpott, *Just and Unjust Peace: An Ethic of Political Reconciliation* (Oxford: Oxford University Press, 2012).

45. Das, *Life and Words*, 57. For more on the distinction between knowledge and acknowledgment, see Stanley Cavell, "Knowing and Acknowledging," in *Must We Mean What We Say?* (Cambridge, UK: Cambridge University Press, 1976), 238–66.

9

Insert Soul Here

LIVED THEOLOGY AS WITNESS

David Dark

*Perhaps this is the mysterious "it" of the common phrase
"it is snowing"—what we are always inside of.*
JOSHUA CLOVER, "The Bubble and the Globe"

The Conned Man

Here's the way it went. I was eating and reading alone at a table in a Nashville location of the Wendy's Old Fashioned Hamburgers franchise when I spotted, out of my periphery, a heavy man at a table nearby with a collection of shopping bags on the floor next to his chair. He ate quickly, but his face registered no agitation as he stared straight ahead. Upon finishing his meal, he made his way to the door. From there, the restaurant's large glass windows afforded me a view of the man's progress across the parking lot, and I was intrigued to note that his next destination was a Domino's Pizza at the nearest corner of a strip mall just a few yards away. Within minutes, he exited with a Domino's bag added to his collection and went directly into a TCBY ("The Country's Best Yogurt"). He followed the same pattern as he exited with a new bag and then finished off, as far as I could tell, with the Subway restaurant next door, disappearing around the corner with bags in both hands. I've seen him around town many times since, always bearing a diversely branded burden that may or may not contain brand products within.

Reflecting upon this episode, I began to concoct a thought experiment. What if the fellow suffered from an emotional disorder that rendered him incapable of incredulity and therefore peculiarly vulnerable to commercial claims, so vulnerable, in fact, that he believed—could not *not* believe—*all* commercials? Whereas most people appear capable of filtering out the myriad forms of sales pitch, guarantee, promise, and false covenant foisted upon public minds via billboards, posters, product placement, and all manner of electronic media, perhaps this unfortunate soul could not. And if this were the case, I reasoned, something as seemingly insignificant as exposure to a three-minute commercial break might suffice to send him on his way searching, enthralled along a perverse pilgrimage that would consume the length of his progressively less healthy life. In this way, he is successfully enlisted in an endless series of faith-based initiatives provoked by and based in the alluringly situated but necessarily insincere signals, the deliberate fictions, of a myriad-minded brand culture which, taken together, render him the subject of what amounts to a kind of cruel psychological experiment. His work, we understand, will be cut out *for* him, and advertising strategies ostensibly crafted to move a few units, to sell a little confidence here and there, will have unwittingly come together to reduce the beleaguered existence of an impressionable mind to a soul-sucking nightmare.

When I spotted this fellow and started writing these sort of things down, I had yet to hear tell of a *habitus*, I'd read zero Certeau, and nobody had taken me aside to propose the PhD state of mind—a strange world where I could do the kind of reading and writing I was already up to during my planning periods at a Presbyterian high school, find out how one is expected to pronounce Walter Benjamin's name, *and* receive a credential that might gain me a *new* teaching gig at a college or university. If you'd asked me for a word on lived theology, I'd have likely channeled my inner Will Campbell to say that I liked the sound of it, that it's the only kind that counts, and that I'd like to think I have a go at it myself on occasion. Somewhere back there, following a lecture I gave in Chicago that involved thinking through the War on Terror, the Barmen Declaration, and the music of Radiohead, a graduate student asked me what my methodology was. The word was new to me, and I didn't know what to say apart from describing how I take notes and collect quotes which I then bring to bear on whatever artist, issue, or event happens to interest me. I did it with letters and stamped envelopes in the days before Internet. A lot of it ends up in books and lectures now. He was satisfied, but if he'd pressed me further I suppose I'd have cited Charles Williams's "way of affirmation" (which Williams saw modeled in Dante), the work of saying what we see, what I'd learn to call, under the burden of a dissertation, the sacramental poetic work of paying attention.

In the case of the conned man I saw—or imagined I saw—at Wendy's Old Fashioned Hamburgers, I took note and it remained in my memory, because I often shared the scene with my students in the hope of cultivating and modeling critical thinking—work I find indistinguishable from the hope of prophetic consciousness within the workaday world, the theological task of discerning the spirits and unmasking idolatry (though I don't always find it fitting to put it that way). My model here, as it often is, is Marshall McLuhan, who posited precisely this particular apocalyptic sensibility in 1951: "Why not assist the public to observe consciously the drama which is intended to operate upon it unconsciously?"[1]

In the context of a PhD program, I found the tale of the conned man serves as an instructive caricature in taking up the problematic of religion, the ways the religious sphere has been conventionally ordained, and how religion, as a category, might be more meaningfully and critically deployed. The mental bind, the illusion, in which the conned man lives, moves, and has his being, need not involve theistic confessions or metaphysical claims to be understood as an ineluctably religious one ("religio" as *binding* influence), and the same goes for the high-budget, high-tech processes of religious formation—renewed, redeployed, and made new every morning—within which his emotional health is continually compromised. He has become what various brand agencies once beheld—and in fact bargained for—when they took a theoretical interest in him (or his type) as a potential target market. Such interest is admittedly limited to his purchasing capacity, but an advertising campaign, to be successful, must seek to address the whole self, the everyday emotional life of individuals, with the imaginative constructions of brand culture (no less binding, we understand, for being mere constructions). The narrative associations of a brand are designed to prey upon and cater to every discerned aspect of the individual's social imagination, conjuring desired behavior by creating, if only momentarily, a loss of identity that can be most reliably recovered by way of accessing a certain proffered product. The conned man has received and incorporated (or has perhaps been incorporated by) these calls to worship, these carefully calibrated mystifications, one after the other, and has come to believe that the answer to his meaning-problem—we all have them—resides within these stories in which he's been successfully enlisted. He will know no lasting satisfaction on his quest, because too much is never enough and, as my caricature has it, he won't stop believing. He is an ensnared civilian immersed in a religious crisis.

How does considering the plight of the conned man through the lens
of religion serve the task of lived theology? By doing so, I believe we're
afforded a tool for looking harder at the kind of immersive campaigns
that go some distance in overcoming his powers of discernment, a space
for raising the question of agency—always a religious question—for this
mobile buyer moving through a fantasized space, *and* a pivot-point for
envisioning the possibility of creative countermeasures. In this way, religion is a term that characterizes the net we are held within, whether will-
ingly or unconsciously, a net that is alternately woven and unwoven. If, as
is the case with the conned man, we see religion as a kind of nightmare
from which we mean to awaken, the awakening itself is also religious.

As a thick accounting of practice, religion names the binding *and* the
loosing of hearts and minds, the entrenched means to status-quo fulfillment as well as the open spaces that lie outside them. All are illumined
and brought into dramatic relief by the problematic of religion. No cultural
form lies outside its scope.

In the interest of widening our sense of the subject matter of lived theology
and observing more consciously those commercially generated dramas which
would otherwise operate upon us unconsciously, the caricature of conned
men and women might be helpfully moved beyond fast-food franchises to
include other forms of brand culture. Consider the ostensibly mature adult
whose waking moments expend primary energy not toward seeking God's
kingdom and righteousness, or discerning and meeting the needs of a close
relative or neighbor, but to feeling rage toward famous strangers: competing
media pundits, celebrity politicians, sports figures, or participants on a tele-
vised dance competition. Imagine the armchair activist e-mailers, anywhere
along the ideological spectrum, who primarily speak in conversation-stoppers,
who can't change their minds and won't change the subject. Consider also the
consumer of luxury goods, the talk-radio enthusiast, the political-party appa-
ratchik, the soul whose emotional life is increasingly enthralled by and conducted through online social networks, or the magnetic pull of an Apple store.

While largely uncoerced and free to weave their way amid distractions,
commodities, and various service options, these figures are obedient to
certain given scripts and symbols of human flourishing characteristic of
brand culture, even as they convert their attention from one distraction to
another many times during a given day. While their consciences evade,
to some extent, the endless moral injury of the conned man, any attempt
to represent these phenomena in a non-compartmentalized fashion will
return us to the question of religion; or, to risk redundancy, the issue of

performed religiosity remains in play, religion *as practice* as opposed to conscious profession. If we think of a brand campaign as a form of proselytization, the strategies and tactics at work within reigning technopolies challenge the popular separation of the merely secular from the ostensibly sacred. Whether geared toward securing votes, moving units, developing a following, selling tickets, or organizing military recruitment, the colonization of the targeted imagination, from whatever sphere, will ignore our habitual distinctions. Frames of mind and forms of consent are being religiously cultivated and maintained whenever successful conscription is performed. This is the exchange of *confidence* connoted in the work of *con* artistry (the con game of the con artist is a matter of selling confidence). If religion is a thick descriptor of the instruction we've received, for better and worse, it is both the terrain of the con *and* the naming of said terrain. Religion is the name of the con game. If to *be* conned is human, confessing to *having been* conned is an act of religious awareness.

Religion is Non-optional, or, You've Got to Be In It to Win It

Against accounts of religion which imply that it operates in a space outside of everyday practices, concerns, and motivations, the lived theology I'd like to think I'm up to keeps the question of religion open, allowing it to designate any number of social bonds, *avowedly* religious or otherwise. Rather than framing religion as a set of propositions to which the critical subject can lend or withhold assent, I define religion as a neutral social fact which includes, rather than eschews, the rational sense we make (or try to make) in our representations of our worlds. I take *religious belief* to be instrumental, formative, and, with the anthropologist Talal Asad, "a constituting activity in the world."[2] Understanding, with Marx, that religion effectively names those forms of consolation (other-worldly and/or market-driven) that anesthetize the popular imagination into submission, the "illusory happiness" of the conned man and his ilk, there is nevertheless more to the picture. Marx also gives us the more comprehensive account in which religion names, as well, the stock inventory of word and image on offer for narrating historical processes, an assemblage of ways of putting matters, explaining the how's and why's of life and how it might yet (or should) be lived:

> Religion is the general theory of this world, its encyclopedic compendium, its logic in popular form ... The wretchedness of religion

is at once an expression of and protest against real wretchedness. Religion is the sigh of the oppressed creature, the heart of a heartless world, and the soul of soulless conditions.[3]

As an expression of material wretchedness that is also a protest against it, Marx views religion as a form of creative labor. This language recasts religion as not merely the opiate of the masses but, more broadly, the poetics of the people. Like ritual, symbol, or ceremony, religion isn't something one can be for or against or decide to somehow suddenly engage. Religious traditions are always already underway; we can never step in the same one twice. Their engagement precedes us, having already formed our imaginaries. It is in this sense that Marx insists "the critique of religion is the prerequisite of every critique."[4] It is that with which we have to do (or the way we do everything we do or think we do). It binds us, for better and worse, until we begin to critique it religiously and relentlessly, in view of the possibility of better boundedness, different and more redeeming orientations, or, to put it a little strangely, less bad religions. Religiosity, in this sense, is a sort of non-optional sociality, an open-ended form which funds the more settled forms we usually have in mind when we speak of religions. And one's religiosity is never not in play in one way or another. It names the patterns, shifting or consistent, avowed or unavowed, of all our interactions. If we let religion, as a descriptive term, be applied more broadly to all narratives and networks that seek to bind hearts and minds, avowedly religious or otherwise, it might even be broad and comprehensive enough to deliver analysis from the myth of critical detachment. To be deployed critically, meaningfully, and helpfully, religion will have to refer to more than the scams we imagine uncritical or unenlightened others consistently fall for. If, within our usage of the category, religion only names the ideological delusions of *other* people, we have yet to deeply realize the pervasiveness of freeing and binding artifice (read religion). As the Palmolive commercial once put it, we're soaking in it. Or as Beck advises us, "Don't believe everything that you breathe." Or as James Joyce's Leopold Bloom posits concerning the inevitable communism of all our imaginings, disavowing a too-knowing knowingness concerning ones own hodge-podge thought processes: "Never know whose thoughts you're chewing."[5] This is the religious situation for alleged informant and alleged researcher alike.

In an articulation of this religious situation that seems to draw Joyce and his student Marshall McLuhan to the table in one fell swoop, Lewis

Hyde offers the following description of the meaning-making scene: "Story and song: these are two of the hypnotics by which social orders maintain their self-enchantment, the radio playing all day in laundries and gas stations, a background hum of catchy ballads to keep an agreed-upon reality in place and seemingly alive."[6] Story and song, we might say, for better and worse. Saturated within and by these twin hypnotics, lived theology, like every form of sacramental poetic, will aim to stir the pot of whatever "agreed-upon reality" lately and momentarily holds sway, but the pot and its contents, the given and received liturgies of a given locale, are never exactly removable. The given social commitments as currently organized are, in this sense, crucial to the liturgical work to be done. Religious commitments, ours and others, conscious and unconscious, are what there is to work with, the game you have to be knowingly *in* to win.

"Every telling has a taling"

As one more reminder that it's embodiment we're talking about, the incarnational posture Mary demands when she tells us our analysis is all too often inadequately fleshed out, I'd like to turn to the poetic task one of Shakespeare's characters describes in *A Midsummer Night's Dream*. Listen here for the witnessing work, the space-making enterprise I imagine will have to be characteristic of a lived theology worthy of the name:

> The poet's eye, in fine frenzy rolling,
> Doth glance from heaven to earth, from earth to heaven;
> And as imagination bodies forth
> The forms of things unknown, the poet's pen
> Turns them to shapes and gives to airy nothing
> A local habitation and a name. (5.1.13-18)

Within Shakespeare's account, that which was inarticulate, not yet storied or lyricized and therefore subjected to futility as unheard and unaccounted for, is now named anew, given flesh, and made at home by the redeeming activity we honor with the name of poetry, the news that stays news, the creative labor of revivifying expression, that which *bodies forth* new social forms, what we might call poetic thinking— the creative work that expands the space of the talkaboutable, a work that I take to be almost synonymous with the raising of prophetic consciousness.

I'm helped here by the experience of reading James Joyce and
W. E. B. Du Bois in classroom collaboration with Hortense Spillers, who
got me thinking of this as the kind of consciousness characteristic of, but
not contained by, what she terms the idea of black culture.[7] Both Joyce and
Du Bois take up the poetic vocation of giving to airy nothing a local habitation and a name, and the critical consciousness they conjure is an activity
to which everyone is invited.

Robert Stepto characterizes Du Bois's narrative method in *The Souls of
Black Folk* as the "transformation of data into metaphor,"[8] an attempt to
join his own scholarship with songs, making sound work against crushing
realities, attempting exorcism, conjuring a space for recognition, analysis,
and a provocative account of what's going on, a space for the bearing of
poetic witness.

As Joyce understood, any voice that hopes to assert itself in the direction of swaying the will of another can only do so only as one inescapably
storied interest among others ("Every telling has a taling and that's the he
and the she of it").[9] In this sense, lived theology has nowhere else to happen but narrative, lyric, or, in Hyde's phrase, the always up-for-grabs, take
and give of story and song; nowhere else to pursue the possibility of the
giving and receiving of witness.

I have in mind here the fluency of "saying," which Levinas distinguishes from the definitively said. "Saying bears witness to the other of
the Infinite which rends me, which in the saying awakens me," instructs
Levinas. "Saying as testimony precedes all the said."[10] It is with this sensibility in mind that I believe tale-tellers like Joyce self-consciously strive
to render human life as lyrically as possible lest it lose, or never discover
to begin with, its saying power. As is often the case in *The Souls of Black
Folk, Ulysses* is an attempt at the lyrical wit of a folk song, because it's
primarily the sung and recited that can hope for a living, imaginative, full-
bodied reception, not argument or analysis as such. It's the songs that
say and live and ring truly. Or as George Russell puts it in the "Scylla
and Charybdis" scene: "People do not know how dangerous lovesongs can
be . . . The movements which work revolutions in the world are born out of
the dreams and visions in a peasant's heart on the hillside. For them, the
earth is not an exploitable ground but the living mother."[11]

Joyce's prioritizing of the lyrical as what the witnessing work at hand
demands brings to mind Walter Benjamin's account concerning the possibility of truth in the task of creative representation: "Truth is not a process
of exposure which destroys the secret, but a revelation which does justice

to it."[12] In Joyce's vision, doing justice to the revelation—the apocalypse—
that is everyday life is both the priestly-poetic vocation Stephen Dedalus
proclaims for himself and the mental hobby Leopold Bloom undertakes
without letting his right hand know what his left hand is doing.

The necessary poeticizing, that creative symbol-making task involved
in such showing business, is an imaginative work that Joyce would have
his readers never stop doing. Joyce's desire to summon his readership
toward the political-poetic possibilities of imaginative magnanimity is a
concern he shares with Du Bois as well as Ralph Ellison, who understood
literary fiction to be nothing less than "the brightest instrument for recording sociological fact, physical action, the nuance of speech, yet achieved."[13]
How might those of us who aspire toward the work of lived theology live
up to the standard of such witness-bearing brightness?

Apocalyptic for the People

In his magisterial volume *Black Reconstruction in America: 1860–1880*,
W .E. B. Du Bois begins with a sober recognition of the stakes confronting
his complex rhetorical task: "In fine, I am going to tell this story as though
Negroes were ordinary human beings, realizing that this attitude will from
the first seriously curtail my audience."[14] Despite his dutiful and painstak-
ing use of primary sources, he knows that those most invested in popular
misconceptions of his subject will distort his narrative witness, the better to reside comfortably within the preferred abstractions of a no-fault,
white supremacist, American history. And even those who emerge from
the reigning willed myopia to pay him heed will have to pay unaccustomed
attention to the tale he tells.

In his account, Du Bois means to bring the difficult past to the rescue
of his ongoingly problematic present, and this work can't begin without
undoing the strategic deceptions of "the fairy tale of a beautiful Southern
slave civilization."[15] How to proceed? Every so often within the text, Du
Bois indulges a poetic form, breaking out of his careful, formalized his-
toriography to draw upon the available mythologies that undergird the
reigning supremacist fantasy to seize upon and deploy them differently.
And to my mind, he does so most beautifully with a bit of apocalyptic
supposition concerning the formal conclusion of the Civil War, the day
"freedom came to America."[16] For all their self-satisfied and often death-
dealing talk of manifest destiny, do Americans actually believe in God? Du
Bois submits a picture for our approval:

Suppose on some gray day, as you plod down Wall Street, you should see God sitting on the Treasury steps, in His Glory, with the thunders curved about him? Suppose on Michigan Avenue, between the lakes and hills of stone, and in the midst of hastening automobiles and jostling crowds, suddenly you see living and walking toward you, the Christ, with sorrow and sunshine in his face?

Foolish talk, all of this you say, of course; and that is because no American now believes in his religion. Its facts are mere symbolism; its revelation vague generalities; its ethics a matter of carefully balanced gain. But to most of the four million black folk emancipated by civil war, God was real. They knew him. They had met him personally ... in the black stillness of the night. His plan for them was clear; they were to suffer and be degraded, and then afterwards by divine edict, raised to manhood and power; and so on January 1, 1863, He made them free.

There is so much here. By out-theologizing the God-talkers, Du Bois calls the fact of their long touted and loudly celebrated faith into question, making clear that the avowedly religious among his audience—presuming they mean to be at all serious in their assertions—will have to adjust their imaginations and play to a different calculus. And his lyrical hermeneutic isn't done. The biblical witness will be made to resonate further and more deeply and more comprehensively than any conveniently de-politicized or spiritualized reading of Scripture will allow:

It was all foolish, bizarre, and tawdry. Gangs of dirty Negroes howling and dancing; poverty-stricken ignorant laborers mistaking war, destruction, and revolution for the mystery of the free human soul; and yet to these Black folk it was the Apocalypse. The magnificent trumpet tones of Hebrew Scripture, transmuted and oddly changed, became a brand new Gospel. All that was Beauty, all that was Love, all that was Truth, stood on top of those mad mornings and sang with the stars. A great human sob shrieked in the wind, and tossed its tears upon the sea—free, free, free.

And in the event that we have yet to receive his drift, Du Bois will have us understand that the coherence of the Christian tradition and the redemptive meaning of America itself are at stake in our reception—or refusal—of the great human sob turned song he discerns:

> A great song arose . . . It was a new song . . . They sneered at it—those white Southerners who heard it and never understood. They raped and defiled it—those white Northerners who listened without ears. Yet it lived and grew; always it grew and swelled and lived, and it sits today at the right hand of God, as America's one real gift to beauty; as slavery's one redemption, distilled from the dross of its dung.[17]

Like Joyce a misbeliever at best, Du Bois nevertheless throws down a metaphysical gauntlet. What meaning is there in the ascension of Jesus of Nazareth to the right hand of the Almighty (*Dextera Domini*, Mark 16:19, Acts 2:34) if *this* song-prayer (Psalm 63:8), ever ancient and ever new, isn't squarely situated within this eternal elevation asserted by the Christian tradition as represented in North America? Is the Christian hope to be understood as a meaningfully human commitment, a *lived* theology, or not? If it is, then Du Bois offers his provocative account on conventionally religious grounds in the hope that it will be received as *actionable* intelligence, a revelation that might serve to overcome the willful amnesia of white supremacist history. In this sense, what I view as the lively apocalyptic of Du Bois's poetic witness, George Shulman calls prophecy: "Prophecy raises the issue of *authority* with unrivaled profundity and intensity. Prophetic voices ask not whether we are ruled by authority, but which authority rules in and through us." Probing the contradiction between our alleged or advertised commitments, our self-image as it were, and the publicly visible facts on the ground, "Prophecy asks, What gods do you already serve? What is your animating faith? . . . Here is my table of values, what is yours?"[18] As I understand it, these are the questions lived theology calls us to self-administer, put to the communities of our sojourn, and lift up repeatedly with candor and wit.

The Way We Look To A Song

It with this open-handed ethic in mind that Du Bois elsewhere speaks of the work of the Fisk Jubilee Singers, whose performances around the world both funded the establishment of Fisk University, and exemplified the ongoing lyrical and prophetic heft of what Du Bois refers to as the

Sorrow Songs. Positioning *The Souls of Black Folk* as an attempt to give voice in sync with these songs, Du Bois describes the hope that breathes within them, a hope upon which the songs and Du Bois's own work, in no small way, bank: "The meaning is always clear: that sometime, somewhere, men will judge men by their souls and not by their skins. Is such a hope justified? Do the sorrow songs ring true?" Eschatologically speaking, these are fearsomely open questions which Du Bois feels compelled to leave unanswered, except by way of throwing them back upon the reader accompanied, we understand, by the expenditure of his own hopes, by his own intellectual efforts, and by the challenge to no longer "stand meekly dumb before such questions." Du Bois demands that the fact of the songs (the witness that is their stand, their very content) demands a reckoning, an according of freedom of opportunity to those "who brought the Sorrow Songs," this genre of *actionable intelligence*, "to the seats of the Mighty."

Having already drawn Shakespeare, Balzac, and Aristotle into his great cloud of witnesses, he broadens his testimony concerning the pluralistic facts-on-the-ground to include the indigenous peoples of the Americas: "Your Country? How came it yours? Before the Pilgrims landed we were here." But lest this particular gauntlet be misunderstood, he again recasts his account to insist that the songs are themselves a manifestation of "our gift of the Spirit." And here we rightly recall the image of African American culture (a category now powerfully broadened) as what seems to Du Bois to be, at least for now, "the sole oasis of simple faith and reverence in a dusty desert of dollars and smartness" which he now situates both as "our gift," awaiting reception, *and* "the hope [not unrelated to the hoped-for reception] that sang in the song of my fathers."[19]

Having launched his open-ended query concerning the fate of the songs (will they sing true?), the specific hope that the songs—among which now resides *his* song—might be received as an ethical summons, that the call would be met with response, is pronounced as a prayer-appeal in Du Bois's conclusion, "The After-Thought":

Hear my cry, O God the Reader; vouchsafe that this book fall not still-born into the world-wilderness ... Let the ears of a guilty people tingle with truth, and seventy millions sigh for the righteousness which exalteth nations, in this drear day when human brotherhood is a mockery

and a snare. Thus in Thy good time may infinite reason turn the tangle
straight, and these crooked marks on a fragile leaf be not indeed

THE END[20]

Into our hands he commits the gift of Spirit. The sign of our reception
will be solely verified (or not) in a posture/practice of universal enfran-
chisement ("the righteousness which exalteth nations") which seeks to
overturn the material conditions which "in this drear day [our day]" give
the lie to "human brotherhood."

As we try to write lived theology, what might it mean to register this
cry, respond to it, and carry on the gift of Spirit we receive in the songs
that ring true? How can writing ring true in the way that songs do? I imagine the truest writing is written along the kind of trajectory or continuum
along which Du Bois means to lift his voice. I imagine it's born out of the
deep reception, alive and signaling, of a call. "The call," Certeau reminds
us, "cannot be known outside of the response which it receives. It has no
expression of its own."[21] Here the fragility of the call, the voice, that which
might yet ring true (or, in Du Bois's parlance, "*sing* true") is especially
evident. Certeau hones down motivations, desires, and beliefs so closely
that the metaphorical, for instance, is *never* a separate issue. To speak of
story or song as an addendum won't do. And to speak of *religious* discourse
would be a redundancy. Discourse, in the thickest sense, is what there
is: "The story does not express a practice. It does not limit itself to telling
about a movement. It *makes* it. One understands it, then, if one enters into
this movement oneself."[22]

Meanwhile On the Lower Frequencies

According to Certeau, it is the knowingly mythological labor of stories that
can transform a place into a space, and this seems to be the relentlessly
narratival process whereby the narrator of Ellison's *Invisible Man* trans-
forms, for the reader, the settled givens of a place into the foreignness of
a space rendered revolutionary, rich, and strange.[23] Rendered invisible by
the alleged givens of a white world and having ranted in a Dostoevsky-
like fashion throughout the novel, he begins a peremptory address that's
been at work all along: "Thus, having tried to give pattern to the chaos
which lives within the pattern of your certainties, I must come out. I must
emerge."[24]

Radical, open-handed telling it as he sees it, we understand, has been his only method and his only hope. "What else could I do? What else but try to tell you what was really happening when your eyes were looking through?" asks the Invisible Man. And here he strikes a note of casual inevitability concerning the only tactic available—tell it *true*—to one whose existence within the reigning economies of meaning is one of practical invisibility "without substance, a disembodied voice, as it were."[25] To tell (or try to tell) what's really happening, to hazard a little cosmic plainspeak, to cobble together your own witness box out of thin air, is one way of giving voice, of making believe, of being social.

"I'll verse you but I won't curse you," observes one self-proclaimed bearer of "shit, grit, and mother-wit,"[26] who crosses the Invisible Man's path, a figure who refers to himself as Blue in one breath and Peter Wheatstraw in the next. By the end of Ellison's novel, we see how this mode of artful communication, this proffering of a verse, this method of *taking care*, has been inherited by the Invisible Man himself. A lively, wide-awake orality, a gift of Spirit, has successfully insinuated itself. The redeeming dialectic of prophetic consciousness has been passed down and received. And from here on out, plurality isn't an issue, but a fact, a fact to be met with receptivity and wit: "Life is to be lived, not controlled; and humanity is won by continuing to play in face of certain defeat. Our fate is to become one, and yet many—This is not prophecy, but description."[27]

Lest we think of his witness as *mere* words or *mere* verse, we're reminded that his account bears the critical heft of observational candor, and if we won't see and get in on the drift of his problematic, we're pulling the wool over our *own* eyes. But it could be that the reader begins to credit his narrative with explanatory power. Maybe we *do* see. Perhaps the call is being successfully transmitted: "Who knows but that, on the lower frequencies, I speak for you?"[28]

With this question (by my reckoning, the best last sentence of any novel I know), a table is set and a site is made ready and available for all takers. Perhaps the form of life I've conjured here, he seems to say, shall *in*-form yours. Maybe it's been happening all along. Might there be a giving, a receiving, a back-and-forth of witness underway? A space is cleared which, to my mind, evokes Du Bois's "After-Thought." In case we've missed it, Ellison's story has all along been nothing less than a presentation of *his* consciousness to ours. And more, perhaps we aren't merely being addressed, spoken *to*—

maybe we even feel we've been spoken *for*. Perhaps we hear our own voice lifted somehow within his. Can he get a witness?

Like Du Bois, Ellison's unexpected opening reminds us that the poetic call banks its existence on response. Only in response can its evocation be kept alive as a living power, and the line of recognition drawn here continue. Everything depends upon the viability of a space of address. Judith Butler carries the matter further by insisting, "No one survives without being addressed."[29]

I suspect we've all heard the popular adage to those who try their hands at making time to write their minds the way they want them to read: write about what you *know*. Perhaps writing in the vein of lived theology could take this advice in a confessional direction with a slightly different admonition: write about that which overwhelms—or overcomes—your sense of critical detachment. Write about what has addressed you, called upon you, and called you out of yourself. I think of Dorothy Day's hope that she would be remembered as one who read Dostoevsky well; and I think of Bob Dylan, who remarked that hearing Johnny Cash sing "A Boy Named Sue" was like hearing an ancient voice ask, "What are you doing there, boy?" Everything depends upon our receiving of the witness of another as a form of life with which we mean to reckon. Isn't all writing, at its best, a form of reckoning? A feat of attentiveness? A response to a call?

This kind of writing differs, admittedly, from the demand for distancing and objectivity associated with most scholarly writing, but perhaps we engage our subject most effectively when we're engaged *by* it, and freely testify concerning our enthusiasm *for* it. When stories and songs speak our language, speak *for* us, when we hear our own voices in someone else's, it won't do to fold our arms tight, or front, when it comes to the fact of someone's witness getting through to us. I don't know what I'd have to offer my students and readers if I felt compelled to argue that the Bible or Ellison or Radiohead only engaged me on the level of detached intellectual interest. I don't just like Radiohead, I like to profess to students aloud, I *believe* them. I want to get in on their act. I want to be up to what they're up to, because I number them among my religious commitments. What are yours?

To take up Certeau's instruction, the witness of a lived theology won't merely express or represent a practice, nor will it limit itself to telling *about* a movement. It *makes* the move. Lived theology takes up the gifts of Spirit on offer and carries them forward. One understands a gift of Spirit when one enters into the movement oneself. Insert soul here.

Notes

1. Marshall McLuhan, *The Mechanical Bride: Folklore of Industrial Man* (London: Routledge & K. Paul, 1967), 2.

2. Talal Asad, "The Construction of Religion as an Anthropological Category," in *Genealogies of Religion: Discipline and Reasons of Power in Christianity and Islam* (Baltimore: Johns Hopkins University Press, 1993), 47.

3. Karl Marx, *Critique of Hegel's "Philosophy of Right,"* trans. Annette Jolin and Joseph O'Malley (Cambridge, UK: Cambridge University Press, 1977), 137.

4. Marx, *Critique of Hegel's "Philosophy of Right,"* 131.

5. James Joyce, *Ulysses* (Oxford: Oxford University Press, 2008), 162.

6. Lewis Hyde, *Trickster Makes This World: Mischief, Myth, and Art* (New York: Farrar, Straus and Giroux, 1998), 218

7. Hortense Spillers, "The Idea of Black Culture," *CR: The New Centennial Review* 6, no. 3 (2007): 17–28.

8. Robert B. Stepto, "The Quest of the Weary Traveler: W. E. B. Du Bois's *The Souls of Black Folk,"* in *From Behind the Veil: a Study of Afro-American Narrative* (Champaign: University of Illinois Press, 1991), 53.

9. Joyce, *Finnegan's Wake* (London: Penguin Classics, 1999), 213.

10. Emmanuel Levinas, "God and Philosophy," in *Collected Philosophical Papers*, trans. Alphonso Lingis (Dordrecht: Martinus Nijhoff Publishers 1987), 170.

11. James Joyce, *Ulysses*, 186–187.

12. Walter Benjamin, *The Origin of German Tragic Drama*, trans. John Osborne (New York: Verso, 1977) 31.

13. Ellison, "Twentieth-Century Fiction and the Black Mask of Humanity," in *Shadow and Act* (New York: Vintage, 1964), 26.

14. W. E. B. Du Bois, "To the Reader," in *Black Reconstruction in America: 1860–1880* ([1934] New York: Free Press, 1998).

15. Du Bois, *Black Reconstruction in America*, 715.

16. Du Bois, *Black Reconstruction in America*, 121.

17. Du Bois, *Black Reconstruction in America*, 123–25.

18. George Shulman, *American Prophecy: Race and Redemption in American Political Culture* (Minneapolis: University of Minnesota Press, 2008), 29.

19. Shulman, *American Prophecy*, 162–63.

20. Du Bois, "The After-Thought," in *The Souls of Black Folk* (New York: Dover, 1994), 165.

21. Michel de Certeau, "The Weakness of Believing," trans. Saskia Brown, *The Certeau Reader*, ed. Graham Ward (Oxford: Blackwell Publishers, 2000), 227.

22. Certeau, "Story Time," in *The Practice of Everyday Life*, trans. Steven Rendall (Berkeley: University of California Press, 1984), 81.

23. Certeau, "Spatial Stories," in *The Practice of Everyday Life*, 116–18.

24. Ellison, *Invisible Man* (Vintage International: New York, 1995), 438.

25. Ellison, *Invisible Man*, 581

26. Ellison, *Invisible Man*, 176.

27. Ellison, *Invisible Man*, 577.

28. Ellison, *Invisible Man*, 581.

29. Judith Butler, "Against Ethical Violence," in *Giving an Account of Oneself* (New York: Fordham University Press, 2005), 63.

PART THREE

Lived Theology as Pedagogy

Lived Theology 101

EXPLORING THE CLAIM "WHAT WE BELIEVE
MATTERS" WITH UNDERGRADUATES

Lori Brandt Hale

*Later on I discovered, and am still discovering to this day,
that one only learns to have faith by living in the full this-
worldliness of life . . . this is what I call this-worldliness: living fully in the midst of life's tasks, questions, successes and
failures, experiences, and perplexities—then one takes seriously no longer one's own sufferings but rather the suffering
of God in the world. Then one stays awake with Christ in
Gethsemane. And I think this is faith: this is metanoia.
And this is how one becomes a human being, a Christian.*

DIETRICH BONHOEFFER, in a letter to Eberhard Bethge

*Both the civil rights and the anti-civil rights movements
were saturated with religion; in every mass meeting, church
service, and Klan rally, God's name was invoked and his
power claimed. White conservatives and civil rights activists, black militants and white liberals, black moderates
and klansmen, all staked their particular claims for racial
justice and social order on the premise that God was on
their side.*

CHARLES MARSH, *God's Long Summer: Stories of Faith
and Civil Rights*

DIETRICH BONHOEFFER, GERMAN theologian and Nazi resister, has
shaped my theology and my theological imagination. The passage in
Bonhoeffer that has always resonated most deeply for me is the one

quoted above, from his famous letter to his friend and theological confidante, Eberhard Bethge.[1] It was written from Tegel prison in Berlin on July 20, 1944, one day after Bonhoeffer's co-conspirators attempted and failed to assassinate Hitler. It is, in ways that I have only recently begun to appreciate, a profound example of *lived theology*.

I have taught semester-length seminars on Bonhoeffer a number of times. In the first few iterations, we marched through the texts and biography chronologically, driving—in my mind, at least—toward this passage, written late in his life, as an apex of sorts. But in the most recent offering of the seminar, I began with this letter. I detailed the place I think it holds in Bonhoeffer's work as well as its importance in my own thinking, and in my own theology. From that starting point, we proceeded to plumb the depths of Bonhoeffer's work and life, unpacking details along the way to best understand the richness and substance of the ideas in the letter. The students and I were engaged in a wholly new way. In an important way, the task at hand changed: from understanding meaning to making meaning; from reading historical texts as such to considering the abiding power of texts to speak in new, changing, and personal contexts and ways. The students, of course, were not expected to reach the same conclusions I did about this particular passage or Bonhoeffer in general, but were free— were set free, I hope—to find their own footing in this story or, eventually, in a different story or different topic of their own choosing. Lived theology had become both the content and the method for our collective work.

This chapter is not pointing to these Bonhoeffer courses. I will detail another course in the pages that follow. Nonetheless, I open with my comments about Bonhoeffer, and teaching Bonhoeffer, because my own lived experience as a member of the faculty at Augsburg College is part of the story. And it is important, I think, to frame my work at Augsburg in the larger context of my work on and passion for the lived theology of Dietrich Bonhoeffer. I came to Augsburg with a sense, perhaps still inchoate, but with a particular sense nonetheless that was informed by that Tegel letter, about the relationship between faith and the world in all its messiness and complications. Exploring the claim "what we believe matters" with undergraduates is nothing if not complicated and messy.

FANNIE LOU HAMER, Sam Bowers, William Douglas Hudgins, Ed King, and Cleveland Sellers: these are the figures of the 1960s American civil rights and anti-civil rights movements described by Charles Marsh in his provocative book *God's Long Summer: Stories of Faith and Civil Rights*.[2]

All five of these individuals self-identify as Christian. All five speak of a sense of calling, a vocation, to their work. And all five bring to life in tangible, even visceral, ways the idea that what we believe matters. Hamer and Bowers, Hudgins, King, and Sellers embody the idea that our commitments, religious and otherwise, truth claims, sensibilities, and values matter because, in fact, those things shape our actions in and for (or against) the world; they inform our relationships with others, even to the point of determining how we see or do not see, embrace or marginalize, others in the first place. These commitments, claims, and values matter because they direct and create the contours of our lived experience. Of course, at the very same time, our lived experience is shaping, creating, and informing those beliefs, sensibilities, and claims to truth.

Every student at Augsburg College, where I teach, is required to take a sequence of two core courses, housed in the Religion Department, titled "Christian Vocation and the Search for Meaning (I and II)." The courses introduce students to the faith claims and lived experiences of Christians, Jews, Muslims, Hindus, and Buddhists. In addition, the courses consider biblical and theological resources of the Christian tradition, in particular and using vocation as a hermeneutic, to approach questions germane to the search for meaning. The second offering in the sequence has long carried the unofficial subtitle "What We Believe Matters." And from the inception of the course in 2003, as part of a new general education curriculum, *God's Long Summer* has been one of its key texts. Lived theology, both as embedded in those five stories and in a myriad of other readings and exercises, has served both methodological and pedagogical purposes in meeting Augsburg's commitment to the theological exploration of vocation, which includes helping students understand and embrace their (theological) identity and its import in the college community, the neighborhood (particularly the diverse Cedar-Riverside neighborhood of Minneapolis where Augsburg is located), and the world. Put more directly, lived theology *is* the methodology-*cum*-pedagogy that makes it possible for students to engage ideas of vocation, and the concomitant notion that "what we believe matters," in a substantive and personal way.

As suggested above, *God's Long Summer*, with its specific concerns regarding religious identity and claims, personal character and vocation, racial justice, social order, and the common good, is a particularly good text to engage students in the proposition "what we believe matters."[3] But more than that, more than disclosing the truth of that claim, *God's Long Summer* also opens up the possibility of addressing the challenges implicit in that claim related to relativism and personal commitment, the cognitive and moral development of students, and institutional commitments that shape the whole conversation. This chapter ventures to address these matters by sharing a particular narrative—a lived theology, or *my* lived theology, as it were—of teaching "Christian Vocation and the Search for Meaning II" at Augsburg College.

The commitment to vocation at Augsburg is long-standing. The college motto, *education for service*, and college mission statement, which maintains that Augsburg educates students to be responsible leaders and thoughtful stewards, are replete with vocational overtones.[4] In 2001, the college received a Lilly Endowment grant to think explicitly about the connections between faith and learning; in particular, the grant funded the theological exploration of vocation. Augsburg was not a lone recipient of this grant; since 1999, Lilly has funded this kind of work at eighty-eight church-related liberal arts colleges and universities. Augsburg, however, is relatively unique in that cohort with regard to the substantial embedding of that exploration in our curriculum, rather than relegating the inquiry about vocation solely to co-curricular events and programs.

In the summer of 2002, a six-person team was charged with the task of redesigning the Augsburg general education curriculum to better reflect our institutional and mission-based commitments and to include, in some way, attention to this new and somewhat daunting task of investigating vocation. I was a member of that team; it was a difficult work, with many, many stakeholders. Nonetheless, we took up the charge and set out, as our own goal, to create a signature curriculum; that is, a curriculum so reflective of the identity and character of Augsburg College that, even if distributed without identifying markers, it would be recognizable as ours. The "Christian Vocation and Search for Meaning" courses were created as signature courses in this new curriculum. In addition, a Senior Keystone signature requirement was also developed. Offered in departments and, sometimes, disciplinary divisions, the Keystone course asks students to return to conversations and inquiries about vocation and purpose in light of their curricular and co-curricular experiences; that is, to look back and look ahead at once.

The Religion Department embraced the challenge of both articulating and teaching this sometimes elusive concept: vocation. With strong ties between the college and the Evangelical Lutheran Church in America, the department turned to Martin Luther's work on vocation as an obvious starting point for conversation. My colleague and director of the Lilly

Program, "Exploring our Gifts (2001–2009)," Dr. Mark Tranvik, claims the following: "vocation (which means to be called) in the Lutheran tradition places us in two important relationships, one involving God and the other involving the neighbor. We are called, forgiven and empowered by God in Christ in order to love our neighbor and serve all of creation."[5] Other voices, including Friedrich Buechner, Parker Palmer, Dorothy Day, and (even) Dietrich Bonhoeffer, found their way into the conversation; there was talk of vocation as that place where the deep gladness of one's heart meets the world's deep need; authentic selfhood; and responsible action. It became increasingly clear that vocation, most simply understood, was to be found in the intersection of God (as caller), the self (with talents and gifts), and the world (with needs). Our Lilly program even ventured a visual image—the "vocation triangle" with God, self, and world inhabiting the corners, respectively, to convey and capture the (dialectical) connections between the three. The triangle has proven to be both a useful starting point and an insufficient ending point for discussion about vocation; while it introduces important and basic elements of the concept, it does not and cannot fully capture the dynamic, contextual, and complex nature of vocation. (And, it certainly does not entertain the Kantian epistemological questions about God, self, and world.) But it is precisely on these points of dynamism, complexity, and contextuality that lived theology as methodology plays a role of critical import in our inquiry.

Lived theology, notes Marsh in his essay "What is Lived Theology?" maintains a direct correlation between proclamation and practice.[6] What we proclaim shapes what we do and how we act in the world. In other words, what we believe matters. To reiterate a point made earlier, the choice to use *God's Long Summer* as a key text in our course was an intentional choice to use lived theology as a methodology to explore vocation and engage the search for meaning. Lived theology allows us to uncover the complexity and dynamism of vocation because it recognizes—even insists—that the self, one's understanding of one's self, one's concept of God, the needs of the community, and the call of the world are *situated*. They are shaped by particularities of time and place; they are understood in a context.

For those well-acquainted with postmodern academic discourse, these ideas are neither sophisticated nor novel; but they are powerful and new to undergraduate students. The details of one's lived experience, the details of one's social, cultural, historical, political, and religious realities shape one's understanding of self, world, and God. The details of one's lived experience shape one's commitments, sensibilities, and proclamations which, in turn, determine one's actions and practices in the world; these, in turn, give shape to real and lived experience. Lived theology discloses the iterative and complicated reality that constitutes the search for meaning and vocation. But, moreover, and on the flip side, lived theology as a methodology makes room, as it were, for all students to have and to find their voice, because lived theology invites them to bring the particularities and details of their own lived experience to the table.

Since the early 2000s, the student body of Augsburg College has become increasingly diverse: in ethnicity; in socioeconomic, generational, immigration, and documented status; in LGBTQIA identification; and in religious identity. In 2003 our incoming day school/traditionally-aged class was 10 percent students of color; the fall term of 2013 marked the fifth consecutive year with an incoming class that was 40 percent students of color. Such diversity simultaneously enriches and complicates those conversations about vocation and meaning. It elicits encounters between students who have or come to very different conclusions about the content of the "what we believe" in "what we believe matters." And it requires students to reckon with those differences.

Augsburg is a church-related (ELCA) college and the religion department is just that, by design, a department of religion. It is not a department of religious studies and it is not a department of theology. In this endeavor of asking students to consider what they believe and why it matters, these distinctions are important.

Our religion classes, perhaps despite persistent misconceptions, are not catechetical. As a church-related college and as a religion department, we have some latitude to ask questions of belief and purpose and meaning that public institutions and religious studies departments, for the most part, do not. In fact, shaped by our own institutional commitments, informed by our exploration of vocation, and emboldened by our use of lived theology, we are willing to engage students with questions that transcend strictly academic pursuits.[7] But, we do not expect conformity in their conclusions. We are not looking for particular answers. Herein lies the key point of departure from a theology department, which is heavily invested in prescribing the content of each student's beliefs.

For us, the point of echoing this refrain, "what we believe matters," is precisely to allow students to fill in the substance of the "what" in many different ways, to reflect critically on their own beliefs and experiences as well as the claims of others, and to recognize that, in the end, what they claim (how they fill out the "what") matters. The details of the "what" do shape students' lives and decisions and actions. Proclamation and practice are intricately linked. But here is the point where things get extremely complicated and messy, especially for a religion department interested in more than studying the "what we believe" claims of other people, not interested in prescribing that "what," but deeply dedicated—out of its own deep roots in the Christian tradition and its openness to other views—to helping students make moral and religious commitments that subvert the easy pull and implicit dangers of relativism, especially nihilistic relativism.

Let me explain by way of example, using *God's Long Summer* to do so. Consider, briefly, the first four figures in the text: Hamer, Bowers, Hudgins, and King.

Fannie Lou Hamer, Sam Bowers, William Douglas Hudgins, and Edwin King

Raised in the cotton fields and subjugated by the harsh realities of the Jim Crow South, Mrs. Fannie Lou Hamer became a catalyzing figure in the civil rights movement. With a deep and abiding faith, a strong sense of call from Jesus, and a vision that Christian discipleship requires revolutionary action on behalf of the disenfranchised, Hamer was, in Marsh's words, "one of America's most innovative religious imaginations."[8]

Sam Bowers, a Baptist Sunday School teacher and honorably discharged Naval Machinist, reinvigorated the Christian identity of the Ku Klux Klan. As the Imperial Wizard of the White Knights of the KKK, he is said to be responsible for at least nine murders, seventy-five bombings of black churches, and more than three hundred assaults, bombings, and beatings. Like Fannie Lou Hamer, Bowers had a strong sense of call from Jesus; but unlike Mrs. Hamer, Bowers described his vocation as "a priestly task of preserving the purity of his blood and soil."[9]

Articulate, meticulous, and stylish, Douglas Hudgins was Mississippi's "preeminent Southern Baptist minister," according to Marsh. Hudgins served as the pastor for the sizable First Baptist Church in Jackson, where he preached messages of personal purity and salvation.[10] With implicit support for the status quo and white supremacy, Hudgins saw no connection between the gospel message and black suffering. "The cross of Christ . . . has nothing to do with social movements or realities beyond the church; it's a matter of individual salvation!" he preached.[11]

Ed King was raised to accept the attitudes and privileges of being a white Southerner in the 1950s. But after helping clean up an African American neighborhood hit by a tornado, he recognized that the damage done by the storm was of little consequence relative to the stark and endemic poverty of that community. Called to the ministry, he committed his life to fighting for equality and integration in communities, churches, and civic life. Knocking on the door of a whites-only church, he called, "we are just letting you know that every single aspect of your Southern Way of Life is under attack."[12]

WITH SURPRISING CONSISTENCY over the years, students conclude that Fannie Lou Hamer, Sam Bowers, Douglas Hudgins, and Ed King have equally valid vocations; that each articulates beliefs and commitments shaped by their respective lived experiences and Biblical interpretations and, therefore, each bears a mark of authenticity that renders their consequent actions legitimate because they are consistent with those beliefs. In other words, the claim "what we believe matters" holds true; proclamation and practice are, in fact, united in each example. In the cognitive and moral development of students, reaching this understanding is an important step. But many are unwilling or unprepared to go beyond this point.

Generally speaking, students are, or at least they have been, reticent to make any claim of their own, even something as simple as "Sam Bowers' violent nationalism and racism is not okay." What happens, in short, is that we bump up against the students' uncritical relativism.[13] Their attempts to be inclusive of many views devolve into a relativism (sometimes nihilism) that gives them no ground, whether cast in ethical or religious or some other terms, to claim as their own. This way of thinking cuts across all religious and ethnic identities. But from my own place, and my own religion department's place, of committed pluralism, this uncritical relativism is a significant problem. Responsible leaders, thoughtful stewards, informed citizens—the mission-driven hopes for who and what our students will be—are in desperate need of more sophisticated ways of engaging, honoring, and critiquing difference. Fortunately, in recent semesters, I see more students willing to take up this challenge. I am doing my best both to give and support such a challenge.

In my most recent offering of "Christian Vocation and the Search for Meaning II," I included a question on the midterm exam to assess my students' ability to engage their moral and theological imaginations relative to the figures in *God's Long Summer*. I included a section called "True or False with Explanation" and explained to the students that I could imagine them answering true or false. I told them to select one or the other and provide an explanation for their choice. The question was this one:

True or False?
   Fannie Lou Hamer, Sam Bowers, Douglas Hudgins, and Ed King each had a sense of calling and vocation; consequently, their positions must be respected.
   Explain.

Fifty-eight percent (thirty-one students) chose *true*. Their answers corroborate my concerns about unfettered and uncritical relativism, and a key locus of their embrace of all four figures seems to lie specifically in the uncritical appropriation of each reported calling from God. One student writes, *"All of these people had some kind of calling or vocation from God or within themselves, which is why they must be respected based on their positions. Out of the four people, Sam Bowers can be classified as the most disrespected, because of what he thought and did. Since he based his actions from his "calling from God," his actions must be somewhat respected."* Another student puts it this way, *"I think that statement is true because even though people didn't agree with what some of the 4 people stood for, it was still their sense of what God was calling them to do. For example, Fannie Lou Hamer and Sam Bowers were basically like complete opposites, but they both felt like God was calling them to do what they did."*

Another focus in these explanations is internal consistency; as mentioned earlier, the proclamation and practice for each figure—Hamer, Bowers, Hudgins, and King—is united. In the words of a student, *"To each of them they were doing what they truly believed was the right thing to do. Whether you agree with what they did, the place that they came from with their opinions must be respected."* And this student combines the two themes: *"Each figure has a right to their opinion and how they want to present their calling. Even if one may not agree with another, by being judgmental of one's belief, one may go against the belief of another. All callings must be respected under God."*

Perhaps most frustrating in this set of responses are from the ones who more or less articulate key pros or cons of the respective positions, but fall back into the idealized notion that to be open-minded is to blindly accept all ideas. Here are two examples: *"I think they all had a calling and vocation and I think they should all be respected, even if you don't like their decisions, at least they did something. Fannie Lou Hamer and Ed King did something for civil rights. Sam Bowers, who was a bad man for being part of the KKK, should still be respected for doing what he believes in. Even Douglas Hudgins should be respected. It doesn't seem like he did anything, but at least he didn't back down and go to one side or the other."* And, *"Although they all had a calling from God towards the Civil Rights Movement, they all varied. Fannie Lou believed her vocation was to stand up against laws constricting voting to Blacks. Bowers believed his vocation was to keep segregation alive. Hudgins believed that the church should not get involved with civil rights, while King used his church to get involved. These all varied, but is one person's vocation wrong? We have to respect them all."*

That said, 42 percent (twenty-two students) chose *false*. Their thoughtful answers indicate a more sophisticated and critical reading of the Marsh text as well as more a productive use of supporting class materials and other named criteria. As with the *true* responses, the specific rationales used by individual students vary, but can be examined around several themes. For example, and in contrast to answers given above, some of these *false* explanations raise critical questions about the authenticity of Bowers's and Hudgins's vocations or senses of calling. One student writes, *"While it is true that they each felt called to act in the way that they did, there is only so far someone can go. When your "calling" is oppressive to others (Sam Bowers and Douglas Hudgins) then it isn't really a calling at all. They may have felt compelled to do what they did, but God doesn't call people to oppress others."*

Another says, *"Despite the argument that Bowers and Hudgins, like Hamer and King, had a sense of vocation, I believe that the vocations of Bowers and Hudgins were unjustified and a "false calling," especially on the part of Bowers. The message of the Bible is love, compassion, and liberation through Jesus and his teachings. Bowers misinterpreted a few verses out of context and missed the inclusive nature of the Biblical text. In his vocation, he should not be respected. And Hudgins, because of his ignorance or dissocial [sic] Gospel reading, also has a skewed vocational message, which should be challenged. Doing nothing can sometimes be worse."* In both examples, raising questions about one's "calling" is only part of the answer. The first student also uses an ethical principle opposing oppression to measure and dismiss the worth of Bowers's and Hudgins's actions in the world. The second student calls on Biblical principles and interpretive integrity to take a stand. This level of complexity marks many of these answers.

Human rights, Biblical interpretation, external sources of authority, and internal sources of authority, respectively, serve as hallmarks in other student responses:

- *While they all believed they had a calling from God, I do not think that earns their positions respect. Sam Bowers's position led to the death and oppression of people, and Douglas Hudgins's position led to people ignoring the death and oppression. When a person's personal position harms others and infringes on rights, it is time to stop respecting differences and start fighting back.*

- *Fannie Lou Hamer, Sam Bowers, Douglas Hudgins, and Ed King each certainly had a sense of calling and vocation. However, I disagree with the notion that each of their positions must be respected. All of these people identified as Christian and believed the Bible is the inspired word of God. However, only Hamer and King acted in a vocation that was actually aligned with Biblical principles. Hudgins chose to ignore a great deal of the Bible's teachings in favor of his own comfort, which is morally ambiguous at best. And Bowers plucked a few verses out of the Bible and used them to create a theology almost entirely against the principles of Christianity. Regardless of his self-perceived calling, I cannot give his position respect. Such a skewed Biblical interpretation merits no respect.*

- *Although I do believe that Hamer, Bowers, Hudgins, and King all had a strong sense of calling and vocation I do not believe that all of their positions should be respected. Bowers, for example, did not show respect for people in the Civil Rights era; therefore, I don't think he should be respected for his discriminatory and often violent actions to others. Just because Bowers believed he was called by God to do this work does not mean it deserves respect. I would go back to what MLK said in his "Letter from Birmingham Jail" and say that Bowers was acting in an unjust way (just as laws can be unjust, I believe people can be unjust too) and I don't think that deserves respect. I think everyone has a sense of calling and vocation and what you do with that deems whether or not you deserve respect.*

- *I respect Fannie Lou Hamer and Ed King's calling for vocation, but I do not agree with the actions of Sam Bowers or Douglas Hudgins. My moral compass leads me to believe that Sam Bowers was an evil man although he used the Bible to justify his actions of "purifying the soil." I still don't think he was right. And Douglas Hudgins was someone that ignored the mistreatments of black people and did nothing to stop it. I lose respect for their vocations for those reasons.*

God's Long Summer: Stories of Faith and Civil Rights is a significant text for me, and for my students, because it raises real and complicated questions about vocation and responsibility, about living and acting in the world, and about faith and Biblical interpretation. Some students need to be jarred out of complacency or apathy, well-intentioned relativism or naiveté. Those students need the juxtaposition of Fannie Lou Hamer with Sam Bowers. They need to read about a poor, uneducated, African American woman who was willing—in the name of Jesus—to endure beatings and risk death, to bring change and justice to her community side-by-side with the account of a white Sunday School teacher, christened the Imperial Wizard of the White Knights, a special branch of the KKK in Mississippi, "called" to eliminate "heretics" like civil rights workers Mickey Schwerner, James Chaney, and Andrew Goodman. Students need to wrestle with the idea that both Hamer and Bowers, as Marsh tells us, stake their claims, and live their lives, on the premise that "God was on their side."[14]

For some students, the book itself, the competing claims and "endorsements" by God, is enough to push them past whatever overt or latent relativism they might harbor. Others, though, as my midterm exam responses suggest, need more; they need more conversation, examples, resources, and practice thinking critically and creatively. Together we read Peter Gomes's *The Good Book: Reading the Bible with Heart and Mind,* Diana Eck's *Encountering God: A Spiritual Journey from Bozeman to Banaras,* and Martin Luther King, Jr.'s "Letter from Birmingham Jail." We listen to the wisdom of Huston Smith and invite a Buddhist practitioner to speak with us in class.

Now more than ever, I maintain that students need to do more than understand that Bowers's or Hamer's or Hudgins's proclamation and practice are united. Drawing on their own religious traditions or familial moral framework or using other resources, students need to be able to make a claim or take a stand. But here is where it really gets messy. This call to commitment, to take seriously the content of their own "what" in "what we believe matters," is not a call to reject all other positions or discourage dialogue across difference. Students also need to recognize that some competing claims can peacefully coexist, can lend mutual insight, can enrich and transform communities, and can be both honored and respected; it is only certain claims that need to be challenged, denied, or protested. Discerning the difference is the real work.

Diana Eck's work, including "The Pluralism Project," at Harvard, is useful in beginning to sort out the broad range of ways people understand their beliefs, particularly in relationship to other beliefs. Her book *Encountering God: A Spiritual Journey from Bozeman to Banaras*, a lived theology in its own right, describes a spectrum of these ways that ranges from hard exclusivism and nihilistic relativism together on one side to committed (and uncommitted) pluralism on the other. Her text allows students to consider the very question suggested above: namely, how is it possible to be open to a diversity of views and beliefs without abandoning one's own claims to truth? But even that question begs more. Even if students realize it is possible, the work is not done. How do you know? How does one adjudicate the difference between positions that are simply different than one's own and ones that are unethical? What are the criteria?

My students who answered *false* to the question about whether Hamer, Bowers, Hudgins, and King should be respected because they felt called by God to their actions suggest that such criteria can take many forms: moral principles, external authorities, even an internal moral compass. But these, too, need substantive ground. Perhaps, as Manuel Vasquez has suggested, the criteria needs be wrapped up with an idea of human flourishing. Dietrich Bonhoeffer suggests that it is always most productive to see the events of history from the perspective of those who suffer, what he calls "the view from below." These ideas might be employed, then, in discerning one's own position vis-à-vis a differing view.

Facilitating student engagement with these questions and decisions is challenging, but ultimately optimistic. A grave concern about this endeavor, and in using *God's Long* Summer in particular, is that religion—on the basis of the presentation of the characters—cannot be trusted as a basis for any claim. Instead of the relativistic conclusion that all beliefs are equally valid, students sometimes conclude that no religious belief can be trusted. None of my students tried to articulate this position on the midterm question. The responses indicated that all the figures should be respected or some of the figures should be respected; no one argued that none of the figures should be respected. Nonetheless, the worry that the book simply confirms rather than challenges students' pre-existing positions stands. Our goal is to challenge students' presuppositions; or, at least, ask them to consider those existing positions (whatever they may be) critically.[15]

To this end, I have embraced lived theology pedagogically as well as methodologically. Every term I have taught "Christian Vocation and the Search for Meaning II," I have assigned a lived theology project, and called it just that: "The Lived Theology Project." The assignments require collaborative work, are most often semester-long endeavors, and have a public dimension. In past years, groups created museum exhibits related to course themes, mounted the varied displays, and opened the museum to the campus community for several days. In other terms, groups wrote hypothetical grant proposals, including theological and ethical rationales, to fund projects addressing real needs in the world. But, I have come to understand that too much is at stake for too many people, including my students, to work hypothetically. My current students are engaged with the campus and neighborhood communities, identifying problems and opportunities, matching needs with solutions, and struggling in concrete ways with the idea that what they believe does, in fact, matter. Maybe they even feel called to their work.

> Vocation is responsibility, and responsibility is the whole response of the whole person to reality as a whole.
>
> Dietrich Bonhoeffer, *Ethics*[16]

Notes

1. Dietrich Bonhoeffer, *Letters and Papers from Prison*, Dietrich Bonhoeffer Works English Edition (DBWE) 8 (Minneapolis: Fortress Press), 486.
2. Charles Marsh, *God's Long Summer: Stories of Faith and Civil Rights* (Princeton, NJ: Princeton University Press, 1997), 3.
3. Marsh, *God's Long Summer*, 4.
4. The Augsburg College Mission Statement: "Augsburg College educates students to be informed citizens, thoughtful stewards, critical thinkers, and responsible leaders. The Augsburg experience is supported by an engaged community that is committed to intentional diversity in its life and work. An Augsburg education is defined by excellence in the liberal arts and professional studies, guided by the faith and values of the Lutheran church, and shaped by its urban and global settings."
5. Mark Tranvik, "What is Vocation?" unpublished essay.
6. Charles Marsh, "What is Lived Theology?" (Project on Lived Theology website).
7. Barbara Walvoord, through extensive surveys of students and faculty across the country, discovered that students studying religion of any kind at institutions of all types, sizes, and affiliations—public and private—are interested in matters of spirituality and personal belief. See her *Teaching and Learning in College Introductory Religion Courses* (Oxford: Blackwell Publishing, 2008).

8. Marsh, *God's Long Summer*, 5.

9. Marsh, *God's Long Summer*, 55.

10. Marsh, *God's Long Summer*, 6.

11. Marsh, *God's Long Summer*, 89.

12. Marsh, *God's Long Summer*, 134.

13. My colleague Russell Kleckley, puts it this way: students sometimes think that holding a belief is sufficient justification for that belief.

14. Marsh, *God's Long Summer*, 5.

15. I wish to thank my colleague Russell Kleckley for conversation on this matter.

16. Bonhoeffer, *Ethics*, DBWE 6: 293.

Teaching to Transform

THEOLOGICAL REFLECTIONS ON THE GIFTS AND CHALLENGES OF SERVICE-LEARNING

Jacqueline A. Bussie

The classroom remains the most radical space of possibility in the Academy.

BELL HOOKS

God is waiting for human human beings.

JURGEN MOLTMANN

Through dialogue, the teacher-of-the-students and the students-of-the-teacher cease to exist and a new term emerges: teacher-student with students-teachers. The teacher is no longer merely the-one-who-teaches, but the one who is herself taught in dialogue with the students, who in turn while being taught also teach. The students become jointly responsible for a process in which all grow.

PAOLO FREIRE

My life is that of a theological worker who tries to tell something of God's pain and God's joy.

DOROTHEE SOELLE

I HAVE SERVED the academy, the church, and my students for more than a decade as a teaching theologian committed to the praxis of lived theology, which the University of Virginia's Project on Lived Theology defines as reconnecting theology with the lived experience of communities embodying their faith traditions. My entire career has been spent at small liberal arts colleges of the Evangelical Lutheran Church of America in the Midwest and upper Midwest, teaching predominately rural, white, Christian students, a large number of whom are first-generation college students, and from farming communities. I have always been troubled by Kathryn Tanner's accurate distinction between academic theology and everyday theology, and have sought through my publishing and pedagogy—especially service-learning pedagogy—to dismantle the divide between the two.[1]

This chapter will reveal that the risks, ambiguities, and challenges encountered in service-learning and a pedagogy of lived theology are many, messy, and mostly unanticipated because of a regrettable absence of serious, authentic, academic discussion in this realm. While the critical literature is replete with excellent, widely read pieces that address the depths of students' resistance to service-learning pedagogical outcomes such as an enhanced understanding of systemic privilege, virtually no critical literature exposes the unique challenges that lived theology professors like myself have faced when our service-learning students actually begin to attain our much-hoped-for learning outcomes. In other words, virtually no one is talking about what happens when students and their theologies begin to be transformed by the lived theologies embodied in underprivileged communities that their lives bump up against via service-learning. This essay, therefore, argues for, and summons serious service-learning practitioners to, a new conversation regarding the immense challenges (and rewards) faced by professors and students when service-learning succeeds rather than fails. As a secondary thesis, I will argue that in spite of the lack of an academic support system, nonetheless the gifts of a pedagogy of lived theology vastly outweigh the challenges, and have helped me to reimagine the role of a professor as that of a "doula," as one who serves and accompanies students on their often painful yet fulfilling perennial journeys to give birth to their liberated and transformed selves.[2]

Early in my career, my religion-department colleagues and I received a generous grant to fund a pedagogical retreat. At the retreat, we performed a bold exercise. We constructed a mock list of the authentic goals and learning outcomes we would put on our Introduction to Religion syllabus if assessment, finances, intellectual objectivity, tenure considerations, colleagues' perceptions, student evaluations and so-called realism were all for the moment suspended and we could just express—in the raw—what we honestly hope for on behalf of our students. My authentic course goals

included: "Liberate you from the fear of difference so that you can celebrate it instead," "Establish those who live in poverty, marginalization
or oppression as your teachers," and "Resurrect your trust in the world as
a place where you and your community matter and all of your actions do
too." And my real learning outcomes expressed the audacious hope that
each of my students would "Grow in compassion for yourself and for one
another, especially people different from yourself," "Unlearn your biases,
prejudices and false assumptions (i.e. all the lies our culture or your privileges have taught you)," and "Become a more human human being (à la
Jurgen Moltmann)."

My construction of this list pulled back the veil and revealed crucial
things about my pedagogical identity. I started teaching more boldly
and innovatively in order that these authentic goals might be reached.
For example, I added the quote found in the above epigraph from Paolo
Freire's *Pedagogy of the Oppressed*[3] to my syllabus, so students would have
some basic insight upfront to my "participatory epistemology"[4] teaching philosophy and some of my more unusual pedagogical practices,
such as having a discussion-based class rather than banking-education-
style lecture,[5] insisting that our chairs be in a democratic circle instead
of rows, engaging every class session in active-learning exercises, and
assigning critical reflection and learning journals on the new reading
for the day, instead of traditional essays or fact-regurgitation quizzes.
Additionally, several colleagues, two of our finest religion majors, and
I formed a working group in which we read Quaker author Anne French
Dalke's text on transformative pedagogy and completely redesigned our
introductory religion courses.[6] My student evaluations provide objective corroboration that all of these changes improved my teaching
exponentially.

Of all of these practices, service-learning transformed the teaching and
learning process more than any other and helped my students to attain
the "real" learning outcomes I most desired. Several colleagues and I who
received service-learning fellowships began teaching service-learning
courses, and constructed the following definition: "Service-learning is a
structured, experiential teaching and learning process that purposefully
combines community service with academic instruction. It connects identified community needs with academic learning outcomes and develops
students' sense of civic responsibility. Concrete opportunities for critical
and reflective thinking about the service experience enhance learning and
self-exploration."[7] We discerned through praxis that critical reflection is

the hyphen of the pairing—for without critical reflection, service is mere volunteerism, and not learning.

Invariably, expeditionary- and service-learning became for my students and me an experience of lived theology. The experiences themselves led me to redefine the term theology in practical embodied and embedded terms that resonate more than brittle "study of God" language with my students and the people of faith we have encountered beyond the classroom. In my book *Outlaw Christian*, I reimagine lived theology as the thoughts, words, and actions people of faith undertake everyday to reconcile the promises of the Gospel and the love of God with the horrors of CNN and the suffering of their own lives.[8]

Over the last ten years, I have taught service-learning courses during which my students and I have served weekly right in our own backyards: at a local homeless shelter, a Lutheran Social Services' food pantry, an urban church's afterschool tutoring program, a settlement house, and a nonprofit organization known as Community Refugee and Immigration Services. The courses I have taught with a service-learning component have included Religion and Nonviolence, Introduction to Religion, Christian Ethics, Problem of Evil, Faith in Dialogue: Interfaith Leadership, and Liberation Theology and Social Justice. Each of these courses offered students multiple options for pairing their gifts and interests with one of several service-partners, so that students could learn from one another's diverse experiences. My students' service-learning activities have ranged from "adopting" and befriending refugee families; tutoring second grade students in math in an at-risk school district; leading a poetry-writing seminar for women at a homeless shelter; playing basketball with urban youth; cooking, serving, and eating meals alongside the homeless; helping clients "shop" at a choice food pantry; and cleaning up a local river post-flood.

Almost all of my courses with a local service-learning component have had an optional complementary global component—and thus my students and I together have pounded rice in an indigenous Bri-Bri village women's co-op in the rainforest of Costa Rica; taught Dominican Republic kindergarteners English; lived with apartheid survivors in the South African township of Khayelitsha and held the frail bodies of AIDS orphans; cleared rocky land by hand and hoe for a much-needed community kitchen in Ensenada, Mexico; and worshipped alongside strangers at a side-of-the-dirt-road church in Nicaragua. Most of the world I have seen, I have been blessed to see through the eyes of my students and in the larger context of a reading-, discussion-, and encounter-based learning emprise. I remain convinced there is no better way to travel the world or to learn from the people in it.

That being said, all of these experiences have offered numerous rewards and challenges, which I want to share with you as we wind our way to wisdom. Teaching with a pedagogy of lived theology that includes experiential-learning, service-learning, and genuine encounters with members of other faith communities who embody their theologies ushers in invaluable rewards and gifts for both students and professors.

Gifts and Rewards of Service-Learning and Lived Theology Pedagogy

First, a pedagogy of lived theology awakens in many students a deeply purposeful sense of vocation, especially to the sublime work of *tikkun-olam*. Within Judaism, the vocation of human beings is to mend or repair of the world, as expressed in the marvelous Hebrew phrase "*tikkun-olam.*" As my students tell it, my service-learning courses and those of my other gifted colleagues have led them to quite literally fall in love with the cross-stitch of mending this needful and wounded world. To name just one example, serving families at the local Lutheran social services (LSS) food pantry through my liberation theology course bestirred in my student Amanda a desire to run her own food pantry one day. Now, only five short years later, Amanda is the director of the very same LSS food pantry where she once served as an undergraduate. Uncountable numbers of my students have gone on to serve in nonprofits such as the Ohio AIDS Coalition, the Peace Corps, Lutheran Volunteer Corps, Jesuit Volunteer Corps, Episcopal Service Corps, and Teach for America, and to work as pastors, teachers, organic farmers, public defenders, and immigration lawyers. The Sufi mystic poet Rumi instructs the faithful, "Be a lamp, lifeboat, or a ladder./ Help someone else's soul heal./Walk out of your house like a shepherd."[9] Many of my students are lamps, lifeboats, and ladders; they walk out of their houses like shepherds.

Create a Solidarity Culture with Resurrection Practices

Second and relatedly, a pedagogy of lived theology sets students free to become people who practice resurrection.[10] Explains Dorothee Soelle, "Where there is solidarity there is resurrection."[11] In the spring of 2009, all semester long my students and I had served at the LSS food pantry closest to our campus, which we learned would be closed for five days over the Easter holiday due to insufficient staffing. Two of my students took the initiative to ask the director if they might open and run the pantry themselves; he said yes if they could procure a dozen volunteers. Because our Lutheran (E.L.C.A) university was officially on break from the Wednesday before Easter through Easter Monday, when my students asked the class for volunteers, I was stunned when ten additional students raised their hands. And so it happened that on a snowy Saturday before Easter, twelve students and I opened up the pantry and served over 150 families who would have gone without that week. Best of all, a local church dropped off goodie bags filled with Easter treats, eggs, and crayons, and my students were able to deliver these straight into the hands of smiling children *before* Easter, rather than after the holiday was over. "*Live resurrection,*" Dorothee Soelle had enjoined in one of our class readings; and my students, by creating a solidarity culture, did exactly that.

Replace Stereotypes with Relationships and Ethnocultural Empathy

Third, my students' compassionate actions were possible only because service- and experiential-learning had helped them replace stereotypes and misconceptions with authentic relationships with people different from themselves in race, nationality, religion, and socioeconomic status. These relationships helped my students gain much-needed ethnocultural empathy. Transformative pedagogy and praxis had put a human face and a real person's name and lived life on otherwise muzzy and diaphanous concepts such as poverty, Islam, homelessness, and immigration. Once during an active learning exercise in which I asked liberation theology students to "dare to be reductive" and distill the message of liberation theology down to a bumper sticker, one student wrote: POVERTY IS A PERSON.[12] Through her service, this student had learned the value of genuine deep listening to the story of the neighbor. While many times my students expressed the desire to be "doing something useful" during their service placement, our community partners were exceptional teachers in reminding them that listening can be most useful of all and a necessary means of de-centering privilege. As one of our service sites had on a sign on the wall in the staff room, "IT'S NOT ABOUT YOU." And as I wrote recently in an article on interfaith dialogue and cooperation, "We all think listening comes naturally to us, like breathing, when really listening is more like swimming, learning not to breathe at the right time."[13]

When my students and I stood in the slums of San Jose, Costa Rica surrounded by light-less shanties, piles of garbage, and human waste that flowed downhill past our feet, we listened as local resident Pastor Roberto exegeted the book of Job and taught us the invaluable lesson, "Humanization is evangelization." In a world that dehumanizes the poor and oppressed, service-learning revealed to us the good news of our common humanity as beloved children of God, and many of my privileged students and I received our own humanity back in the process of recognizing our complicity in all these processes of dehumanization.

A liberation theology graduate of mine once emblazoned his graduation cap with the words of Galatians 2:10: REMEMBER THE POOR. The career paths many of my students have chosen indicates that they have not forgotten the faces of the people whom they loved and learned from, whom they served and who served them, and whom they learned to humanize even as they were humanized by them. On those days when my own arthritic, tired hands fumble to pick up their own needle and thread and resume the horizonless task of unsewing prejudice, the words REMEMBER YOUR STUDENTS breathe enough hope in me to "keep on keeping on" for a lifetime. Once in my liberation theology class, where hope-cultivation became intentional everyday practice, I asked students to write down on one side of an index card something to share with the class that caused them despair or anguish, and on the other side something that gave them hope. I participated in the activity myself, as I always do in my active-learning moments in the classroom. On the side where I expressed my primary resource for hope, I found myself writing in all capital letters: YOU.

Awaken Consciousness of Privilege and Complicity

Fourth, a pedagogy of lived theology awakens in privileged students a consciousness of their privilege that is essential for compassionate living and the pursuit of social justice. My students were shocked to discover that the inner-city youth they tutored not only did not know what college was but also compared it to "jail," because "you had to live and eat there and are forced to read books all the time." Though many students in my class did consider a college education a privilege, none of them had considered that *not* learning from their communities that college was shameful or evil was also a privilege. Likewise, when my students and I lived with families in their homes in a township outside Capetown, South Africa—most without showers, sinks, toilets or roofs other than scrap metal or tarp—we realized as we brushed our teeth outside at the pump every night and hauled heavy buckets that water that flows anywhere inside your house is pure privilege. Street signs, street lights, garbage pick-up, mattresses, grass, drinking water you do not have to boil for twenty minutes: also privileges my students came to name as such. Like never before, my students understood the words we had read in class by Peggy McIntosh in her now classic text on privilege: "I have come to see white privilege as an invisible package of unearned assets I can count on cashing in each day, but about which I was "meant" to remain oblivious . . . To redesign social systems we need first to acknowledge their colossal unseen dimensions. The silences and denials surrounding privilege are the key political tool here. They keep the thinking about quality or equity incomplete, protecting unearned advantage and conferred dominance."[14]

Back home in Columbus, my students who "adopted" refugee families developed relations with immigrants who were often non-Christian, and they were stunned by the amount of prejudice and bullying that, to name only one example, Muslim Somalis encountered on a daily basis. This was another important example of privilege—namely, Christian privilege. Most of my students had never even heard the phrase "Christian privilege" until I introduced it to them.[15] The hallmark of any privilege is its insidious constructed invisibility to those who benefit from it; the hallmark of effective praxis-based service-learning is its relentless exposure of all such invisible pathogens to the glare of daylight and hence, critique.

Rediscover Lament as Spiritual and Sociopolitical Practice

A fifth gift bestowed on the service-learning practitioner is the rediscovery of lament as a spiritual and communal practice. Service-learning and a participatory epistemology have helped me as a teacher fulfill the disconcerting call of Jeremiah 9:20, "Teach your daughters how to wail, teach one another a lament." While serving, my students and I often encounter members of faith communities whose lived theologies still incorporate lament, a practice largely lost in middle-class North America. When we stayed, for example, with the indigenous women of Yorkin, Costa Rica, we learned that almost all of the women were widowed in their late twenties. The women explained that their husbands had died on the US-owned banana plantations, many of which still use the cheap pesticide DDT that, though known to be lethal, is not illegal in Costa Rica. Indeed, while we were there, a fifteen-year-old boy on the banana plantation died while the banana company denied all responsibility. As an act of resistance, the women had formed an agricultural/artisan co-op that effectively saved all of their families and children from ever having to work on the multinational plantations again. More persuasive than any bullet, these beautiful, strong womens' public tears taught us communal lament's possibility to function as an impetus for social change.

Embodying a politics of love for the women they had met, my students came home from our Costa Rica trip and embarked on a successful campaign to get our dining services to serve only organic bananas, for they realized that our culture's systemic demand for cheap bananas had in a very real way widowed the women of Yorkin. I now create a space in most of my courses for the practice of lament. When I was teaching my Problem of Evil course this past semester, we wrote our own laments and spoke them aloud on the college lawn. We pondered together the oddity that the first thing most people in our culture do when they begin to cry is say, "I'm sorry." My students vowed as a class to no longer apologize for our tears and vulnerability, and reconceived of lament as a way of fulfilling Jurgen Moltmann's call to become "the more human human beings" for whom God is waiting.[16] Learning from the incredible human human beings whom we have met who have transformed their afflictions into an ethic of compassion and care for others, service-learning has helped my students to become stewards of their own suffering.

Challenges for Students of Service-learning and Transformative Pedagogies
Disenchantment, Disillusionment, and Despair

Alongside all of the above extraordinary benefits reaped by teaching service-learning and employing a transformative pedagogy, a different and disturbing trend also emerged in my students' lives—one that I had not anticipated or heard discussed: namely, a profound disenchantment. Over and over again, my excited, predominantly white, Christian, liberation theology students would run home to share with roommates, parents, and boyfriends all that they had learned from liberation theology through their burgeoning relationships with Mexican immigrants, Muslim Somali war refugees, underprivileged African American youth, and homeless men and women in our community. Likewise, my "Faith in Dialogue: Interfaith Leadership" students would eagerly share with significant others stories of encounter with Native Americans, Bah'ai, Hindus, and Buddhists whom they had served alongside in the community, working together for the common good. And over and over again, my once elated students would return to class deflated by the inordinate amount of resistance they had encountered in others to the heartfelt stories they had shared. I found myself struggling to even find literature, let alone pedagogical resources, on kinds of privilege other than race, in particular Christian privilege. In other words, when transformative pedagogy actually worked, alongside all of the wonderful, positive consequences listed above in this chapter, my students also experienced serious feelings of estrangement and alienation from family, friends, and their own culture and religious tradition, as well as a profound disillusionment with the United States' consumerist, materialistic, and individualistic culture.

Equally distressing for many of my students as they discovered the depth of their white, middle-class, Christian privilege and its role in oppression, was the alienation many of them began to perceive from themselves, which often took the form of expressions of shame and disgust toward their personhood, their whiteness, or Christianity itself. As my students grew to recognize their complicity in systems of oppression, they often expressed feelings of self-loathing, disempowerment, and despair, for they realized—rightly, I think—that changing *systems* is a much more gargantuan and formidable task than changing *yourself*, which is hard enough.

As a result of these experiences being shared over and over again in my classroom, certain questions began to float, insuppressible, to the surface of my mind: was transformative pedagogy rendering my students unhappy and despairing? Was it shattering some of their closest relationships, rendering them lonely and alienated from the people who claimed to love them most? Would all of this resistance eventually lead them to abandon their activist stance long after our class was over? What are our theological and pedagogical responsibilities toward students whose learning leads them unwittingly into this kind of estrangement and ambiguity? How do we best accompany young people through the process of disenchantment and re-enchantment? In the same theology-as-bumper-sticker activity I mentioned above, one student wrote: ACTIVELY BROKENHEARTED. To this day, I have never really been part of a pedagogical conversation where professors were honest about brokenheartedness as a consequence of experiential learning. While there is a remarkable amount of literature on privileged students' resistance to learning about privilege, particularly with regard to race,[17] I found myself wondering, where is the literature that describes the challenges that result *when service-learning actually **sticks** rather than gets resisted?* That is a conversation I hope this chapter will spark into being.

Living Into New Identities and Consciousness of Privilege

Julie Lindquist writes, "When people learn, they don't take on new knowledge as much as a new identity."[18] Truer words were never spoken, but very few service-learning scholars or lived theologians (with the notable exception of Dorothee Soelle) seem to address the fact that a fresh identity often leads to fresh rejection by those around you, who preferred the never-challenge-the-status-quo identity you formerly possessed. What resources are we providing our students to manage the severe cognitive dissonance, disenchantment, and disillusionment that can ensue when all that their privilege once led them to believe is called into question, when they realize that evil is not simply moral and therefore conveniently "other," but is rather systemic and is therefore ours?

While I would never want to be so theologically arrogant as to claim that the dissonance experienced by privileged students as their privilege is unmasked is tantamount to the everyday dissonance and marginalization experienced by those whom society oppresses, I find that ignoring or dismissing this dissonance as nonexistent or irrelevant is deleterious to my classroom and student-learning. I feel horror at the possibility that this paper could devolve into a treatise on pity for the privileged ("look at how hard it is on privileged students to learn!"), but such fear could explain the dearth of scholarship on this risky yet real issue. That being said, to delegitimize the privileged students' strong grief reactions that accompany the peculiar collapse from an "epistemology of ignorance"[19] into knowledge might be dangerous, as it could preclude the achievement of other desirable outcomes. Among those desirable learning outcomes include: 1) a recognition that those who live in poverty, oppression, and marginalization have become remarkably efficacious teachers in students' lives (in other words, that learning has happened in service-learning and not just service!); and 2) related feelings of solidarity with the oppressed and lament for their daily struggles that run alongside the concomitant lament of knowing we are still complicit in the system of oppression. The difficulty arises from the fact that feelings and stories have a legitimate place in service-learning, namely because the vast majority of what we are learning in this kind of pedagogy are the feelings and stories of communities of people whom many have been taught to ignore as irrelevant or inferior. How, then, can we not admit a place for the feelings and stories that accompany the privileged students' growing consciousness of privilege?

One of my finest theology students, Ken, once proclaimed in his senior chapel talk, "The most dangerous class at Capital University is liberation theology." He went on to explain that though liberation theology was his favorite class, the course texts we had read and the relationships he had built with the immigrants he served had forever altered his worldview, and for him, there was no turning back. Raised in a military family, Ken had shared with the class earlier in the semester that he and his girlfriend had broken up as arguments metastasized over the more nuanced, humanizing worldview he had adopted toward our refugee and immigrant brothers and sisters. His parents wanted to know "what liberal nonsense" he was learning in college.

Ken was far from alone. When Ken shared his story that day in class, our first day back after Thanksgiving break, I remember being taken aback as ten hands shot up in the air at once, heads bobbing in empathic understanding. One student, citing that our course had helped her to find the courage to "betray" privilege and love across traditional boundaries, shared her parents' adamantine rejection of her new boyfriend who was of a different race and class than herself. A stunning number of other students in the class reported deep disappointment and aching arguments with loved ones with whom they had always previously seen eye-to-eye, explaining that when they heard with consciousness-awakened ears racist, classist, oppressive, and heterosexist comments uttered by dads, cousins, aunts, grandpas, and stepmoms around the dinner table, they had chosen to speak out in agapeistic solidarity with the oppressed. My students' non-violent loving speech had earned from their loved ones epithets such as "socialist," "bleeding-heart liberal," "fanatic," "extremist," "idealist," and "un-American" with one sibling commenting, "If you despise this country so much, why don't you just leave it?"

As the students shared their stories, I reminded them that we had discovered the truth about why, in one of our course readings, Dorothee Soelle renamed liberationist theologies "wide-open-eyes" theology.[20] Once a liberationist perspective opens your eyes to the injustices of the world, you can never close them again in good conscience, nor can you close them toward your own complicity or believe in your own "innocence" in the same way ever again. The students declared that they would not want to, even if they could, which comforted me greatly. The students recalled the following passage they had read from Soelle: "Love has its price. God wants to make us alive, and the wider we open our hearts to others or the more audibly we cry out against the injustice which rules over us, the more difficult our life in the rich society of injustice becomes . . . The more you grow into love, into the message of Jesus . . . you enter into loneliness, often you lose friends, a standard of living, a job, or secure career, but at the same time you are changed."[21] But the students also stated unequivocally that we needed to be honest about the fact that to walk around with your eyes that open all the time leads to a lot of tears and pain and shattered foundations, especially when you live in a culture that systemically protects privilege and the status quo through the intentional inculcation of prejudice.[22] Again I found myself asking, where are the pedagogical resources to help me manage these challenges with my students? Why are we not talking about this?

Righteousness or Heroism

While all of the above is true, I also paradoxically and simultaneously worried that, in these alienating interactions with significant others, my students might lapse into righteousness and anger—an attitude I myself am guilty of—and assume an uncompassionate attitude toward those who did not see the world the way they did.[23] I also sometimes asked myself, are my students' service activities allowing them to feel good about themselves so that they forget that systemic change happens gradually and almost invisibly and requires the cooperation of all? I told the students that when I feel frustrated and exasperated toward someone on the other end of the ideological spectrum, I remind myself that I used to think exactly like my ideological opponents do. I then ask my students to ransack their memory banks to recall what methods or practices others once used to help them best genuinely to hear a divergent point of view. We do an exercise in which we all must name a time we learned something, and then unpack *why we were able to learn it.* Unfailingly, this helps students to recall that righteousness and anger almost never helped them to learn anything, and thus cannot be the best approach toward others. In almost all of my classes, I bring in a trainer of nonviolent communication, as this can help considerably with the challenges ushered in by service-learning.

Once when a local Muslim immigrant friend shared with my class the true definition of *jihad* as spiritual struggle, a Christian student became livid to the point of tears and confessed, "My very favorite high school teacher stood up in front of the class and taught us all that jihad means 'holy war' and that Muslims want to kill us because we are unbelievers. What am I supposed to think of her and my school now?" Those of us professors whom education has already transformed must not forget that many of our students will never see the world, themselves, or their communities the same way once those who live in marginalization, poverty, or oppression, become their teachers. To teach to transform means to give our students an experience to which they feel they must bear witness. With this revelation comes great enlightenment, but also immense responsibility. In my view, these spiny experiences of shame, disillusionment, alienation, cognitive dissonance, and frustrated trust are among the greatest challenges for those of us who teach service-learning to largely privileged students.

Possible Strategies for Dispelling Despair and Disenchantment

When service-learning works, it hurts. Yet what are we doing as faculty to name and address these messy issues and preclude student learned despair and social paralysis? Don't those who disenchant young people have a responsibility to point them toward re-enchantment, or if that is not possible, at least toward compassionate activism? If we are going to deconstruct our students *weltanschauung*, we surely must practice a theology of accompaniment with them throughout the process as well as model the possibility of a reconstructed *weltanschauung*.

One helpful strategy I have implemented is the student-led daily hope meditation, wherein students bring to class local wisdom, personal stories, and vernacular models and means of resistance to despair. This enables students to grasp that their own experience is a source of lived theology and to practice plumbing its theological depths. I also regularly teach one of Dorothee Soelle's extraordinarily constructive essays on hope, in which she provocatively argues that hopelessness—despair—is the luxury of the privileged.[24] A second useful strategy involves the forthright naming and pre-emptive discussion of the potentially iconoclastic nature of service-learning. These days my students and I openly discuss the following questions: what happens to you psychologically, emotionally, and spiritually, when what you have been taught to hate and fear turns out to be utterly other than what you were taught? How do you feel toward the people who taught you these things? What happens to your spiritual landscape when you come to see what was once called "justice" as injustice, people once termed lazy, "less-than" or "inferior" as the beloved children of God, or when you come to see yourself not as morally innocent but as a beneficiary of oppression? Though many of us professors may have forgotten it, in the course of our lifetime and careers many of us have had to answer these questions for ourselves. In order to keep student disillusionment from becoming one more "expert blind spot" in our teaching, we would do well to reacquaint ourselves with our own journey and to "profess" it to students.[25]

A third strategy of accompaniment thus involves modeling vulnerability and authenticity. I now practice authenticity with students and confess that I am a person who was transformed by my education, that I am someone for whom college "worked." I confide in students that I am no longer the same person who believed that homeless people are lazy drug addicts, or that I was genuinely "poor" as a college student, or that it would be "weird"—as I once said to a friend in high school—to have a female pastor at my church. At the same time, I discuss honestly with my students the ways in which I am still complicit with my own educated, white, Christian privilege. My students' jaws drop at all of these disclosures and my honesty tends to usher in more truthfulness about their own preconceptions and misassumptions. I also share that my actions and transformed worldviews have led to alien-ation from my own family and I am forever trying (and often failing) to maintain unrighteous loving relationships with people on the other ideolog-ical and theological side of the fence. Writes bell hooks, "When professors bring narrative of their experiences into classroom discussions it eliminates the possibility that we can function as all-knowing, silent interrogators. It is often productive if professors take the first risk, linking confessional narra-tives to academic discussions so as to show how experience can illuminate and enhance our understanding of academic material."[26]

Challenges for Faculty Who Teach Service-Learning and Lived Theology Pedagogy
Micro-aggressions and Resistance from Administration or Colleagues

So far, all the challenges I have discussed have dealt with students who should of course be our primary concern. It bears mentioning, how-ever, if only in brief, that successful transformative pedagogy and service learning can also exact a price from the professor herself, often in the form of administrative opposition, professional envy, or workplace micro-aggressions from colleagues who resist challenges to the status quo of the patriarchal, teacher-centered classroom.

For example, when my radically empowered religion and nonviolence students (who had learned from black apartheid survivors they met in South Africa what lived nonviolence can actually accomplish) realized that our university exclusively used paper products from a multibillion-dollar company that had a toxic, cancerous dump in a local underprivileged neighborhood, they embarked on a nonviolent, multistage campaign to end our university contract with this company. During honors convocation, they wrapped their right arms—the one facing out from the stage and visible in all event photos—in university toilet paper which they marked in black sharpie with the no symbol ⊘ slashed through the company's initials. They wrote a petition on a roll of white paper towels, got over six hundred purple ink signatures (our school colors were purple and white), then unrolled the entire thing on the floor in front of the facilities management office and slept on it until administrators would grant them a meeting. My students succeeded. Not only did the university stop using products from that company, but the administration asked my students to select a green, sustainable company for our new contract. I have many more examples just like this, and each one fills me with respect and admiration for my students' ethics of care.

But as this one example cautions, justice-seeking students can cost institutions money and potentially cause administrators to lose face. We are naïve to think that such actions are without consequences for professors, whom administrators perceive as the inspiration for such subversive activities. We are also naïve to think that repercussions for such actions are the same for privileged white Christian professors who teach at Christian colleges as they are for adjunct faculty, faculty of color, or faculty who hold a minority religious or non-religious worldview who teach at these same colleges. (I, after all, still received tenure, and eventually, a position at an institution far more hospitable to my service-learning pedagogy.)

At an institution where I once worked early in my career, however, when several of my female junior colleagues and I began to engage in lived, transformative pedagogy both within and beyond the classroom walls, some of our senior male colleagues seemed threatened by the high enrollment in our courses, the serpentine lines outside of our doors during office hours, and the campus-wide buzz generated by our global and local service-learning activities. Naïvely confused at the time as to why, we became frequent victims of micro-aggressions from several administrators and department colleagues. For example, one day the male honors director of my institution chided us with the comment, "Service-learning is Mickey Mouse," by which we assumed he meant, "lacking in academic rigor," the shopworn default accusation leveled against professors whose students dare express joy in learning or aspire to real-life application of classroom theory. Recent research on service-learning indicates that our anecdotal experience is symptomatic of a larger problem, "At the institutional level, the most serious obstacle [to expanding and sustaining service-learning programs] is faculty resistance to service-learning . . . Many are skeptical of the educational value of service-learning."[27] In my view, given that a lived feminist theology has no difficulty discerning and embracing the value of service-learning, much critical research still needs to be done regarding resistance to service-learning and possible correlations with gender and other factors of privilege.

In the meantime, we learn much from the sage words of bell hooks:

> Certainly teachers who are trying to institutionalize progressive ped-
> agogical practices risk being subjected to discrediting critiques . . .
> There is a major backlash that seeks to delegitimize progressive
> pedagogy by saying, "This keeps us from having serious thoughts
> and serious education" . . . How do we cope with how we are per-
> ceived by our colleagues? I've actually had colleagues say to me,
> "Students seem to really enjoy your class. What are you doing
> wrong?" . . . Teachers who love students and are loved by them are
> still suspect in the Academy . . . The Academy is not paradise. But
> learning is a place where paradise can be created. The classroom . . .
> remains a location of possibility. In that field of possibility we have
> the opportunity to labor for freedom, to demand of ourselves and
> our comrades . . . that . . . we collectively imagine ways to move
> beyond boundaries, to transgress. This is education as the practice
> of freedom.[28]

We would all do well to be honest with ourselves and our colleagues about the real risks we are taking professionally—especially those who are unten-ured or not in the majority with regard to race, religion, gender, or political leaning—when we dare to allow our teaching to incarnate a pedagogy of lived theology. For those of us who are senior faculty, we have a respon-sibility to serve as allies, and mentor the junior untenured members who are intrepid enough to teach in a way that is true to themselves and their theologies, and who dare to transgress traditional pedagogies as the practice of freedom.

Conclusion

In the end there can be no question that all of the rewards—personal, communal, global, and systemic—of a pedagogy of lived theology immeasurably outweigh the challenges. For this reason, I could not teach otherwise than to teach for transformation and freedom. Because I strive to practice a companioning ministry of presence to my students before, after and during the transformation, I consider myself not only a midwife, but also a doula. Scripturally speaking, the greek word "doula" designates a woman who serves.[29] In contemporary English, a doula has come to mean a trained and experienced professional companion who accompanies a woman before, during, and after the birth of her child. A complement to the medically trained midwife, the doula serves needs beyond the act of physical labor including emotional, spiritual, and informational needs and embodies a lived theology of accompaniment. "Liberation is thus a childbirth, and a painful one," writes Paulo Freire.[30] As a theologian who teaches to transform and liberate, I am both doula and midwife. And what I hope to help students give birth to is themselves.

Notes

1. See Jacqueline Bussie, *The Laughter of the Oppressed: Ethical and Theological Resistance in Wiesel, Morrison, and Endo* (New York: T&T Clark International, 2007), 4.

2. For this metaphor, I am indebted to Anna Mercedes who redescribes Christ as doula in "Who are You?: Christ and the Imperative of Subjectivity," in *Transformative Lutheran Theologies*, ed. Mary Streufert (Minneapolis: Fortress, 2010), 87–95. Writes Mercedes, "A 'Doula' is a woman who assists a pregnant woman in childbirth, helping the birthing woman to know her own strength . . . This wise female companioning in childbirth can call to mind a deeply active and empowering form of service" (90).

3. Paolo Freire, *Pedagogy of the Oppressed* (New York: Continuum, 1981), 67.

4. The phrase "participatory epistemology" comes from Owen Barfield, quoted in Laura I. Rendon, *Sentipensante (Sensing/Thinking) Pedagogy: Educating for Wholeness, Social Justice and Liberation* (Sterling, VA: Stylus Publishing, 2009), 134.

5. See Paolo Freire, *Pedagogy of the Oppressed* (New York: Continuum, 1981): "Banking education attempts to conceal certain facts which explain the way men [*sic*] exist in the world; problem-posing education sets itself the task of demythologizing. Banking education resists dialogue; problem-posing education regards dialogue as indispensable to the act of cognition which unveils reality. Banking education treats students as objects of assistance; problem–posing education makes them critical thinkers" (71).

6. Anne French Dalke, *Teaching to Learn/Learning to Teach: Meditations on the Classroom* (New York: Peter Lang, 2002).

7. Jacqueline Bussie, Lisette Gibson, and Sally Creasap, "From the Bottom Up: Building a Service-Learning Program at the University Level," paper presented at the International Conference on Civic Education, Orlando, Florida, January 19–21, 2006.

8. Jacqueline A. Bussie, *Outlaw Christian: Finding Authentic Faith by Breaking the "Rules"* (Nashville: Nelson, 2016).

9. Coleman Barks, trans., *Rumi: The Big Red Book* (New York: Harper One, 2010), 295.

10. See "On Living Resurrection" in Dianne L. Oliver, ed., *Dorothee Soelle: Essential Writings* (Maryknoll, NY: Orbis, 2006), 128–40.

11. "On Living Resurrection," 136.

12. The phrase "dare to be reductive" comes from Gerald Graff, *Clueless in Academe: How Schooling Obscures the Life of the Mind* (New Haven, CT: Yale University Press, 2003), 10–11. "Much of the problem lies in the belief that to *simplify* academic inquiry is to vulgarize it, whereas simplification is a necessary feature of even the most complex kinds of work . . . Translating academic ideas into nonacademic terms is already internal to successful academic communication itself. 'Dare to be reductive' is one of my maxims for academics."

13. See Jacqueline Bussie, "Reconciled Diversity: Reflections on our Calling to Embrace our Religious Neighbors," *Intersections* 33 (Spring 2011): 30–35.

14. Peggy McIntosh, "White Privilege and Male Privilege: A Personal Account of Coming to See Correspondences Through Work in Women's Studies," in *Privilege: A Reader*, ed. Michael S. Kimmel and Abby L. Ferber (Boulder, CO: Westview Press, 2003), 148, 159.

15. The best essay I have found on Christian privilege to use for teaching students is only in blog form: see Caryn Riswold, "On Christian Privilege and Being an Atheist Ally," Feminismxianity, September 6, 2012, http://www.patheos.com/blogs/carynriswold/2012/09/on-christian-privilege-being-an-atheist-ally/.

16. Jurgen Moltmann, *The Source of Life: The Holy Spirit and the Theology of Life* (Minneapolis: Fortress Press, 1997), 41.

17. For some excellent references on this, see Barbara Applebaum, *Being White, Being Good: White Complicity, White Moral Responsibility, and Social Justice Pedagogy* (Lanham, MD: Lexington Books, 2010).

18. Quoted in Graff, *Clueless in Academe*, 24.

19. This phrase comes from Charles Mills, quoted in Applebaum, *Being White, Being Good*, 35.

20. Oliver, *Dorothee Soelle*, 200.

21. Oliver, *Dorothee Soelle*, 109–10.

22. See James W. Loewen, *Lies My Teacher Told Me: Everything Your American History Textbook Got Wrong* (New York: Simon & Shuster, 2007). This incredible text is recommended background reading in the majority of my courses.

23. Speaking of race relations, Audrey Thomson labels this undesirable attitude the "lone white hero stance," and urges us to resist such a position. See her intriguing article, "Resisting the 'Lone Hero' Stance," in *Everyday Antiracism: Getting Real about Race in School*, ed. Mica Pollock (New York: The Real Press, 2008) 328–333.

24. "Seen from the perspective of the poor, hopelessness itself is the kind of luxury for those who are not caught up in the struggles." Dorothee Soelle, *Stations of the Cross: A Latin American Pilgrimage* (Minneapolis: Fortress, 1993), 135.

25. For the phrase "expert blind spot" I am grateful to the excellent pedagogical resource, Susan A. Ambrose, Michael W. Bridges, Michele DiPietro, Marsha C. Lovett, and Marie K. Norman, *How Learning Works: Seven Research-Based Principles for Smart Teaching* (San Francisco: Jossey-Bass, 2010), 99.

26. bell hooks, *Teaching To Transgress: Education as the Practice of Freedom* (New York: Routledge, 1994), 21.

27. M. J. Gray, E. Ondaatje, R. Fricker, S. Geschwind, C. A. Goldman, T. Kaganoff, A. Robyn, M. Sundt, L. Vogelgesang, & S. P. Klein, *Combining Service and Learning in Higher Education: Evaluation of the Learn and Serve America, Higher Education Program* (Santa Monica, CA: RAND, 1999), 103.

28. hooks, *Teaching To Transgress*, 141,145, 198, 207.

29. This term is used to describe Jesus's mother Mary in Luke 1:38, where it is often translated as "handmaid."

30. Freire, *Pedagogy of the Oppressed*, 33.

12

Public Discipleship, Constructive Theology, and Grassroots Activism

Jennifer M. McBride

"WHAT DOES MAKING gravy have to do with lived theology?" asked Murphy Davis, cofounder of the Open Door Community, as she was teaching me how to make gallons of it for the Thanksgiving meal being served to our friends living on the streets of Atlanta. "Everything," I responded as we smiled knowingly, alert to our shared conviction about the vital relationship between theological insight and grassroots activism.

Davis's embodied commitment to a life centered on action-reflection began in the late 1970s. It was sparked by a Bible study in a tiny urban congregation that began to take Jesus's call to discipleship more seriously and was fueled by a persistent struggle to make sense of her identity as a white Southern Presbyterian who had come of age during Jim Crow. Deeply influenced by the witness of the civil rights movement, the theology of Martin Luther King, Jr., and the vision of the Beloved Community, she and her husband Ed Loring heard the call, reinforced through the writings of Dietrich Bonhoeffer, "to rigorously follow Christ" in "unlimited discipleship."[1] They responded to this call by turning away from traditional academic careers as church historians and toward more costly and immediate relationships with those who are poor and marginalized.

Although a generation or more removed from their formative experiences, my growing commitment to a life centered on action-reflection has similar contours. I, too, trace the origins of my call to discipleship to a Bible study in a tiny urban Christian community, the Southeast White House, a Washington, DC urban hospitality house where I worked for two years after college and where I first wrestled with my formation as a privileged white Southern evangelical, well removed from the lives of those who struggle under forces of racial and economic injustice. Davis's and Loring's commitment to embodied discipleship led to the founding of the Open Door, an intentionally interracial, residential, Christian activist and worshipping community, which for thirty-five years has been engaged in works of mercy and justice on behalf of those who are homeless and in prison. The theology that grows out of their daily work finds verbal expression in the community's deeply liturgical life—in sermon, song, and celebration of the Eucharist in their dining room-turned-worship space; in the prayer and Bible studies before and after the morning soup kitchens; in death row visits, anti-death penalty vigils, and protests on the steps of the state capitol; and in the monthly newspaper *Hospitality* and in a handful of books published through their in-house press over the last three decades. The theology arising from my much more limited experience in places of deep struggle—in a DC urban neighborhood, in a women's prison, and at the Open Door—is finding expression in the traditional academic spaces that Davis and Loring intentionally left behind, in books published by university and church presses and in classrooms of higher education. The manner in which Davis and Loring have ordered their lives and used their gifts as writers, teachers, pastors, and agitators—modeled after Dorothy Day and Peter Maurin's Catholic Worker Movement—cannot help but give pause to those of us in the academy who are driven by similar questions, influenced by similar figures and movements, share similar gifts, yet write and think from the academy.

The privileging of active engagement over traditional academic argument, or better, the productive tension between active engagement (as demonstrated by the witness of Davis and Loring) and theological production bound to the demands of the academy is something I wish to explore in this chapter. Is there a manner in which constructive academic theology may, with integrity, be understood as "discipleship," and, if so, what are the characteristics of that theology? Davis's gravy-making comment reflects two interrelated commitments that have arisen for me as I attempt to abide in this productive tension: First, that my academic writing should develop out of organic immersion in specific social and political struggle, and second, that the experience of struggle—being placed in the midst—should be an end in itself, basic to the life of discipleship, rather than a means toward scholarship or intellectual ingenuity. My engagement with the Project on Lived Theology has helped me envision this possibility, and my conviction that constructive theology must be tied to immediate, this-worldly engagement has deepened as a result of my participation at the Open Door.

The scholarship that has emerged from attending to grassroots activism, both mine and others, took shape first as "theological ethnography," that is, writing rooted in the mutually beneficial relationship between theology and ethnography, and now it is deepening in the direction of practice, specifically in the direction of my own continual discipleship formation. To be deemed discipleship, I argue, participation in the incarnate word must take precedence over the written word, with writing becoming a manifestation of, but not a substitute for, active discipleship. This dynamic is modeled in the lifework of two figures celebrated by the Project as quintessential lived theologians: Dietrich Bonhoeffer and Martin Luther King, Jr. Bonhoeffer and King were not ethnographers, after all; they were pastor-theologians who found themselves immersed in sociopolitical struggle and whose work was held accountable to that struggle. I offer this developing "method"—lived theology as personal and communal discipleship through this-worldly engagement—as one, albeit not the only, possibility for writing lived theology.

With Bonhoeffer as a primary representative of lived theology, it is fitting to turn to his definition and description of discipleship to guide our analysis. Bonhoeffer examines the concept most thoroughly in *Discipleship*, where he makes his famous distinction between cheap and costly grace. While leading the Confessing Church's struggle against Nazi totalitarianism, he contrasts cheap grace, which exonerates the Church from the demanding work of transformative activity in the world, with costly grace, which he equates with discipleship, or more accurately, with the personal and social transformation that happens on account of following Jesus. Bonhoeffer's critique of cheap grace is directed toward Christians who share his social location and whose lives effortlessly uphold an unjust status quo. For them, grace had become "bargain-basement goods" and "cut-rate comfort," "a cheap cover-up for sin," "grace that we bestow on ourselves" that lets us "remain as before in [our] bourgeois ... existence," and that serves as "a denial of God's living word, a denial of the incarnation."[2] While he describes cheap grace with a variety of these vivid phrases that link Christian passivity to Christian complicity in social sin, fundamentally, cheap grace is the privileging of disembodied belief or intellectual ideas over active response to Jesus's gospel commands. Seeking to give specificity and weight to the notion of discipleship, which has become for

Protestants more metaphor than command, Bonhoeffer reflects on Jesus's call to the first disciples (Mk. 2:14): "The call goes out ... The disciple's answer is not a spoken confession of faith in Jesus. Instead it is the obedient deed."[3] A spoken confession of faith, "an idea about Christ, a doctrinal system," does not require discipleship, Bonhoeffer contends. It does not require a relationship of obedience to the living Jesus but only loyalty to an idea it calls Christ. A mere idea, however, lacks the redemptive power of costly grace. Theological claims alone are inadequate and incomplete since "the grace and the command" are one.[4]

Bonhoeffer's discussion of cheap and costly grace in *Discipleship* echoes his earlier 1933 Christology lectures where he similarly juxtaposes the person of Christ with ideas about Christ—that is, the incarnate word (the divine logos) with the spoken and written word (the human logos). Although Bonhoeffer affirms that the human logos may participate in the divine logos through Jesus Christ, who is both fully God and fully human, he draws a sharp contrast between the two. The living Jesus is the "*counter*-Logos," under which all ideas about Christ stand in judgment.[5] As living Word, the counter-Logos is truth revealed in the historic, concrete moment and thus requires the response and responsibility of discipleship to be known and rightly understood. At stake in this distinction between embodied discipleship and disembodied idea is the ability for Christians and church-communities to recognize and promote truth over self-deception. Bonhoeffer defines self-deception as a self-chosen path in the name of Jesus that permits privileged Christians to acquiesce to unjust social arrangements from which they benefit and from which they have little "desire to be set free."[6] Whereas ideas about Jesus, however faithful, inspiring, or sincere, may be articulated at a safe distance, discipleship demands that Christians reduce the distance between themselves and others and follow the living Jesus of the Gospel narratives into costly solidarity with those whom society oppresses and neglects, with "the outcasts, the suspects ... the reviled," as Bonhoeffer writes in prison.[7] From that place of increased solidarity, Christians—who otherwise would have been distant from the real needs of the world—may participate in its concrete redemption.

One way in which theological scholarship may reflect costly grace—thereby privileging the incarnate word and transformative action in the world over disembodied idea—is through ethnographic research attentive to the embodied discipleship of others. This was the approach I took when writing my dissertation and book, *The Church for the World: A Theology of Public Witness*, which holds together two very different styles of scholarship—philosophical theology and ethnography—as it examines how North American Protestants may offer a non-triumphal witness to the lordship of Christ in our pluralistic society.[8] The book draws on philosophical theology through an analysis and appropriation of Bonhoeffer's thought on Christ, the world, and the Church, and argues that church-communities may witness to Christ in a non-triumphant manner through an overlapping confession of their own sin and the sin of broader society, which finds public expression in repentant activity in sociopolitical life. The book also draws on ethnographic research as it examines two case studies of communities—the Southeast White House and the Eleuthero Community—whose work exemplifies ecclesial commitments and practices born out of a disposition of confession and repentance. Church-communities may demonstrate Christ's redemptive work and become vehicles of concrete redemption, I argue, when their mode of being in the world is confession unto repentance.

The ethnographic chapters in *The Church for the World* privilege embodied discipleship over disembodied idea. They serve as a response to the interested layperson's understandable desire that the abstract insights of philosophical theology (in this case, the insights of Bonhoeffer's Christology, ecclesiology, and theology of this-worldliness) be expressed concretely "in the language of reality," as Bonhoeffer himself put it.[9] As a response to the common question voiced by the nonspecialist, "But what does this look like in real life?" my chapter on the Southeast White House depicts an interracial Washington, DC urban ministry that intentionally has made itself present in "the forgotten quadrant" of the nation's capital.[10] I show how the ministry is consciously correcting society's neglect, and how its very presence in the neighborhood stems from an initial act of repentance, as the cofounders turned toward the forgotten quadrant and moved into the neighborhood in order to encounter the neighbor. I also argue that the ministry's work may be viewed as an ongoing activity of repentance—a making right—as it fosters relationships and draws others into its communal life together, connecting people normally divided by race, religion, politics, economics, social standing, geography, and culture. My study of the Eleuthero Community depicts another model of ecclesial witness; when taken together, Eleuthero and the Southeast White House demonstrate that confession and repentance may be embodied communally in various ways.

Eleuthero is an example of a church-community that recognizes that the way North Americans live is unsustainable and damaging to both the environment and the world's vulnerable populations. In response, they fashion right relationships with the earth and with a population of Sudanese refugees in Portland, Maine. This community of white evangelical Episcopalians confesses that North American evangelicals have not given the full narrative of scripture its due and have told fractured, false stories leading to disobedient action. Through the priest's teaching and through the life of the community, they construct "a holistic biblical narrative ... that can handle all of life." As they unlearn and learn anew, Eleuthero members undergo continuous conversion to the life of Christ and to a full vision of scripture.[11]

As concrete examples, these case studies are not comprehensive ethnographies, nor do they aim, like most ethnographies, to ascertain what these particular communities reveal about society as a whole. Rather, I chose communities that I thought offered a possible interpretive frame that would help me better understand public witness and that could be in mutually productive dialogue with Bonhoeffer's theology. Just as I chose Bonhoeffer's writings to guide my theology of public witness, discerning him to be an appropriate interlocutor and a trustworthy figure for many US Protestants, so, too, did I choose church-communities that I intuited were on to something, so to speak, based on my analysis of Bonhoeffer's writings and prior personal engagement with the communities and their leaders. Although the chapters on these two communities are not comprehensive ethnographies, my relationship to the Southeast White House and the Eleuthero Community is best described in classic ethnographic terminology as "participant-observer." I was a participant-observer, though, not simply in the scholarly sense as one who enters fully into the life of the community she is studying, but, notably, in a more ordinary sense, as one who, prior to my scholarly training, chose to be an intern at the Southeast White House and sharing the social location of Eleuthero, would have felt quite at home as a congregant in that worshipping community. Whereas a traditional ethnographer would privilege objectivity over subjectivity—the ethnographer is an observer who also participates—my posture toward these communities was more subjective. I was a participant—they were my people—and so my critical analysis had elements of reflexivity.

Thus, the ethnographic sketches of the Southeast White House and the Eleuthero Community serve as more than concrete examples. They serve as a window through which I could evaluate my own theological commitments and discipleship formation through something akin to an action-reflection hermeneutic. My practice—my participation as a staff member at the Southeast White House—preceded any formal theological training and led to my becoming an academic. Still, even though I was determined to maintain my practitioner status and speak of those two formative years in DC, at the time I privileged right belief, or proper thinking, over active engagement in the world. Impassioned and disoriented from working in that urban context, I entered the academy with concerns and questions about the church's identity and mission in society that I could barely articulate. I became a scholar in large part in an attempt to speak to the realities I had encountered, which necessitated that deliberative, renewed thinking replace those aspects of my embedded theology that bolster cheap grace. Bonhoeffer's theology offered me a foundation for thinking through complex issues surrounding Christology, ecclesiology, and soteriology, particularly in relation to my experience in DC at the Southeast White House. Just as Bonhoeffer's theology offered a lens and language in which to analyze and articulate the practices of this lived community, as discipleship communities, the Southeast White House and Eleuthero at times challenged the terms of my constructive theology and reoriented what I was in the process of developing. While it is true that I prioritized theological reflection, which preceded and guided my ethnographic research, at times the ethnographies qualified the claims of philosophical theology and guided my interpretation of Bonhoeffer's complex and abstract discourse. For example, the work and witness of these communities made me more alert to the fact that a narrowly defined understanding of repentance based on the crucified Christ alone was unfaithful to Bonhoeffer's insistence that the incarnation, crucifixion, and resurrection should never be separated in Christological thinking. Likewise, they made me more aware that, as public witness and social engagement, repentance entails much more than remorse over sin. The communities, in other words, made me a better reader of Bonhoeffer's theology.

Furthermore, the ethnographic studies reached beyond concrete examples in that for neither of the communities I chose to study were "confession" and "repentance" prevalent terms used by the majority of members to describe the community's identity and mission. Rather, their embodied life together reflected commitments and practices that arose out of a *disposition* of confession and repentance. Their repentant posture toward each other and the world was so integral to their formation as disciples that they were not fully conscious of it themselves. This fact, combined with Bonhoeffer's open and creative understanding of the meaning of repentance, paved the way for an expansive and holistic reimagining of what repentance encompasses and entails, with my reading of Bonhoeffer influencing my interpretation of the communities and my reading of the communities influencing my interpretation of Bonhoeffer.

Bonhoeffer's early understanding of the nature of theological discourse captures this dynamic and the methodology undergirding the ethnographic chapters in *The Church for the World*. Given our overarching inquiry into the productive tension between academic theology and embodied engagement, it is interesting to note that Bonhoeffer had this methodological insight about the vital relationship between theory and practice well before his own conversion in Harlem from a distant academic to an engaged disciple. His conviction, cited below, proves to be authentic though, made evident as his theology develops through various stages of his active resistance to social evil. In his 1930 habilitation thesis, *Act and Being*, he writes,

> The fact is that, as a theologian, I cannot resist the lure of intellectual works righteousness except by locating my theology within the community of faith (which is the theologian's humility), allowing the community of faith to allocate its place and bestow meaning upon it. Thinking, including theological thinking, will always be "systematic" by nature and can, therefore, never grasp the living person of Christ unto itself. Yet, there is obedient and disobedient thinking (2 Cor. 10:5). It is obedient when it does not detach itself from the church, which alone can "upset" it as "systematic" thinking and in which alone thinking has meaning...Think boldly, but more boldly still, believe and rejoice in Christ.[12]

Bonhoeffer argues that all systematic thinking has a limit, and for theology that limit is the Church, which he defines as "Christ existing as community." Theology obedient to the living Christ locates itself within the discipleship community and receives into itself all the messiness, complexity, and imperfection intrinsic to the actual Church. Thus, the theologian must guard against attempting to construct a closed system that seals theology off from the Church. Instead, the theologian must welcome lessons learned from church-communities engaged in transformative activity in the world. When this occurs, when academic theologians allow the practical wisdom of actual communities to break open their theologies, they, in effect, recognize that these ethnographies *are* theology—they are an integral part of theological understanding. Just as philosophical theology offers a lens and language to analyze and articulate the practices of lived communities, discipleship communities also, as Bonhoeffer says, "bestow meaning" on philosophical theology—by troubling the waters of systematic thinking, or in my case, by breaking open my theology of public witness to the lived realities of redemptive communal practice.

I discovered this organic connection and mutually beneficial relationship between theology and ethnography through my work with the Project on Lived Theology. The Project operates with the rationale that academic theologians and practitioners, pastors, and activists need one another to engage more fully the task of cultivating just and redemptive communities. Thus, Lived Theology creates space for sustained conversation and collaboration among these groups. The Project invites conversation by organizing workgroups and institutes around particular topics of common concern. Methodologically, lived theology creates conversation between theology and ethnography by attending to the concrete social implications of academic theology. As a scholarly practice, lived theology suggests that academics may gain theological insight by reading a discipleship community in a similar manner to a theological text; reciprocally, the ministry may gain self-understanding when a scholar presents a theological narrative of its work, drawing from the myriad resources within philosophical theology, theological ethics, and related disciplines. Although there are good reasons to move beyond this metaphor of text, first suggested by the philosopher Paul Ricoeur, given that it does not adequately capture the performative quality of lived communities, referring to communities as text does serve the important purpose of emphasizing that knowledge gained from them may be placed on the same authoritative ground as philosophical or theological works, within a subfield where abstract discourse has been the norm.[13]

This mutually beneficial dynamic played out when, in 2001, I returned to the Southeast White House to examine the theological dimensions of their biweekly "reconciliation luncheons." Through the lens of Søren Kierkegaard's discussion of Luke 14 in *Works of Love*, where "a person . . . prepare[s] a banquet and invite[s] as his guests the [outcasts of society]," I examined how this interracial ministry—which is characteristically middle-class in appearance, values, influence, and relational networks— loves its impoverished, African American neighbors through elaborate meals, particularly given social and economic inequities.[14] The Southeast White House's practice of eating with its neighbors, and its articulation of that practice, both illuminated and complicated Kierkegaard's discussion of loving the neighbor amidst the "dissimilarity" of earthly life.[15] In doing so, the ministry proved to be an authoritative theological interlocutor.

Equally significant, my paper was received enthusiastically by the Southeast White House, whose leaders thanked me for giving them additional scriptural and theological language in which they could understand their ministry. The paper expanded into the chapter discussed above in which I present the Southeast White House as a positive example of Christian public witness, and I was pleasantly surprised when staff and neighbors effortlessly referred to the importance of the "banquet" in interviews with me four years later. This discovery impressed upon me how valuable the interconnection of theology and ethnography can be not only for theological scholarship but also for Christians involved in grassroots ministry. It demonstrated how theological scholarship may directly serve and positively influence the work and witness of discipleship communities.

While constructive theology may both influence and be influenced by the active engagement of others through ethnographic research, it would be wrong to deem such scholarship discipleship itself, as Bonhoeffer understands the notion. To be discipleship, constructive thinking would need to be tied to the theologian's immediate this-worldly engagement. My growing conviction that theological thinking should be a direct manifestation of discipleship has deepened as I have lived within the movement of Bonhoeffer's thought and, like him, struggled to make decisions that prioritize immediate this-worldly engagement over academic distance. This prioritizing of practice is not a denigration of the life of the mind or of the real and urgent need for sophisticated theological thinking among US Christians. Instead, it is a recognition that, as Bonhoeffer argues, the call to discipleship is not a specific vocation for a chosen, adventurous few or for those who seem particularly gifted in works of mercy, peace, and justice. Rather, discipleship is a way of life for all who claim faith in Christ, including, of course, the academic theologian. In the opening chapters of *Discipleship*, while still discussing cheap and costly grace, Bonhoeffer addresses a false and widespread assumption about the exceptional nature of discipleship. He asks, "Is Christianity, defined as following Christ, a possibility for too small a number of people?" and answers,

The expansion of Christianity and the increasing secularization
of the church caused the awareness of costly grace to be gradually
lost ... Monastic life thus became a living protest ... against the
cheapening of grace.... Monastic life became the extraordinary
achievement of individuals, to which the majority of church members need not be obliged ... [But] God showed [Luther] through
scripture that discipleship is not the meritorious achievement of
individuals, but a divine commandment to all Christians.[16]

As the Nazi state gains total control over the church in Germany,
Bonhoeffer seeks for his listeners nothing less than conversion—the conversion from mere believers to disciples, a conversion in which location
matters, a conversion that arises from continually placing one's body in
costly situations of social and political struggle. This is the conversion he
experienced himself as he turned from "the phraseological to the real"—
the conversion from a theologian who was full of miraculous theological
insights (as Karl Barth called his early work) yet distant from communities
of distress, to a disciple poignantly aware that location matters when writing theology that will have lasting, transformative value for the Church
and world.

Bonhoeffer's critique of cheap grace in its various formulations (including, for example, in his prison correspondence on religionless Christianity)
is precisely what draws many academic theologians to his work, particularly those of us who are concerned about the Church's public witness and
social commitments. Even if we do not use the term, many of us engaged
in theological writing today appeal to costly grace to counter theologies
rooted in cheap grace, which bolster Christian complicity in a multitude of
interrelated injustices in our nation and around the world. However, the
irony, of which I have come to be poignantly aware, is that Bonhoeffer's
distinction between discipleship and disembodied belief—between the
incarnate and written word—applies as much to my work as an academic
theologian as it does to the average North American Christian. Indeed, it
arguably applies more. For, as an academic, I am perhaps most prone to
the Protestant temptation to turn Christian faith into right belief—into
proper thinking—and leave it at that. I am tempted to use my particular
sense of calling as a writer and professor as an excuse to avoid discipleship, to avoid obeying Jesus's straightforward commands, in the Sermon
on the Mount, to make peace and do justice. The temptation is especially
strong when my writing allows me to live vicariously through the costly

discipleship of others. At stake is my capacity as a writer or thinker to recognize and promote liberating truth over "pious self-deception," the latter allowing me to benefit from unjust social arrangements, even as I tell myself that I write for the sake of their eventual demise.[17] While self-deceit results from the privileged academic remaining distant from the devastation wrought by injustice and oppression, Jesus, the liberating truth, calls the constructive theologian into places of distress and active struggle—into productive tension between embodied discipleship and the written word.

The conviction that theological analysis might be a direct expression of discipleship creates tension for the constructive theologian, because it includes within it a call to costly social engagement *and* an affirmation of the importance of the written word. In his introduction to Dorothy Day's selected writings, Robert Ellsberg recalls Day's understanding of the relationship between the two, specifically her "reluctance" as an activist to make a distinction between the "act" of writing and the "act" of doing. "Both can be part of a person's response, an ethical response to the world," she said.[18] Dorothy Day is, of course, the quintessential writer-activist; her theological insights, published in the *Catholic Worker* newspaper for half a century, are a seamless extension of the community's unremitting and costly discipleship. Still, even for Day, the writing produced an inner tension, because being present to the written word meant being absent for that time from the difficult daily grind of hospitality—work that was then left to the other members of the community. It meant retreating from the primary space where she had been called, the space where Jesus, in the guise of the poor, made his most concrete claim upon her.

The academic theologian, however, abides within a different space. How the scholar-disciple negotiates the tension between writing and embodied social engagement will be as various as the particularities of individual circumstance, including academic location and sense of call to specific social and political struggle. As I have attempted to negotiate this tension, I have identified at least two standards to which my writing must be held accountable in order to claim it—with any integrity—as discipleship.[19] My writing must be held accountable (1) to the needs of the concrete, historic moment, and (2) to unexpected opportunities that make a claim on me and potentially redirect my academic path. What follows gives flesh to these standards of accountability in relation to the particularities of my own academic journey.

First, recall that for Bonhoeffer, the living word (or counter-Logos) requires discipleship in order to be known and understood, because Jesus as living word is revealed in the concrete, historic moment. The writings of lived theologians like Bonhoeffer and Dorothy Day have dynamic power—both now and then—because they express what needed to be said in the present moment. Dorothy Day's intimate proximity to those who were destitute meant that she heard their cries with terrible clarity and that her theological insights could not help but be their echo—cries that she understood to be those of Jesus in the guise of a stranger. By following the voice of Jesus himself and reflecting it in her writing, Day avoided the theologian's primary pitfall as expressed in the words of Martin Luther: "If I profess with the loudest voice and clearest exposition every portion of the truth of God except precisely that little point which the world and the devil are at that moment attacking, I am not confessing Christ, however boldly I may be professing him."[20] In other words, if the constructive theologian fails to say what needs to be said in *this* moment, she is not following Jesus closely enough to hear his concrete word. Like Day, Bonhoeffer is also admired and read because the integrity of his life and thought enabled him to speak to the concrete moment in theologically transformative ways. All of his well-known writings, from *Discipleship* to *Letters and Papers from Prison*, grow out of his discipleship journey, from his leadership within the ecumenical movement and Confessing Church to his conspiracy activities and time in prison. Yet we can also see in Bonhoeffer's work points where the writing does not arise from concrete experience—from hearing the living word in the present moment—and thus falls flat, failing to have the lasting redemptive power that characterizes the majority of his work. Juxtaposing two passages related to prisons demonstrates this point.

In a 1933 Advent sermon on Luke 21:28—"look up and raise your heads, because your redemption is drawing near"—Bonhoeffer describes God's coming as divine rescue from a situation from which we need redemption. He begins by describing a mining accident in England that made front-page news, and then asks of the biblical text, "To whom might these words be spoken? ... Who would get excited on hearing something like this? Think of a prison." Bonhoeffer mentions "the humiliation and punishment" of prison, "the misery of heavy forced labor," the occasional escape attempt, and the majority of inmates bearing "their chains with sighing and tears." Then, with fantastical language and imagery reminiscent of the *deus ex machina* theology he explicitly criticizes a decade later, Bonhoeffer soars:

Then suddenly a message penetrates into the prison: Very soon you will all be free, your chains will be taken away, and those who have enslaved you will be bound in chains while you are redeemed. Then all the prisoners look up, in chorus, with a heartbreaking cry: Yes, come, O Savior![21]

Although Bonhoeffer gains an embodied understanding of the relationship between prison and Advent ten years later—he writes to Bethge in 1943: "Life in a prison cell may be well compared to Advent; one waits, hopes, and does this, that, or the other . . . the door is shut, and can be opened only from the outside"—his words in this 1933 sermon stand in striking contrast to the insights he gains in prison.[22] I noticed this contrast when I read the sermon in preparation for my chapter on Advent in *Radical Discipleship: A Liturgical Politics of the Gospel*, a book that investigates how Christians may become disciples of, as opposed to simply believers in, Jesus, by drawing on my interrelated experiences as a full-time participant at the Open Door and as a teacher in an academic theology program at a Georgia women's prison. During Advent in 2008, I was invited to teach a class period on Bonhoeffer for the pilot course of the program. Although it was my first time in a prison and I had no idea how the women would respond, I ended the session with a passage from Bonhoeffer's prison correspondence. His theological reflection proved not only to cross "time and space" as it spoke directly to these women—reflecting their experiences of God and self—it also knit us together through our mutual affirmation of the shared words. "He's talking about us," said Natalie, with visible emotion and measured surprise, after reading Bonhoeffer's words of December 17, 1943:

From a Christian point of view there is no special problem about Christmas in a prison cell. For many people in this building it will probably be a more sincere and genuine occasion than in places where nothing but the name is kept. That misery, suffering, poverty, loneliness, helplessness, and guilt mean something quite different in the eyes of God from what they mean in the judgment of human beings, that God will approach where humans turn away, that Christ was born in a stable because there was no room in the inn—these are things that a prisoner can understand better than other people; for her they really are glad tidings, and that faith gives her a part in the community of the saints, a Christian fellowship breaking the bounds of time and space.[23]

Over time, as my friendship with Natalie and the other women deepened and as our study of Bonhoeffer progressed, many of them shared how much his critique of the *deus ex machina* theology and his call for a "religionless Christianity" applies to them, not just the privileged Christians Bonhoeffer had in mind. Many of the women shared how they have struggled to move beyond the otherworldly hope Bonhoeffer inadvertently reinforces in the 1933 sermon, which distracts them from the urgent work of learning to find God's sustenance in the painful details of their present incarceration.[24] Arguably, the whole of Bonhoeffer's theology, including his 1933 sermon, is concerned with concreteness or "this-worldliness," yet his writing fails and potentially even injures at those points where it is abstracted from the actual experiences of real human beings. Theological reflection that is rooted in a discipleship characterized by engaged social struggle, by contrast, is dynamic, empowering, unifying, living—as well as lived. In other words, it has transformative power for oneself, others, and the world.

Second, recall that as costly grace, discipleship for Bonhoeffer is both gift and task—"the grace and the command" are one, he says. Thus, as a disciple, the constructive theologian must be open to the new command—the unexpected situation—that may make a claim on her and potentially redirect her away from the path of received wisdom about academic progress and success. Again, one needs only look as far as Bonhoeffer's professional discernment to recognize that discipleship involves risk and demands courage to go against accepted norms. Although this quick jump from Bonhoeffer's life and context to ours may be disconcerting, we need not presume the vast historical differences disqualify his life from challenging our own. Our society is plagued with social evils, too, like mass incarceration—grave injustices by which we are slow to be alarmed. While social evils are always irreducible, in that the unique experiences of those who suffer them require we respond with specific concern and detailed remembrance, they often share mechanisms of escalation: from identifying a particular group as a problem; to ostracism and isolation; to confiscation of rights, property, and persons; to concentration in prisons or camps; and finally to annihilation, as argued in the award-winning documentary *The House I Live In.*[25] Thus, the disciple's small acts of courage today may serve as vital preparation for more costly acts of resistance tomorrow.

The unexpected situation that made a claim on me came in the form of the prison theology program, or more accurately, in the form of my relationships with the women in it. As the pilot course transitioned into the program's inaugural year, I transitioned with it, as unexpected opportunities arose allowing me to remain engaged in the work of teaching and then also directing the program under the vision and leadership of Emory ethicist Elizabeth Bounds. Although comparatively quite minor, the opportunity to serve as program director was not without risk; it meant turning down a short term teaching appointment at the height of the economic downturn before it was clear that the monies would come through for a full time director. At the time an agonizing decision, I undeniably desired to remain with these women to whom I felt increasingly called. My first sustained interactions with them, spending approximately eight hours at the prison every Friday while teaching the theology foundations course and directing afternoon study hall, is what finally drove me to worship at the Open Door. I needed a church-community "on the outside" that understood what I was encountering for the first time and that, I later found, could sustain me as I lived my life inside and outside the prison for two and a half years. Over time I had a growing desire to become more involved in the work of the Open Door beyond worshipping with them on Sunday afternoons. This led to my spending a year as a full-time community member with the support of a Lived Theology writing grant, while also continuing to work with the prison theology program. Notably, just as Bonhoeffer's decisions to take certain risks were made not in a vacuum, but rather within shifting frameworks of institutional and professional support (be it the alternative institutional structure of the Confessing Church or the more traditional institution of Union Theological Seminary), the creative vision of the Project on Lived Theology and its material support enabled me to encounter the Open Door as an academic who also sought to be a disciple. Thus, the path of discipleship is made straight (Mk 1:3)—the way is prepared—in part through nontraditional academic spaces that offer alternatives to the institutional structures of the academy that impede sustained connection between theological reflection and concrete social engagement.[26] The Project enabled me to be an academic-disciple who desired to deepen my engagement with unjust realities and the people affected by them as I pursued this basic and vital question of Christian faith: what is the gospel the church proclaims—given homelessness, mass incarceration, and capital punishment—and how may Christians be formed as disciples who faithfully embody that gospel?

This driving question is directed as much to me as to my readers, for I cannot ask of them something I am unwilling to do myself. *Radical Discipleship* argues that learning to follow the living Jesus requires entering the gospel narratives in real time though the liturgical calendar, and the book seeks to inaugurate the process by structuring the chapters according to the liturgical seasons that move readers through the gospel texts. At the same time, discipleship requires reducing distance between one's own place of privilege and places of social struggle and distress, or as Bonhoeffer says, between the old and new situation. "A call to discipleship," he argues, "immediately creates a new situation. . . . Jesus could have given the tax collector new knowledge of God and left him in the old situation." If he had not been the word incarnate, the old situation would have sufficed. But the incarnation demonstrates that "his word is not a doctrine. Instead, it creates existence anew." "The point," Bonhoeffer concludes, is "to really walk with Jesus."[27] For me, the women's prison and the Open Door Community together became the new situation that led me deeper down the path of discipleship, farther from the old situation and its tendency to privilege theological reflection over active engagement. Whereas my theology of public witness was rooted in Bonhoeffer's writings, thus making Bonhoeffer the privileged conversation partner in my first book, the Open Door and its liturgy is the privileged conversation partner in the second. By "liturgy" I mean literally "the work of the people," which envelops not only the community's worship but also its daily activism and theological reflection. As a member of this discipleship community, the Open Door's liturgical activism includes my engagement with the women in prison who are drawn into the beloved community of the Open Door when, for example, their voices echo in the prayers of the people or when they receive the newspaper *Hospitality* and are reminded that they are not forgotten. It includes the women themselves who have become my teachers and guides, as I witness their lives and hear their voices through the theology program and subsequent correspondence.

Given the broad expanse of the Open Door's liturgy, *Radical Discipleship* examines discipleship *through* the Open Door rather than *at* the Open Door. In other words, the Open Door is not an object of ethnographic study but is the primary *space*—the new situation—through which I discover how Christians may be formed as disciples who embody good news. By emphasizing the centrality of the new situation for discipleship, Bonhoeffer anticipates the theological turn toward embodiment, practice, and placement that lived theology and the Open Door Community manifests: where I place my body matters. We learn through our bodies; our practice shapes our understanding. Therefore, awareness and critical reflection on the location of our bodies is nonnegotiable for writing constructive theology that seeks also to be discipleship.

Notes

1. Dietrich Bonhoeffer, *Discipleship*, ed. Geffrey B. Kelly and John D. Godsey, trans. Barbara Green and Reinhard Krauss. Vol. 4 of *Dietrich Bonhoeffer Works*. 16 vols. (Minneapolis: Fortress Press, 2003), 53, 39.

2. Bonhoeffer, *Discipleship*, 43–44, 50.

3. Bonhoeffer, *Discipleship*, 57.

4. Bonhoeffer, *Discipleship*, 59.

5. Dietrich Bonhoeffer, *Christ the Center*, trans. Edwin H. Robertson (New York: HarperCollins, 1978), 27–37.

6. Bonhoeffer, *Discipleship*, 43.

7. Dietrich Bonhoeffer, *Letters and Papers from Prison*, trans. Reginald Fuller (New York: Touchstone, 1997), 17.

8. I began to articulate my methodology more specifically in terms of theology and ethnography when asked to present about the relationship between the two in my book, *The Church for the World: A Theology of Public Witness* (New York: Oxford University Press, 2011) at a consultation for *Practical Matters*, an online journal sponsored by Emory University's Initiative in Religious Practices and Practical Theology. See Jennifer M. McBride, "Bestowing Meaning: A Reflection on Philosophical Theology and Ethnography," *Practical Matters: A Transdisciplinary, Multimedia Journal of Religious Practices and Practical Theology* (Issue 3). This paper is a revision and expansion of what appears there and material is used with permission.

9. Dietrich Bonhoeffer, *Barcelona, Berlin, New York: 1928–1931*, DBWE 10, ed. Clifford J. Green (Minneapolis: Fortress Press, 2008), 186.

10. McBride, *The Church for the World*, 179–205.

11. McBride, *The Church for the World*, 153–178.

12. Dietrich Bonhoeffer, *Act and Being: Transcendental Philosophy and Ontology in Systematic Theology*, DBWE 2, ed. Wayne Whitson Floyd, Jr. (Minneapolis: Fortress Press, 1996), 132, 135.

13. Paul Ricoeur, "The Model of the Text: Meaningful Action Considered as a Text," in *Interpretive Social Science: A Reader*, ed. Paul Rabinow and William M. Sullivan (Berkeley: University of California Press, 1979), 73–101. See also Manuel Vásquez, *More Than Belief: A Materialist Theory of Religion* (New York: Oxford University Press, 2011), 216.

14. Søren Kierkegaard, *Works of Love*, ed. and trans. Howard V. Hong and Edna H. Hong (Princeton, NJ: Princeton University Press, 1995), 81.

15. Kierkegaard, *Works of Love*, 61–90. See Jennifer M. McBride, "A Theology of the Southeast White House Hospitable Meals," <http://www.livedtheology.org/pdfs/mcbride_hospitable.pdf>.

16. Bonhoeffer, *Discipleship*, 46–47.

17. Bonhoeffer, *Discipleship*, 64.

18. Robert Ellsberg, ed., *By Little and By Little: Dorothy Day Selected Writings* (New York: Orbis Books, 2005), xviii.

19. Although there is not enough space to develop it here, my writing also must be accountable to the persons about whom I write. More specifically, it must be accountable to the principle of respect for persons that prohibits me from using them as means to my end, even when that end is a noble one—the attempt to gain transformative theological insight that may serve the church. A question of central importance for any work that involves ethnographic method is how to avoid objectifying the community or the particular persons with whom I am engaged. I have found that placing authentic discipleship (instead of intellectual production) as a primary goal helps guard against exploitation.

20. *D. Martin Luthers Werke. Briefwchsel*, 18 vols. (Weimer, 1930–), 3:81f. Cited in George Hunsinger, *Disruptive Grace: Studies in the Theology of Karl Barth* (Grand Rapids: Eerdmans, 2000), 89.

21. Dietrich Bonhoeffer, *London, 1933–1935*, ed. Keith Clements, trans. Hans Goedeking et al., vol. 13 of *Dietrich Bonhoeffer Works*, 16 vols. (Minneapolis: Fortress Press, 1996), 338.

22. Bonhoeffer, *London, 1933–1935*. See editor's footnote.

23. Bonhoeffer, *Letters and Papers*, 166. The quote appears here as I typed it on the handout. I took the liberty of changing the male pronouns to female pronouns and of not using brackets so that the passage would speak to the women as clearly as possible.

24. They and I understand the inherent relationship between eschatological hope and its daily concrete manifestations, but this acknowledgment alone does not settle the question of how to live in hope in the context of an unjust and dehumanizing prison system.

25. Eugene Jarecki, *The House I Live In*, FilmBuff Studio, 2012.

26. See Jennifer M. McBride, "Introduction: Communal Receptions and Constructive Readings for the Twenty-First Century" in *Bonhoeffer and King: Their Legacies and Import for Christian Social Thought*, ed. Willis Jenkins and Jennifer M. McBride (Minneapolis: Fortress Press, 2011), 8–9.

27. Bonhoeffer, *Discipleship*, 62.

I3

Organizing as a Theological Practice

Susan M. Glisson

ONE OF THE defining moments of the 2008 presidential campaign was the "unveiling" of Sarah Palin as vice presidential candidate for the Republican Party. In her first major address at the Republican Convention, Palin laid out what would become her trademark "attack dog" style, which undergirded her tough mom/hunter/fearless potential leader persona. As a signature of her speech at the convention, Palin contrasted her experience as a small-town mayor with, as she described it derisively, the relative lack of experience one would gain as a community organizer—which Barack Obama had previously been. The way in which her derision was embraced by many in this country revealed a disturbing attitude toward community organizing, in a country that purports to celebrate small-town values and local community strength. The problem lies not just in the hypocrisy of our country; it rests also in what has occurred to the concept of community organizing over time.[1]

As it was taught and understood by activists like Ella Baker to the young people of the Student Nonviolent Coordinating Committee (SNCC), community organizing is concerned with empowering local people to challenge their own oppression, to have the greatest control over the decisions that affect their lives. As exemplified in SNCC, it was collaborative, non-hierarchical, non charismatic, tedious, everyday, often-unrewarded work. Baker identified it as "group-centered leadership," rather than a "leader-centered" group.[2] It was meant to create leadership that would continue long after activists were gone.

Despite the fact that many of those strategies of grassroots leadership were implemented in other movements for change in the 1970s, from women's issues to gay rights, a different narrative of social change took hold, often encouraged by traditional civil rights organizations and unchallenged in scholarship until the 1980s and 1990s. That legend was the savior narrative, and it focused all attention on Martin Luther King, Jr., as the sole defender and achiever of civil rights protections. The problem with that narrative, over and above its lack of historical accuracy, is that, as it is taught to children, it communicates that social change must wait on a savior, rather than being something we can secure for ourselves.

Ironically, some groups did study the lessons of grassroots leadership modeled in the civil rights movement, but such study came from a perhaps unexpected quarter. Political operative Ralph Reed built the Christian Coalition, which undergirded the rise of the Religious Right, by appropriating the strategies of the civil rights movement.[3] Not only did he help build a movement to undermine the accomplishments of the black struggle for freedom; his efforts helped obscure the origins of one of the country's central modern movements—namely, the commitment to maintain white supremacy—by claiming the legacy of Martin King for themselves. Such developments are but one of the ironies of the legacy of community organizing since the 1960s, such that while community organizing for many in the civil rights movement was a spiritual practice, the group that has most effectively studied and implemented its tactics are not organizers on the left, but rather those on the religious right. As historian Joseph Crespino has shown, Reed and others like him were able to tap into an essential desire of folks to act out of their religious beliefs—beliefs that they felt were being disregarded and destroyed.[4] Thus, a dangerous cocktail of religion, patriarchy, and white supremacy manipulated the tools of grassroots organizing to ensure the maintenance of their power.

How does such a process happen? How do the seemingly natural inheritors of an organizing tradition abandon those strategies and, in that vacuum, leave a space for those who oppose social justice to appropriate those tools for their own ends? There is a valuable conversation to be had about fatigue and burnout, about the sometimes debilitating allure of celebrity, about identity politics and what was useful and what was not in those efforts. In the aftermath of these developments, community organizing has too often become a more professionalized program and inward-focused career, rather than work that seeks to organize and empower people. Historian Theda Skocpol has noticed the lack of democratic depth in what often passes for community organizing.[5] Community organizers themselves have contributed to the perception of a professionalized "expert-client" relationship, rather than one that seeks to learn from community wisdom. The evolution of service learning as focused on serving "clients," rather than learning from fellow citizens, is but one example. A recent Kettering Foundation study noted such changes in many community organizations, revealing that some organizations that purport to serve the public do not even like the public.[6] It is impossible for community members not to perceive such disdain.

What would it mean for community organizations, institutions of higher learning, and religious organizations to truly value the wisdom in community, especially in those communities that are marginalized? Instead of learning from those we serve, we too often think we have all the answers they need. Or, perhaps even more dangerously, as with the Christian Coalition, tools to build a just society are misappropriated to ensure that power relations do not change. We need to be specific about the kind of community organizing that is life-affirming, socially just, racially inclusive, people-centered, transformative work, rather than its opposite. The use of a tool—namely, community organizing—that is meant to be empowering, egalitarian, and justice loving, to create a movement that is hierarchical, exclusive, and judgmental is not only ironic, but cannot help but do some damage to the tools it manipulated to ensure its strength. Democracy is best when citizens have maximum control of their own lives, and that is what authentic community organizing should aspire to.

Is there an antidote to all this professionalism and decentering of community from community organizing? Perhaps it resides in the practices of spirituality? The practices of communities that embody and enact their implicit lived theological commitments also inform and sustain movements for social change in precisely the ways that are the most long-lasting and transformative. They also, sadly, seem to be the tools most attacked in our modern world and least valued by progressive activists today. Philosopher Roger Scruton argues that,

> Citizenship is precisely not a form of brotherhood, of the kind that follows from a shared act of heartfelt submission: it is a relation among strangers, a collective apartness, in which fulfillment and meaning are confined to the private sphere. To have created this form of renewable loneliness is the great achievement of Western civilization, and my way of describing it raises the question of whether it is worth defending and, if so, how.[7]

He advances, "yes, it is worth defending, but only if we recognize the truth that ... citizenship is not enough, and it will endure only if associated with meanings to which the rising generation can attach its hopes and its search for identity."[8] Scruton suggests that in the Western world's ever-expanding desire for the new, we have too often sloughed off the traditions of previous generations, some of which may be valuable. He goes on to say,

> This culture of repudiation has transmitted itself, through the media and the schools, across the spiritual terrain of Western civilization, leaving behind it a sense of emptiness and defeat, a sense that nothing is left to believe in or endorse, save only the freedom to believe. And a belief in the freedom to believe is neither a belief nor a freedom. It encourages hesitation in the place of conviction and timidity in the place of choice.

"What is needed," Scruton suggests, "is not to reject citizenship as the foundation of social order but to provide it with a heart. And in seeking that heart, we ... return to the gifts that we have received from our Judeo-Christian tradition."[9]

One gift, Scruton asserts, is forgiveness. "In the Judeo-Christian tradition, the primary act of sacrifice is forgiveness. The one who forgives sacrifices resentment and thereby renounces something that had been dear to his heart."[10] It is this gift that some of us are attempting to explore through a grassroots process in Mississippi to create a truth and reconciliation commission (TRC). Truth commissions, of which there have been over thirty around the globe, have often nodded toward reconciliation as a correlative goal, if not in the title of the commission, then within its mandate. And yet, however laudable a goal reconciliation might be, it is often cast by the wayside in the pressing effort to tell the truth—another process that generally remains incomplete but at least attempted. Most other commissions have contexts that impel stressing the truth: they are generally undertaken in countries in transition from dictatorships to democracies. There is an urgency to prevent civil war, and to restore or create working judicial systems, law enforcement, and governing bodies that will not repeat the atrocities of the past. With these pressing and necessary objectives, reconciliation on a national or individual level is too often overlooked. It may, in fact, not even be possible until a sufficient passage of time. Which brings us to Mississippi.

In the midst of organizing a grassroots effort to create a TRC in Mississippi, civil rights activists from the 1960s-era Mississippi movement have expressed concern that a Mississippi commission should not repeat what have been seen as failures of the South African process. One activist was concerned that we might attempt to offer amnesty or prevent further trials. Another claimed the South African process was "too religious," underscoring a concern that justice is often sacrificed on the altar of reconciliation. It is perhaps more useful not to think of truth commissions as either/or propositions. They are not replacements for criminal prosecutions; neither are they very effective agents of reconciliation. They are useful to both, but unique in what they can accomplish.

The Mississippi Truth Project began in June 2005, at the conclusion of the first state prosecution of one of the murderers of James Chaney, Andrew Goodman, and Michael Schwerner, who were killed in 1964 in Neshoba County. At a press conference upon the rendering of a guilty verdict for Edgar Ray Killen, the multiracial group the Philadelphia Coalition, whose work had prompted the new trial and conviction, declared that, "These three brave young men were not murdered by a lone individual. While a vigilante group may have fired the gun, the State of Mississippi loaded and aimed the weapon. The Mississippi State Sovereignty Commission monitored and intimidated civil rights activists to prevent black voter registration. The White Citizens' Councils enforced white supremacy through economic oppression. And decent people remained silent while evil was done in their name. These shameful actions have been little understood by Mississippi citizens. We must now seek the truth. We call on the State of Mississippi, all of its citizens in every county, to begin an honest investigation into our history."[11]

This challenge to the state was not simply an orchestrated media event; rather, it had grown out of intentional and purposeful, and often painful, community conversations by thirty citizens who rose above their fears and suspicions to seek connection and to change their community's narrative. In the fall of 2003, two old friends ran into each other on the courthouse steps. One was black, one white. They had gone to school together and worked at *The Neshoba Democrat* as interns to Mr. Dearman the editor. Both had grown up in the shadows of the murders. Leroy Clemons had just been elected to chair the county NAACP, having campaigned on the platform of addressing the murders. Jim Prince had just returned home to run the newspaper. The two men quickly determined to pressure local leaders to acknowledge the upcoming fortieth anniversary of the murders in an appropriate way.

Early in 2004, Clemons and Prince formed a task force with the full support of the city, county, and the Mississippi Band of Choctaw Indians. They invited the Winter Institute—a university-based nonprofit specializing in racial reconciliation of which I am the founding director—to help facilitate the task force's work. They initially identified its work as commemorating the fortieth anniversary of the murders. But they both hoped for more—specifically, for a call for justice—but they weren't sure the larger community would join in that goal. And so, at the first meeting in April of the new task force, blacks and whites sat around a table and began to talk about the public secret.

For the African Americans in the room, this new discussion had been long overdue. Each year Mt. Zion United Methodist Church, which had been burned to lure the civil rights workers to town, held a memorial service for the victims and demanded an accounting for the murders. Few local whites attended these services. So, at the first meeting, local blacks were eager for action, for a public demand for accountability. They suggested a march through town. The whites in the room shrank visibly in their seats. For them, marches meant direct protest and rioting. They countered with a proposal for a community resolution. Now it was the black participants' turn to resist. Resolutions were just words on a page—they wanted action. It was clear that while both groups had come to the same table, unanimity about next steps would be difficult.

The task force opened its meetings to the public, with Jim Prince initiating a series of editorials and articles about the upcoming anniversary as one way to raise awareness in the town and to clear the air, so to speak. We moved from the local Chamber of Commerce boardroom to the fellowship hall of the First United Methodist Church, and in one session asked the attendees to say why they were there. The stories that tumbled out were powerful and moving, and were immediately grounding to the work necessary to bring the town forward.

Jewel Rush McDonald is the daughter of Georgia Rush and sister to John Thomas Rush, members of Mt. Zion beaten by Klansmen the night of the church burning in 1964. She wept as she spoke of her family's fear that summer, that Klansmen would return to "finish the job," to keep them from identifying their assailants. She told of hiding clothes in the chicken coop in case the house was burned and they needed to make a quick escape. And she spoke of leaving Mississippi and its racism behind, only to return decades later when her mother fell ill. She was determined now to make it home but wanted justice, not just for "those three boys," but for her mother and brother, too.

Nettie Cox Moore, an African American woman from Philadelphia, joined at the urging of Leroy despite her deep distrust of whites. Nettie had been a schoolteacher in the local system and began teaching civil rights history and wearing dashikis to class. Rumors of militancy preceded her firing, so Nettie was not inclined to believe that any whites shared her beliefs. She was quiet in the early meetings but soon learned that the whites in the group were as outraged over the murders as she. When she told Leroy that she might, in fact, like white folks, she helped transform a fragile peace into a lasting civic bridge.

After reading of the now-named Philadelphia Coalition in the newspaper, Deborah Posey decided to see "if it was for real." Posey is a white, rural, working-class woman who married into the family of one of the murderers. She initially believed her husband's family and her culture that the three workers were "Communist infiltrators," "dirty" and not worth grieving over. But one day, she saw a picture of the three men. They looked clean and decent and she began to question everything she had ever believed in. Weekly prayers at a stone memorial she built by hand at the murder site just off Highway 19 cemented her determination to do something, hoping that faith would help cleanse her community.

Fent DeWeese had been one of the few whites who regularly attended the Mt. Zion memorial service. He spoke of how in 1989, Mississippi's secretary of state Dick Molpus's apology for the murder of the civil rights workers had begun to relieve some of the guilt experienced by whites of his generation. And he consistently pushed the group to be aggressive in pursuing a trial. James Young was one of the first black children to integrate Philadelphia Elementary, just two years after the 1964 murders. It was a difficult experience and one that could have caused Young to forever hate whites. Yet he does not, and he rose to hold the chairmanship of the Neshoba County board of supervisors—the first African American to do so—and later became the town's first black mayor. His attendance in the Coalition underscored the new political clout held by black Mississippians, and his belief that the relationships built between Coalition members are its most important accomplishment.

Guy Nowell is a white banker, quiet, reserved. He spoke of shame as he shared why he became a member of the Coalition, shame that whites hadn't stood up against the Klan, and had allowed murderers to go free. In June 2004, at the Coalition's public appeal for justice, Nowell attempted to apologize to David Goodman, Andy's brother, for the murder. Goodman, in his gentle way, assured Nowell that no such apology was necessary. It was, as Nowell recounted the next day, the first time he hadn't felt ashamed to be from Neshoba County. Each member had a powerful story and we spent a majority of the early Coalition meetings listening to the words being said publicly for the first time, watching as relationships formed and deepened across racial lines.

It was in these stories that the path to unity became quickly apparent. The group decided it must issue a call for justice to the State of Mississippi and pressure local officials to join them. It did so, demanding and getting unanimous votes from the Chamber of Commerce, the City Council, and the County Board of Supervisors. The group then became even stronger in its connections to each other, as it bore the suspicion of some civil right veterans and family members of victims who did not trust this new push for atonement from the long-silent community. In one contentious meeting in which some of these veterans challenged the motives of the group, members literally sat with their arms around each other as they responded to the charges. But, armed with clear community support for a trial, the Coalition met with the local district attorney. And in September, 2004, it invited Carolyn Goodman and her son David to join in a meeting with the state attorney to push for a trial. In that meeting, the community again shared its stories. It wanted the attorney general to understand the cost of silence, shame, and murder to the town's moral well-being. The attorney general has credited this meeting with cementing his commitment to bring the case to trial. On January 6, 2005 (the Day of Epiphany in the Christian calendar), the State of Mississippi brought the first murder charges in the 1964 murders. And forty-one years to the day of the murders, a jury of his peers found Edgar Ray Killen guilty in the murders; he was sentenced to sixty years in prison.

Underneath the decades of silence about the murders, there were citizens who were waiting for someone to speak up, to tell the story of the boys' lives, and to condemn their deaths. Within a week of the trial in 2005, then-Governor Haley Barbour declared "closure" for Mississippi's racial past; his stance solicited a forthright letter from Rita Schwerner Bender, the widow of Mickey Schwerner. She asserted that, "Restorative justice can only come with recognition of the past, acknowledgement of wrongdoing, and acceptance of responsibility in the present by government and individuals to ameliorate the harm done. People in positions of public trust, such as you, must take the lead in opening the window upon the many years of criminal conduct in which the State, and its officials, engaged. Only with such acknowledgement will the present generation understand how these many terrible crimes occurred, and the responsibility which present officials, voters, and indeed, all citizens, have to each other to move forward."[12]

Emboldened by her letter and by the courageous plea from the Philadelphia Coalition, and on the heels of the tremendously positive press received by the Neshoba conviction (which had even country music radio stations in the state calling for honest investigations into the past), the Winter Institute convened a group of civil rights veterans, progressive activists, and religious leaders to discuss and began planning a statewide truth and reconciliation process to understand and redeem Mississippi's racist past in order to create a more inclusive and equitable future. The ad hoc group met for several weeks, pondering what Mississippi might look like if it were a social justice state, and we imagined the mechanisms by which we might transform it in that way. However, on August 29th, Hurricane Katrina cut shorts its momentum.

For the group, the debacle of the response in the aftermath of the storm underscored the need to understand the history of structural racism in our country. But very quickly, Haley Barbour (most assuredly planning his public-relations campaign before a potential presidential bid) moved to craft a narrative of storm recovery in Mississippi that hinged on resiliency and triumph of the human spirit and on proving how far Mississippi had come, especially cast as a "white" story of success as opposed to the "black" story of failure in New Orleans. It was clear that a process of truth and reconciliation would not be sanctioned or supported by Mississippi officials and so we began to look for other models. And yet, in the spring of 2006, we were able to exploit the momentum of the Killen verdict in one important way; we spearheaded the successful passage of a bill mandating teaching civil and human rights history in all Mississippi classrooms in the legislative session that year.

Over the course of 2006, the ad hoc group reached out to youth leaders to engage in a process with us and continued discussions as to what steps forward might be possible. We learned that far too many of our young people did not know the racial history of our state, making the curriculum bill all the more necessary. In 2007, the group decided to initiate a year-long, statewide conversation called "The Welcome Table," which would promote open and honest dialogue on race. Over three hundred citizens gathered on the steps of the capitol on June 21st, the forty-third anniversary of the Neshoba murders, to launch a pilot year meant to "test the waters" of the readiness for such dialogue throughout the state so that a more comprehensive initiative might be engaged. The Methodist Conference of Mississippi led the most wide-ranging effort for that Welcome Table year, with Bishop Hope Morgan Ward insisting that every church engage in racial discussions and with a focus on race in the 2008 Lenten publication by the conference. What they learned was crucial to our steps forward: on the whole, blacks and whites alike were anxious to engage in open dialogue on race, but unsure how best to do so, and thus avoided such discussions for fear of failure. Because many saw the need for tools to engage in ways that moved beyond those anxieties to create trusting and respectful relationships as a basis for positive social change, we sought out colleagues at the Fetzer Institute's Generosity of Spirit initiative to provide training to us.

Simultaneously in 2007, we came together with a number of civil rights veterans, as well as scholars engaged in examining Mississippi's past, to explore the creation of a truth and reconciliation commission. By April of 2008, we were able to host several statewide meetings. Without official sanction from the State of Mississippi, we had learned from the Greensboro, North Carolina, model that collective community can create the authority to call for a commission. By outlining our intentions and then inviting Mississippians to endorse the document, we could legitimize ourselves through grassroots endorsement.

By January of 2009, we were able to convene a signing ceremony, where hundreds of Mississippians came forward to endorse the declaration of intent. The ceremony signaled our first public announcements about the work, and signees organized a five-region structure for the state, with elected representatives, including youth, from each region to direct the next phase of writing a mandate for a commission. As community leaders worked, our academic partners began securing funding for an intensive research project in Mississippi that would place scholars and students in four communities to digitize existing records related to the racial history of Mississippi, so that patterns of abuse in education and criminal justice might be discerned. Truly, in that moment we felt invincible.

Next, a few of us were able to attend a conference, "Beyond Reconciliation," hosted in Cape Town in December of 2009. Friends introduced us to Reverend Peter Storey, one of the architects of South Africa's Truth and Reconciliation Commission. We spent several hours with Storey, learning from his assessment of South Africa's TRC, which provided a cautionary tale for our work in Mississippi. Storey shared with us that while many have charged his country's TRC with failure, he believes instead that, "the country failed the TRC."[13] He advised us to drill down as deeply into communities as possible, and to not overlook the ordinary and the quotidian. Too often, practitioners of truth and healing work have been distracted by a single large event: the massacre by police of hundreds or murders of well-known resistors to the status quo. But such a narrow focus misses the micro-aggressions, the bystanderism, the activities of everyday people to create the lived experience of a society proscribed by oppression. Thus the focus on super-events fails to hold everyone accountable on a day-to-day basis for activities that cumulatively escalate to the super-event. This advice lingered with us as we returned to Mississippi in 2010, especially as the work of the Mississippi Truth Project, as it had become known by then, began to stall.

The steering committee charged with writing a mandate could not seem to agree on the substantive issues around a mandate. Would we provide oral histories to police investigations? One week, the group wanted to do so, asking us to reach out to the newly created Department of Justice civil rights cold cases effort to seek partnership. With that partnership secured, the group decided it did not want to share information with investigators, for fear that those with incriminating information would refuse to come forward to share their stories. And so the tension between truth and justice thwarted forward movement. At the same time, the country was reeling from two forces: a deep recession that made many in the state feel that trying to tell stories of the past had no place in the real-world efforts to just get by economically; and the election of Barack Obama in 2008, which had many declaring our entrance into a "post-racial society," where discussing civil rights history was seen as rude, no longer necessary, or downright un-American in the midst of our new progress. And yet, we saw the FBI report that revealed the increase in the creation of anti-black hate groups in the wake of Obama's election, and we continued to live in a state where 34 percent of all our children live in poverty, so we were not quite ready to declare victory over white supremacy.

And so we went back to the stakeholders engaged in the process and asked, "what should we do?" And they answered, "collect our stories, because no one seems to remember the history enough to understand how it shapes us today.[14] By recovering these local memories and stories, we are learning more about the microaggressions that secured the edifice of structural inequities in our state. Likewise, advocates are now working more effectively to teach about "micro-progressions," as Winter Institute staffer Jennifer Stollman has called them, or the everyday actions the collectively create a more just and inclusive society. We believe this approach more effectively enables ordinary people to understand and act on their roles as change agents in their own communities. While it captures the separations and discriminations imposed in a white supremacist system, it also highlights the connections and systems of support of dignity, self-determination, and resilience, of spiritual resources that far outshined the lack of financial wealth and enabled communities in poverty to topple an entire system of segregation.

In 2010, a second decisive conversation happened, this time with George Vickers at the Open Society Institute (OSI). Vickers had been involved in the Guatemalan Truth Commission process and a mutual friend connected us as we sought our way forward. Vickers's advice was initially shocking but came to hold sway: "Stop working for a truth commission," he said. "Most, if not all commissions produce reports that sit on shelves and collect dust." He went on to suggest that they very rarely change policies and they do not necessarily create a framework for progressive activism that changes structures. "Spend your energy," he said, "on creating a coalition of progressive groups who can work together for policy change in the state."[15] It was in this exchange, and with OSI's support, that the idea of deconstructing the elements of a truth and reconciliation process began to emerge for us. Thus, where Michael Ignatieff has argued that the main contribution of truth commissions has been to "limit the range of permissible lies,"[16] we offer as an improvement the deconstructed and more multifaceted truth process approach which, as our Winter Institute staffer Charles Tucker has described, "increases the range of voices of those who are deemed credible enough to tell the truth." Rather than creating a truth commission and report, we now work to create a culture of truth-telling in Mississippi.

In support of this work, we now offer our community process, the evolved "Welcome Table," which creates civil and respectful sacred spaces to consider the "everydayness" of oppression and healing, which is then infused with community building and structural reforms to more effectively ensure that oppressive histories do not repeat themselves. It supported recent efforts in Oxford in which the First Baptist Church there—an historically white Southern Baptist church, which enacted a closed door policy in 1968 to exclude blacks—undertook a self-examination of that policy and its implementation over decades and then decided to condemn

itself and offer an apology to their black neighbors. Now they are all working together to repair the community harms that resulted from that policy.

What does all this have to do with community organizing and its potential connections to spiritual disciplines? Much of what might be useful
about community organizing, beyond its focus on grassroots attempts to
help people help themselves, is that it is most useful when it resembles
the practices of spirituality. Knowing the truth brings us freedom, we are
told by the disciple John. Bearing witness to the pain of others can provide healing. Justice is an integral and perhaps prerequisite part of seeking reconciliation, and justice can be both retributive and restorative. And
reconciliation, as the historian Tim Tyson has said, is what allows us to
live together in the knowledge that justice will always be incomplete—
thus, the importance of forgiveness. The excommunicated priest Matthew
Fox asserted that, "All work worthy of being called spiritual and worthy
of being called human is in some way prophetic work. It contributes to
the growth of justice and compassion in the world; it contributes to social
transformation, not for its own sake but for the sake of increasing justice."[17] Community organizers can learn something from that admonition.

So too, can they learn from Thomas Merton. In a letter to a young
activist, Merton advised him not to be caught up in the cause for which he
fought, but rather in the lives of those he served:

> Do not depend on the hope of results. When you are doing the sort
> of work you have taken on, essentially an apostolic work, you may
> have to face the fact that your work will be apparently worthless and
> even achieve no result at all, if not perhaps results opposite to what
> you expect. As you get used to this idea, you start more and more to
> concentrate not on the results but on the value, the rightness, the
> truth of the work itself. And there too a great deal has to be gone
> through as gradually you struggle less and less for an idea and more
> and more for specific people. The range tends to narrow down, but
> it gets much more real. In the end, it is the reality of personal rela-
> tionships that saves everything[18]

This means letting go of preconceived notions of what we can lead people
to do. It means not having expectations for people, but rather providing
a space so that people may determine for themselves what they need, as
Thomas Aquinas suggested was the meaning of true friendship. So, in the
end, what might community organizers do to be most effective? As with

the Good Samaritan, they can help rescue people from places of danger by moving them to places of safety. What rescued folks do with themselves once in a safe place is up to them. As Margaret Wheatley says, for every trauma, community is the answer.[19] So, racial healing work must be about reuniting us. And at its core stands relationship.

Writer David Foster Wallace understood the need for meaning and the necessity of finding meaning together. In a commencement address to Kenyon College, he said,

> This, I submit, is the freedom of a real education, of learning how to be well-adjusted. You get to consciously decide what has meaning and what doesn't. You get to decide what to worship. Because here's something else that's weird but true: in the day-to- day trenches of adult life, there is actually no such thing as atheism. There is no such thing as not worshipping. Everybody worships. The only choice we get is what to worship. The really important kind of freedom involves attention and awareness and discipline, and being able truly to care about other people and to sacrifice for them over and over in myriad petty, unsexy ways every day.[20]

Community organizing is not about living other people's lives for them. It is simply about loving them. And of course that is the most sacred practice of all.

Notes

1. Huge appreciation to Winter Institute Research Associate Megan McRaney, who assisted in the research for this chapter.
2. Manning Marable and Leith Mullings, eds., *Let Nobody Turn Us Around, Voices of Resistance, Reform and Renewal* (Lanham, MD: Rowman and Littlefield, 2000), 347; Barbara Ransby, *Ella Baker and the Black Freedom Movement: A Radical Democratic Vision* (Chapel Hill: University of North Carolina Press, 2002), 83.
3. At the "Road to Victory Conference" in 1995, Reed distributed Christian Coalition pledge cards modeled after Martin Luther King, Jr.'s pledge for the Southern Christian Leadership Conference Convention in 1964. He also borrowed the rhetoric and techniques of the 1960s movement. See David John Marley, "How the Christian Right Borrowed the Rhetoric of the Civil Rights Movement" in George Mason's History News Network, http://historynewsnetwork.org/article/5398; Linda Kintz, *Between Jesus and the Market: The Emotions That Matter in Right-Wing America* (Durham, NC: Duke University Press, 1997), 24; Daniel Marcus, *Happy Days and Wonder Years: The Fifties and Sixties in Contemporary Cultural Politics* (New Brunswick, NJ: Rutgers University Press, 2004), 184.

4. Joseph Crespino, "Civil Rights and the Religious Right," In *Rightward Bound: Making America Conservative in the 1970s*, ed. Bruce J. Schulman & Julian E. Zelizer, (Cambridge, MA: Harvard University Press, 2008), 90–105.

5. Theda Skocpol, *Civic Engagement in American Democracy: From Membership to Management in American Civic Life* (Norman: University of Oklahoma Press, 2003).

6. Peter Pennekamp and Anne Focke, "Philanthropy and the Regeneration of Community Democracy," Kettering Foundation (December 2012), http://the-commons.kettering.org/news/philanthropy-and-the-regeneration-of-community-democracy/.

7. Roger Scruton, "Forgiveness and Irony: What Makes the West Strong," *City Journal* (Winter 2009), http://www.city-journal.org/html/forgiveness-and-irony-13144.html.

8. Scruton, "Forgiveness and Irony: What Makes the West Strong."

9. Scruton, "Forgiveness and Irony: What Makes the West Strong."

10. Scruton, "Forgiveness and Irony: What Makes the West Strong."

11. "The Philadelphia Coalition. Recognition, Resolution, Redemption: Uniting for Justice," www.neshobajustice.com.

12. Rita Schwerner Bender's letter to Governor Haley Barbour, published in *The Clarion Ledger*, July 17, 2005.

13. Interview with Peter Storey at his home in Simon's Town, South Africa in December, 2009.

14. Mississippi Truth Project, Steering Committee Meeting, held in the spring of 2010.

15. Phone call between Susan Glisson and George Vickers in the spring of 2010.

16. Michael Ignatieff, "Overview: Articles of Faith," *Index on Censorship* 25 (May 1996): 113.

17. Matthew Fox, *The Reinvention of Work* (San Francisco: Harper, 1994), 13.

18. William Shannon, ed., *Thomas Merton: The Hidden Ground of Love, Letters on Religious Experience and Social Concerns* (New York: Farrer, Straus, Giroux, 1985).

19. Margaret Wheatley, "The Big Learning Event," http://www.margaretwheatley.com/articles/Wheatley-The-Big-Learning-Event.pdf.

20. David Foster Wallace, "Commencement Address to Kenyon College," delivered May 21, 2005.

Epilogue

LIVED THEOLOGY IS BEING LED INTO MYSTERY

John W. de Gruchy

OUR ELDER SON, Steve, tragically died in a river accident on Sunday, February 21, 2010. He was forty-eight years old and, at the time of his death, a professor of theology at the University of KwaZulu-Natal. In the weeks and months that followed I sought the words to express my grief, and, at the same time, developed a dogged unwillingness to surrender hope. I knew that the enemy of faith is not doubt, but rather an unwillingness to acknowledge doubt. I had also learned over the years that hope is not wishful thinking or optimism, but rather a question posed by faith in a world that gives so much cause for despair and lament. As I struggled with my grief, I found help through reading Nicholas Wolterstorff's book *Lament for a Son,* in which he reflects on his grieving the death of his son Eric in a climbing accident in Austria in 1983. Sometimes it was too painful to read. But it helped, as Nick put it in his Preface, to "own my grief."[1] That phrase struck me then, and has stuck with me ever since.[2]

Owning Grief: A Step into Mystery

To grieve is to be human; grief binds us all together in the solidarity of our human frailty. For that reason, while owning grief is always an intensely personal and often a lonely journey, it is often also a communal experience in which one is embraced and held tight, and in which new relationships are formed and old ones deepened, not least with others who have also experienced the death of a son or daughter. The week Steve died four other young men of his age known to us also died tragically. We had unexpectedly and unwillingly joined the company of so many others who have lost children, something which contradicts what should be the natural order of things. Children should not die before their parents die. But they often do—even, in this day and age, at birth.

Since Steve's death I have often thought of the many parents who daily grieve the death of their children in countless places where disease, war, terror, and genocide have shattered their lives. Or the parents of those children who starve to death before their eyes, in the barren landscape of perpetual drought. Or those dying painful deaths because drugs are unavailable to cure or soothe the pain. Or those who mourn the death of a loved one who committed suicide. The possible scenarios are endless. Everybody has to own their own grief, but I cannot begin to imagine how those do so who have no support, those who have lost all hope and those unable even to shed tears. That Jesus wept over Jerusalem and wept before Lazarus's tomb makes the necessary connection between the grief we should feel for the victims of injustice, oppression, and violence in our world, and the personal grief of those who suffer the death of a loved one.

There are neurological explanations for the process of grieving. Traumatic experiences trigger chemicals in the brain that enable us to cope. Tears are a biological reaction to pain, just as they are to ecstasy. This is part of being human and why repression of grieving and tears is unhealthy; in doing so, we are preventing the brain from functioning normally. But grieving cannot simply be explained as the activity of molecules at work in the brain. Grieving is the activity of my "self," or more meaningfully my "soul," understood not as a discrete ghostlike being located somewhere in my body, but in complex, dynamic, and relational terms.[3] This accords with the biblical view that human beings are constantly changing, psychosomatic wholes in relation to God, the world, and others. We grieve because relationships that give meaning to our lives come to an end as we have known them, even if they may continue in a new way and may be restored in ways beyond understanding.

Grief accompanies us through life, and not only in times of death; it is part of the human condition. We grieve if we have hurt others, especially those we love. We shed tears when our children leave home, or when we move from a house of wonderful memories in which we have lived for years, or when we say goodbye to family and friends after holidays together, or when we say farewell to colleagues with whom we have worked over many years. George Eliot reminds us that, "in every parting there is an image of death."[4] For death is the defining moment of parting. Yet if we grieve in hope, we do not have to accept that our relationship with those who have died has ended. The idea that the process of grief comes to an end, that there is some kind of final closure, is only partially true.[5] Yes, there will come a time when the dead move beyond our horizon as our memory grows dim and fails us, for grief is contingent on remembering.[6] But we cannot dis-own our grief anymore than we can get over loving someone we truly loved.[7] If we truly own our grief it becomes part of our journey in life, an expression of love that endures even though it changes character as we weave new futures, and maybe enter new relationships. It is a journey into the mystery that lies at the heart of the universe, the mystery to which we refer when we utter the word "God," inadequate as it is to encompass all that it is meant to convey.

Writing my book *Led into Mystery* was one of the ways I attempted to "own my grief," to examine and express my faith and hope through an ongoing conversation with Steve, but it was also an experience of being led into this mystery. Writing a book is a very public way to go about owning grief. As such, it carries with it the danger of abusing the process through lack of sensitivity to others who mourn differently, and requires prudence in exploring the issues to prevent sentimentality gaining the upper hand. There is also the danger of turning even the sense of grief and being led into mystery into a mental, academic exercise, perhaps the most likely and dangerous of all for a theologian. After all, do we not like to think we are the experts when it comes to talking about God and life after death? Yet if the truth be known, doing theology raises as many questions even as we seek—as we must—answers to those posed. After all, is everything that I hold true and that has given purpose and direction to my life false, an illusion or what neuropsychologists call a confabulation, an explanation we construct which is a fantasy of the imagination?[8] Or is it the case that in struggling with the questions that face us in our grief, we are being led into a mystery that is ultimately beyond explanation? Are the answers always questions precisely because they lead us deeper into the mystery we name God—deeper perhaps into silence before the mystery that encounters us?

Christian (and any good) grief counselling involves learning how to sit alongside those who grieve without trying to offer advice or answer questions until the appropriate time, and even then we do so with circumspection and caution. Rowan Williams has rightly said that the words of faith we try to speak to those who have experienced loss "have to emerge from whatever we can do to inhabit" their territory, "to move as far inside as we can." Even though we may not be able to move very far inside, this is not only sound counsel but consistent with our "belief in God who heals only by inhabiting the world of death and grief."[9] The much-maligned Job's comforters knew that, as the author of the book tells us:

> They sat with him on the ground seven days and seven nights, *and no one spoke a word to him*, for they saw that his suffering was very great. (Job 2:11–13)

When Jesus was confronted by the agonizing cries of the Canaanite woman whose daughter was possessed by demons, so Matthew tells us, "he did not answer her at all" (15:23). Was he callous and uncaring; or was he listening intently to her cry for help, waiting for the moment when his words and actions might become a means of grace and healing? Maybe God is silent more often than not because God is overwhelmed by human suffering, perplexed by the pain that cries out accusingly to him: "Why have you forsaken me?" God is silent not because God is absent, but because God grieves with us. God knows even more than we do that grief is beyond words. Our inhumanity to others, our crimes against humanity, our unbearable suffering, reduce God to silence. But it is not the silence of uncaring absence; it is the silence of solidarity in suffering, a presence beyond words.

The early Christian fathers and mothers well knew that theology, like grief counselling, begins in silence, not in asking questions and demanding answers. Not the stony silence of hostility, or the silence experienced by those who are totally deaf, those unable to hear even the gentle song of a small bird at dawn. It is the silence that enables us to listen to that song, to hear the "still small voice," listening for the Word of grace. Grieving teaches us to listen in the silence to the heartbeat of those who weep, and discern in their pain the heartbeat of the vulnerable God who grieves in solidarity with them and a world in need. This is the first step into the mystery of God embodied in human flesh. The world lay in solemn silence when the Word came to dwell among us, and Mary's joyful contemplation was tempered by the anticipation of sorrow and grief.

Mystery Hidden and Disclosed

The word "mystery" has multiple, layered meanings. Mystery is used to describe detective novels, the Internet, God and the universe, the Christian sacraments, and anything that puzzles us and for which we are at a loss for words. It is also, as Karl Rahner tells us, "one of the most important key-words of Christianity and its theology."[10] Doing theology, he says, is being drawn back into mystery. But it is not a shortcut to solving problems akin to obfuscation, nor should we take refuge in mystery too soon when faced with the challenges presented to faith by reason and science. Rather, it is the acknowledgment that doing theology is more than intellectual enquiry; it is exploring—no, better—*participating* in something that transcends and ultimately overwhelms us as we struggle with matters of life and death, love and justice, faith and hope. But the journey into mystery is not one that takes us into the realm of the ethereal. It is neither otherworldly nor a-historical; it is being encountered by and engaging reality differently as human beings in solidarity with all creation, with all living beings, with God.[11]

My sense of being led into mystery began in a new way the day I sat beside the river right where Steve drowned and where his body still lay trapped. In stumbling along the valley of death I experienced a desolation that could only be expressed in inarticulate groans. I experienced "fear and trembling," overwhelmed, as Rudolf Otto describes it, by the mysterious beyond my "apprehension and comprehension."[12] But from early on my brain chemistry began processing and interpreting my experience in a particular way, calling forth a theological response. At one level, my response was simply faith seeking answers, and therefore no different from what we normally do when thinking theologically, whether in the seminar room or in parish ministry. Of course, to begin with there was no systematic attempt to answer the questions, no possibility that I could stand back and reflect on the painfully raw data of my experience. The best I could do was to let the questions come and go, neither repressing or trying to answer them, but bracketing them, putting them into cold storage and holding them in abeyance for the time being. I had to allow the resources of faith hold me together rather than trying to make sense of what had happened.

The same is true for others who grieve. Even though we sit in silent solidarity with them as we must, questions are already implicit even if not expressed. Why does God permit such suffering? Is this God's will? What is the meaning of life if it all leads to this sad conclusion? Is there a God? Why did she die so young? Did my sin bring this about? And, behind all these inevitable questions, did God raise Jesus from the dead? Is there good reason to love God or only reason to despair and fear God, even hate God, even hate the word "God" and all that it has come to signify? These are all important questions, they take us to the heart of theological enquiry, but the answers of conventional wisdom are inadequate, especially when pronounced with dogmatic certainty and uncritical biblical proof-texting.

Of all the questions the most perplexing into which we are inevitably led in our grief is that of the mystery of God's agency and the mystery of evil. Why is destruction not covered by insurance policies referred to as an "act of God?" Why does God seem so impotent in the face of human suffering? Is tragedy God's will? There are reasonable responses to the problem that carry some explanatory weight. If God is God then surely somehow, somewhere amidst such tragic events God must be present even if hidden, otherwise, as Desmond Tutu has said, "God is God's Worst Enemy."[13] But there is no "solution" this side of eternity, [14] for the problem "remains unjust and inexplicable, haphazard and cruelly excessive," or at the very least, a mystery "impenetrable to the rationalizing human mind."[15] That is why any genuinely Christian theodicy, that is, any attempt to justify God's permitting of human suffering, must surely begin with the suffering of God in Christ as the revelation of the mystery of who God is.

It has become almost commonplace to speak of the crucified God, the suffering God, the God who stands in solidarity with all who mourn—perhaps too commonplace. One of the prayers in the Volmoed prayer book speaks of God as the "vulnerable God who stands in solidarity with the suffering people of the earth." These words often perplex those who hear them, for how is it possible for the almighty creator of heaven and earth to be vulnerable and suffer? Before rushing into glibly answering that question, we do well to remember that the idea that God could suffer was a major problem for ancient theologians. This is neither the time nor place to engage in the debate that led the early Church to reject the idea that God the *Father* suffered on the cross (*patripassianism*), or to enter the world of Greek metaphysical thought and note how the terms *apatheia* and *pathos* were understood differently to the way in which we now speak of apathy or express pity.[16] But at the very least, we should pause on the threshold of this perplexing question, for we stand before what is undoubtedly at the heart of the mystery of God, which led the ancient Fathers to speak of the mystery of the triune God.

The narrative of the Trinitarian God paradoxically affirms God's freedom and power, and God's kenotic love and compassion as distinct yet
inseparable. God is neither subject to the passions of the ancient divini-
ties, nor incapable of suffering with humanity.[17] The shift from a divinity
who is impassive to the incarnate mystery of the crucified God provides
a penultimate clue as to why God so often seems silent, as we previously noted. God is silent for the very same reason we are silent when
in the company of those who suffer, except that God's love is such that
he enters fully and redemptively into our pain. God's silence is not the
silence of absence or apathy, but rather the silence of one who grieves
totally because God loves absolutely. It is part of the mystery into which
we are led, the mystery of the cross as the outpouring of love. "For God
loved the world so much that he gave his only son" (John 3:16). How
could God not grieve?

Bonhoeffer expressed God's own grieving in relation to ours in his
poem, written in prison, entitled "Christians and Heathens." In the first
verse he writes about how we all turn to God in our time of need, and in
the third, how God in turn comes to us. But in the middle verse it is about
us going to God in God's need:

> People go to God when God's in need,
> find God poor, reviled, without shelter or bread,
> see God devoured by sin, weakness and death.
> Christians go to God in his hour of grieving[18]

The journey into the mystery of God's grief, and therefore love, is integral
to the journey of the "self" or "soul" from brokenness into wholeness, the
reintegration of body, mind and soul in Christ. In other words, to return
to where we began, the process of grief should not be understood as
something distinct *from*, but rather distinct *within* the journey of both life
and faith, of dying and rebirth, of death and resurrection. Christian grief
counselling that is theologically informed is not simply about enabling
people to work through their grief and own it but also to enable those
who grieve to be led gently and over time into the mystery of the God
who grieves and, eventually to discover a presence in their lives that is
infinitely loving and indescribably beautiful. But this is only after a long
and sometimes painful journey along what is sometimes described as the
"way of unknowing."

The Way of Unknowing

The way of "unknowing" begins when it dawns on us that God is beyond our knowing, and therefore that the answers to ultimate questions are also beyond our grasp. To say that the answers are ultimately beyond our grasp is not the same as saying that there are no penultimate intimations that shed light on our path. Christian faith in the mystery of God revealed in Jesus is not irrational and blind, it is not fideism, for while it acknowledges that reason cannot proceed without faith, it also insists that faith needs reason to understand itself. In the same way as Bonhoeffer made the connection between our struggles for justice in the penultimate now, and our ultimate justification by grace alone, so we need to recognize that our theological enquiry into the questions of life and death in the penultimate, and the insight that we are given now, are connected to the ultimate even though not yet final or complete. The meaning of life and death are inseparably connected; the meaning of death is discovered in the meaning of life. This is what eternal life as present reality is about.

There is a connection, then, between what reason illumined by faith enables us to discern now and the ultimate revelation of the mystery when we know even as we are known, for now "we only know in part; but then we will know fully" (I Cor. 13:12). It is only in the end that the mystery is revealed in its fullness, when we know even as we are known. Now, as we journey through life, the revelation of the mystery of God in Jesus Christ does not mean that everything we want to know is disclosed to us, but that everything we need to know for each step of the way is made known to us as we travel. That is why we can only be justified by the faith that we share with Abraham who went out not knowing where he was going but trusting in the God of promise and hope—and the God who grieves in solidarity with us.

The journey along the path of unknowing into this mystery is not first of all about doing theology in the classroom; it is about lived theology whether in ordinary time or on boundaries of human experience, and about being drawn painfully yet joyfully into the embrace of a love and beauty that is both disclosed yet always exceeding what we can fathom. Only this ultimate reality is worthy of the name God, and therefore of our worship, that which makes us "pause to wonder and stand rapt in awe."[19] Only then, in contemplation and reflection, can we begin to discern honest answers to the questions that confront us through theological enquiry.

But always knowing that those that trip off our tongues are inadequate, specious, and sometimes downright unhelpful and even hurtful. At best they can only be preliminary, penultimate. We know that, because our answers to the questions of others do not necessarily convince us when we suffer or grieve, so why would they convince anyone else who wants to know why God has forsaken them? Such questions may not bother those who do not believe that we humans are unique within the animal kingdom—only flesh and blood, just meat, even though wondrously evolved. It is only believers who can get angry with God and struggle with doubt. Atheists and agnostics who ask questions that imply the existence or presence of God, meaning, or purpose, are not true to their convictions, and must surely be closet or would-be believers. But a genuine, lively faith in God does not answer all our questions; it makes them more complex, urgent, and demanding.

In owning my grief and counseling others I soon discovered that in asking questions, more questions, rather than neat answers, became part of the quest, an opening up and a deepening of the mystery into which I was being led. Is not this Job's experience? In answer to Job's questions, God confronts him with even more, virtually assaulting his agonized consciousness with a torrent of demands:

who is this that darkens counsel by words without knowledge?
... I will question you, and you shall declare to me. (38:2–3)

Those of us who are theologically trained may think we know the answers, until we shift from being Job's comforters to being Job himself, from sitting with others who grieve, to being those who grieve. Initially we cannot even begin to answer the questions they are asking even for ourselves. We have to travel deeper into mystery with them as we listen to their anguished cries for answers, and shed tears with them. And maybe only when we have haltingly begun to own our own grief, uttered our own cries of desolation and shed our own tears, do we really know there are no easy answers. We may declare the mystery of our faith at the Eucharist, but can our faith ever be strong enough to carry us through? Is it not, rather, that somewhere deep within us we acknowledge that the profound and mysterious reality we have embraced in "faith" was holding on to us?[20] Christians refer to this as the mystery of God's grace disclosed in the life, death, and resurrection of Jesus Christ. Yet God remains unfathomable mystery even when revealed, for what is revealed is what we need to know about God, not everything there is to be known, or that we would like to know. Jesus as the revelation of God is truly God but not the whole of God; in Jesus God is at the same time hidden and revealed from the cradle to the cross.

Faith in God as unfathomable mystery disclosed yet hidden in Christ, far from being an abstraction unrelated to our experience of reality, implies a commitment to the journey into God as the one "in whom we live, move and have our being." This journey leads us deeper into reality, not away from it, for whatever else the word "God" might mean, it refers to ultimate reality. And in the course of that journey we discover with St. Paul that all that finally counts "is faith working through love" (Gal. 5:6). Such faith is therefore a commitment to love that has to be made everyday within the realities of the world. It is not a certainty that we possess, but a certainty that comes to possess us, the mystery of grace that makes believing and loving possible in the first place.

The unending quest of science and the theological sense of being led along the path of unknowing into mystery are analogous and converge even though they usually are expressed differently. When Einstein says that the "most beautiful thing we can experience is the mysterious," and that this is "the source of all true art and all science," he is referring to that ultimate mystery which transcends art, science, and theological enquiry itself. Being led into mystery requires openness to the possibility of such transcendence. When religion or science turn in on themselves, close the door of the sanctuary or laboratory to mystery, lose their ability to wonder, their childlike capacity to trust, they become idolatrous, dehumanizing, and destructive. "The lack of mystery in our modern life," wrote Bonhoeffer, "means decay and impoverishment for us. A human life is of worth to the extent that it keeps respect for mystery."[21] To lose respect for mystery is to lose respect for life, for the creation, for the other, for God. It is to become cynical, nihilistic, incapable of hope—to wash our hands of political responsibility and action. To respect mystery is to remain hopeful that what has been revealed will be fulfilled, even if in ways that take us by surprise, for that is the nature of mystery.

Grieving in Hope

In *Led into Mystery*, I examine in some detail how I understand Christian hope, and how this connects, on the one hand, to our life in the world and the struggle for justice and peace and, on the other, to the integrity of

creation and the ultimate restoration of all things. Believing in the resurrection of Christ means that in the darkest times of personal tragedy or political violence, we affirm that God's purpose for the well-being of creation will
not finally be thwarted. In exploring this hope I also examine such notions
as the immortality of the soul, the meaning of heaven and its connection
with the earth, the resurrection of the body, and political reality. This is not
the place to repeat all that I say there, but what I say there provides the background for these final comments. For when Paul tells the Thessalonians
that we grieve but always in hope, what is he telling us about grief?

Paul's description of the whole of creation groaning in labor pains,
waiting for the birth of a "new creation," or a "new heaven and a new
earth," evokes in us an awareness that our grieving is cosmic in dimension. The whole cosmos, it would appear, is grieving its own degradation
at the hands of humanity and, in doing so, recognizes that its future well-
being is bound up with the hope of humanity's redemption (Romans
8:18–25). This hope is firmly planted on the earth yet cosmic in expectation, intensely personal but at the same time interconnected "in Christ."
Christian hope, in other words, is penultimately related to all our struggles
for justice and peace in this world, and ultimately to the restoration of all
things. It is only within this framework that we can make sense of the New
Testament data and the personal confession of faith in the "resurrection
of the body and the life eternal." The hope that resides within us is profoundly related to the hope of creation as a whole.[22]

What happens to you or me, or anyone else after death, Bonhoeffer
reminds us, is not the central, framing question of the Bible.[23] There are,
he says, "more important things than this question."[24] The Christian belief
in the "resurrection of the body" has to do with the continuity of identity
in relationships within the context of a new creation, not with the resusci-
tation of our physical bodies of bone, flesh, and blood in individual glory.
John Polkinghorne, a physicist and a theologian, writes:

> In natural terms, the pattern that is me, whatever form it actually
> takes, will be dissolved at my death, as my body decays and my rela-
> tionships are reduced simply to the fading retention of memories
> by others. Yet it seems an entirely coherent belief that the everlast-
> ingly faithful God will hold that pattern perfectly preserved in the
> divine memory, and then embody it in the ultimate divine eschato-
> logical act of resurrection at the last day, as the new creation enters
> into the unfolding fullness of time.[25]

If this is so, then "God's remembering, recognizing, and relating to me," is, as Nancey Murphy says, "essential to my post-resurrection identity."[26] But she adds that the continuity of personal identity is only meaningful if it includes "*self-recognition, continuity of moral character,* and *personal relations,* both with others and with God."[27] This is what resurrection hope "in Christ" is all about within the new creation, for this is what the resurrection of Christ means for us.

The disclosure of God's mysterious purpose is the substance of Christian hope, as can be seen in passages where Paul speaks about the glory that is still to be revealed, and for which the whole of creation "waits with eager longing." (Romans 8:19). Likewise, to the Colossians, Paul writes about the "riches of the glory of this mystery" revealed in the gospel, "which is Christ in you, the hope of glory" (1:27). He also writes about our waiting in hope for the "redemption of our bodies" which we do not yet see, and concludes with the rhetorical question: "for who hopes for that which is seen?" Believers know that what is not yet seen has already been disclosed in the gospel. But even then, it remains unfathomable mystery: "for who knows the mind of the Lord?" asks Paul (Romans 11:34). His judgments are unsearchable and his ways inscrutable. There are things not revealed, things that remain hidden until the end. Yet the end has already been anticipated. The mystery still to be revealed will not be contrary to that already disclosed in Christ; it will be the unveiling of that mystery in its entirety.

Acutely aware of the destruction that was daily taking place in Berlin and throughout Europe, while in prison Bonhoeffer came to accept the fragmentary character of life and his own impending death. But he also discerned that "that which is fragmentary may point to a higher fulfillment, which can no longer be achieved by human effort." That was the only way he could think about the death of so many of his former students in the war.[28] In doing so, Bonhoeffer refers to Irenaeus's doctrine of recapitulation, in a passage to which I have frequently returned since the death of Steve.

Nothing is lost; in Christ all things are taken up, preserved, albeit in transfigured form, transparent, clear, liberated from the torment of self-serving demands. Christ brings all this back, indeed, as God intended, without being distorted by sin. The doctrine originating in Ephesians 1:10 of the restoration of all things, – *re-capitulatio* (Irenaeus), is a magnificent and consummately consoling thought.[29]

In the end, Christian hope is the anticipation that the fragments of life, the fragments that we are as human beings, the fragments that we become in death, will be brought to completion as we are finally led into in the ultimate mystery of an unfathomable love that embraces us in life and death. That is our hope, a hope that does not repress grief, does not exclude tears, does not deny pain, but enables us to see beyond them and live in anticipation with the whole of creation of the magnificent work that God is yet to do. Hope is, after all, imagining something different than despair and death. If our belief in God means anything at all, it will transcend all expectation and open up a totally new dimension to our relationship with those we continue to remember and love within the memory and love of God. Only then will the mystery into which we are being led be fully and finally fulfilled. And only then, as John of Patmos perceived as he gazed into the mystery of God's future for us, will "mourning and crying and pain be no more" (Rev. 22:4).

Notes

1. Nicholas Wolterstorff, *Lament for a Son* (Grand Rapids, MI: Eerdmans, 1987), 5.
2. My understanding of grief has been confirmed and enriched further by the essays edited by Stephen Oliver in *Inside Grief* (London: SPCK, 2013).
3. See John de Gruchy, *Led into Mystery* (London: SCM Press, 2013), 159–65.
4. George Eliot, *Scenes from a Clerical Life* (Oxford: Clarendon Press, 1985), bk. 1, chap. 10, 70.
5. See Oliver, *Inside Grief*, 11.
6. See Sheldon Vanauken, *A Severe Mercy* (London: Hodder & Stoughton, 1977), 231.
7. See Allen Verhey, *The Christian Art of Dying: Learning from Jesus* (Grand Rapids, MI: Eerdmans, 2011), 342.
8. See S. A. Graziano, *God, Soul, Mind, Brain: A Neuroscientist's Reflections on the Spirit World* (Teaticket, MA: Leapfrog Press, 2010), 61–65; David Eagleman, *Incognito: The Secret Lives of the Brain* (New York: Pantheon Books, 2011), 101–50.
9. Oliver, "Foreword," *Inside Grief*, x.
10. Karl Rahner, "Mystery," in *Encyclopedia of Theology: A Concise Sacramentum Mundi*, ed. Karl Rahner (London: Burns & Oates, 1975), 1000.
11. See "Karl Rahner," in *The Making of Modern Theology*, ed. Geffrey B. Kelly (Minneapolis: Fortress, 1992), 335.
12. Rudolf Otto, *The Idea of the Holy* (London: Oxford University Press, 1931), 28.
13. In the first Steve de Gruchy Memorial Lecture, held in the Rondebosch United Church, Cape Town, April 24, 2012.

14. John Hick, *Evil & the Love of God* (London: Macmillan Fontana, 1968), 398.

15. Hick, *Evil & the Love of God*, 371.

16. See Jürgen Moltmann, *The Crucified God* (London: SCM, 1974), 267.

17. See David Bentley Hart, *The Beauty of the Infinite: The Aesthetics of Christian Truth* (Grand Rapids, MI: Eerdmans, 2003), 166–67.

18. Dietrich Bonhoeffer, *Letters and Papers from Prison*, Dietrich Bonhoeffer Works, vol. 8 (Minneapolis: Fortress, 2010), 461. I have used an earlier translation of the last line, that from the 1971 enlarged edition of LPP, p 349. In DBWE 8 it reads: "Christians stand by God in God's own pain (leiden)."

19. Albert Einstein, back cover of *Inside the Mind of God*.

20. Oliver, "No one ever told me," *Inside Grief*, 9.

21. Dietrich Bonhoeffer, *London, 1933–1935*, Dietrich Bonhoeffer Works, vol. 13 (Minneapolis: Fortress Press, 2007), 360.

22. See Romans 8:18–25.

23. See N. T. Wright, *urprised by Hope* (London: SPCK, 2011), 197.

24. Bonhoeffer, *Letters and Papers*, 373.

25. John Polkinghorne, "Eschatological Credibility," in *Resurrection: Scientific and Theological Assessments*, ed. Robert John Russell, Ted Peters, and Michael Welcker (Grand Rapids, MI: Eerdmans, 2002), 52.

26. Nancey Murphy, "The Resurrection Body," *Resurrection*, 213.

27. Murphy, "The Resurrection Body," *Resurrection*, 208.

28. Bonhoeffer, *Letters and Papers*, 301.

29. Bonhoeffer, *Letters and Papers*, 230.

Selected Bibliography

Adorno, Theodor W. "Minima Moralia." In *Gesammelte Schriften*, 20 vols., ed. Rolf Tiedemann. Frankfurt am Main: Suhrkamp Verlag, 1970–1986.

Adorno, Theodor W. *Minima Moralia: Reflections from a Damaged Life*. Trans. E. F. N. Jephcott. New York: Verso, 1978.

Agamben, Georgio. *Homo Sacer: Sovereign Power and Bare Life*. Redwood City, CA: Stanford University Press, 1998.

Asad, Talal. *Genealogies of Religion: Discipline and Reasons of Power in Christianity and Islam*. Baltimore: Johns Hopkins University Press, 1993.

Barth, Karl. *The Word of God and the Word of Man*. Trans. Douglas Horton. Gloucester, UK: Peter Smith, 1978 [1928].

Bonhoeffer, Dietrich. *Discipleship*. Dietrich Bonhoeffer Works. Vol. 4. Ed. Geffrey B. Kelly and John D. Godsey Minneapolis: Fortress Press, 2003.

Bonhoeffer, Dietrich. *Letters and Papers from Prison*. Dietrich Bonhoeffer Works. Vol. 8. Ed. John de Gruchy. Minneapolis: Fortress Press, 2010.

Bourdieu, Pierre. *Outline of a Theory of Practice*. Cambridge, UK: Cambridge University Press, 1977.

Bourdieu, Pierre. *The Logic of Practice*. Redwood City, CA: Stanford University Press, 1990.

Bourdieu, Pierre. *Pascalian Meditations*. Redwood City, CA: Stanford University Press, 1997.

Bretherton, Luke. "The Duty of Care to Refugees, Christian Cosmopolitanism, and the Hallowing of Bare Life." *Studies in Christian Ethics* 19, no. 1 (2006): 39–61.

Brettel, Caroline. *When They Read What We Right: The Politics of Ethnography*. Westport, CT: Bergin & Garvey, 1993.

Bussie, Jacqueline A. *Outlaw Christian: Finding Authentic Faith by Breaking the "Rules"*. Nashville: Nelson, 2016.

Cannon, Katie G. "Sexing Black Women: Liberation from the Prisonhouse of Anatomical Authority." In *Loving the Body: Black Religious Studies and the Erotic*. Ed. Anthony B. Pinn and Dwight N. Hopkins, 11–30. New York: Palgrave, 2004.

Cheng, Patrick S. *Radical Love: An Introduction to Queer Theology.* New York: Seabury Books, 2011.

Christ, Carol. "Embodied Embedded Mysticism: Affirming the Self and Others in a Radically Interdependent World." *Journal of Feminist Studies of Religion* 26, no. 2 (2008): 165.

Christ, Carol. *She who Changes: Re-Imagining the Divine in the World.* New York: Palgrave Macmillan, 2003.

Claussen, Detlev. *Theodor Adorno: One Last Genius.* Trans. Rodney Livingstone. Cambridge, MA: Belknap Press, 2008.

Cone, James. *Black Theology and Black Power.* 20th anniversary ed. San Francisco: Harper, 1989.

Das, Veena. *Life and Words: Violence and the Descent into the Ordinary.* Berkeley: University of California Press, 2007.

De Certeau, Michel. "Story Time." In *The Practice of Everyday Life.* Trans. Steven Rendall, 77–90. Berkeley: University of California Press, 1984.

De Certeau, Michel. "The Weakness of Believing." In *The Certeau Reader.* Ed. Graham Ward. Trans. Saskia Brown, 214–43. Oxford: Blackwell Publishers, 2000.

De Certau, Michel, *The Writing of History,* Trans. Tom Conley. New York: Columbia University Press, 1988.

Du Bois, W. E. B, *John Brown.* Ed. David Roediger. New York: Modern Library, 2001.

Dykstra, Craig, and Dorothy C. Bass, "A Theological Understanding of Christian Practices." In *Practicing Theology: Beliefs and Practices in Christian Life.* Ed. Miroslav Volf and Dorothy C. Bass, 13–32. Grand Rapids, MI: Eerdmans, 2002.

Dykstra, Craig. *For Life Abundant: Practical Theology, Theological Education, and Christian Ministry.* Grand Rapids, MI: Eerdmans, 2008.

Farley, Edward. *Theologia: The Fragmentation and Unity of Theological Education.* Minneapolis: Fortress Press, 1983.

Frederick, Marla F. *Between Sundays: Black Women and Everyday Struggles of Faith.* Berkeley: University of California Press, 2003.

Freire, Paulo. *Pedagogy of the Oppressed.* New York: Continuum, 1981.

Fulkerson, Mary McClintock. *Places of Redemption: Theology for a Worldly Church.* Oxford: Oxford University Press, 2007.

Geertz, Clifford. *The Interpretation of Cultures: Selected Essays.* New York: Basic Books, 1973.

Gray, M. J., E. Ondaatje, R. Fricker, S. Geschwind, C. A., Goldman, T. Kaganoff, A. Robyn, M. Sundt, L. Vogelgesang, & S. P. Klein. *Combining Service and Learning in Higher Education: Evaluation of the Learn and Serve America, Higher Education Program.* Santa Monica, CA: RAND: 1999.

Hall, David D., ed. *Lived Religion in America: Toward a History of Practice.* Princeton, NJ: Princeton University Press, 1997.

Healy, Nicholas M. *Church, World and the Christian Life: Practical-Prophetic Ecclesiology.* Cambridge, UK: Cambridge University Press, 2000.

Holman, Susan R. *Beholden: Religion, Global Health, and Human Rights*. New York: Oxford University Press, 2015.

Hooks, Bell. *Teaching to Transgress: Education as the Practice of Freedom*. New York: Routledge, 1994.

Ivory, Luther. *Toward a Theology of Radical Involvement: The Theological Legacy of Martin Luther King, Jr.* Nashville, TN: Abingdon Press, 1997.

Jantzen, Grace. *Becoming Divine: Toward a Feminist Philosophy of Religion*. Bloomington: Indiana University Press, 1999.

Jenkins, Willis. *The Future of Ethics: Sustainability, Social Justice, and Religious Creativity*. Washington, D.C.: Georgetown Press, 2013.

Marable, Manning, and Leith Mullings, eds. *Let Nobody Turn Us Around: Voices of Resistance, Reform and Renewal*. Lanham, MD: Rowman and Littlefield, 2000.

Marsh, Charles. *God's Long Summer: Stories of Faith and Civil Rights*. Princeton, NJ: Princeton University Press, 2008.

Marsh, Charles. *The Beloved Community*. New York: Basic Books, 2006.

Martin, Calvin Luther. *The Way of the Human Being*. New Haven, CT: Yale University Press, 1999.

McBride, Jennifer. *The Church for the World: A Theology of Public Witness*. New York: Oxford University Press, 2011.

McClendon, James Wm. *Biography as Theology: How Life Stories Can Remake Today's Theology*. Eugene, OR: Wipf and Stock, 2002.

Milbank, John. *Theology and Social Theory: Beyond Secular Reason*. Oxford: Basil Blackwell, 1990.

Nabhan-Warren, Kristy. "Embodied Research and Writing: A Case for Phenomenologically Oriented Religious Studies Ethnographies." *Journal of the American Academy of Religion* 79, no. 2 (June 2011): 378–407.

Niebuhr, H. R. *Kingdom of God in America*. Middletown, CT: Wesleyan University Press, 1988.

Norgaard, Kari. *Climate Change, Emotions, and Everyday Life*. Cambridge, MA: The MIT Press, 2011.

Oliver, Stephen. *Inside Grief*. London: SPCK Publishing, 2013.

Orsi, Robert. *Between Heaven and Earth: The Religious Worlds People Make and the Scholars who Study Them*. Princeton, NJ: Princeton University Press, 2005.

Ransby, Barbara. *Ella Baker and the Black Freedom Movement: A Radical Democratic Vision*. Chapel Hill: University of North Carolina Press, 2002.

Sandoval, Chela. *Methodology of the Oppressed*. Minneapolis: University of Minnesota Press, 2000.

Scruton, Roger. "Forgiveness and Irony: What Makes the West Strong." *City Journal* 19, no. 1 (2005). http://www.city-journal.org/html/forgiveness-and-irony-13144.html.

Shannon, William, ed. *Thomas Merton: The Hidden Ground of Love, Letters on Religious Experience and Social Concerns*. New York: Farrer, Straus, Giroux, 1985.

Shulman, George. *American Prophecy: Race and Redemption in American Political Culture*. Minneapolis: University of Minnesota Press, 2008.

Slade, Peter. *Open Friendship in a Closed Society: Mission Mississippi and a Theology of Friendship*. New York: Oxford University Press, 2009.

Smith, Ted A. *The New Measures: A Theological History of Democratic Practice*. Cambridge, UK: Cambridge University Press, 2007.

Smith, Ted A. "Troeltschian Questions for 'Ethnography as Christian Theology and Ethics.'" *Practical Matters* 6 (2012). http://practicalmattersjournal.org/2013/03/01/troeltschian-questions/.

Smith, Ted A. *Weird John Brown: Divine Violence and the Limits of Ethics*. Redwood City, CA: Stanford University Press, 2014.

Sobrino, Jon. *No Salvation Outside the Poor*. Maryknoll, NY: Orbis Books, 2008.

Spillers, Hortense. "The Idea of Black Culture." *CR: The New Centennial Review* 6, no. 3 (2007): 17–28.

Tanner, Kathryn. "Theological Reflection and Christian Practices." In *Practicing Theology: Beliefs and Practices in Christian Life*, 228–44. Grand Rapids, MI: Eerdmans, 2002.

Tanner, Kathryn. *Theories of Culture*. Minneapolis: Fortress Press, 1997.

Troeltsch, Ernst. "What Does the 'Essence of Christianity' Mean?" In *Ernst Troeltsch: Writings on Theology and Religion*. Trans. and ed. Robert Morgan and Michael Pye, 141–98 Atlanta: John Knox, 1977.

Vigen, Aana Marie, and Christian Scharen, eds. *Ethnography as Christian Theology and Ethics*. New York: Continuum, 2011.

Volf, Miroslav. *Exclusion and Embrace: A Theological Exploration of Identity, Otherness, and Reconciliation*. Nashville, TN: Abingdon Press, 1996.

Wacquant, Loïc J. D. *Body & Soul: Notebooks of an Apprentice Boxer*. New York: Oxford University Press, 2004.

Ward, Peter, ed. *Perspectives on Ecclesiology and Ethnography*. Grand Rapids, MI: Eerdmans, 2012.

West, Cornel. *The American Evasion of Philosophy: A Genealogy of Pragmatism*. Madison: University of Wisconsin Press, 1989.

West, Cornel. *The Cornel West Reader*. New York: Civitas Books, 1999.

West, Traci. *Disruptive Christian Ethics: When Racism and Women's Lives Matter*. Louisville, KY: Westminster John Knox Press, 2006.

Index